A Society in the Making

Zsuzsa Ferge

A Society in the Making

Hungarian Social and
Societal Policy 1945-75

Zsuzsa Ferge

M. E. Sharpe, Inc.
White Plains, New York

Published in 1980 by M. E. Sharpe, Inc.,
901 North Broadway, White Plains, New York 10603

Library of Congress Catalog Card Number: 80-80116
International Standard Book Number: 0-87332-155-3

Printed in the United States of America

Contents

Preface

This important book is the product of a remarkable experience. A sociologist domiciled in Hungary, Zsuzsa Ferge has intermittently taught and studied in France, Britain and the United States. Few social scientists of the post-Second World War generation have had this range of experience. And, as we know from the history of theoretical physics, psychoanalysis, economic and other fields, Hungary is the incubator of great talents.

A Society in the Making can be read on three levels: as a study of Hungarian social structure, as a case-study in comparative social policy, or as a contribution to the theory of social policy.

As a study of Hungary, Dr Ferge's book is one of the small but growing number of analyses of Eastern Europe and the Soviet Union which avoid denunciamentos and apologetics. It is a sympathetically critical account (as she says 'In social science, there is no neutral act') from which much can be learned. The book builds on Ferge's researches into Hungarian social structure (only pieces of which have appeared in English) which are outstanding studies in their own right.

Her mode of analysis is influenced by Lukács, the Hungarian Marxist, who invented the young Marx before the pre-1848 philosophically humanist manuscripts were discovered. The Marxism of Lukács and his interpreters is about the shaping of consciousness, the search for wholeness, the activity or the praxis of people in their self-development. It seeks to connect historically based social structures to the emergence of varied consciousness. The goal is the emancipation and extension of potentiality that Hegel wrote about. The coming of socialism does not deliver these conditions; it provides the rudiments of the framework for their possible emergence. This orientation is what some have termed an 'open Marxism', recognizing the impact of economic forces but not ignoring the importance and variability of subjectivity. It offers questions, ways of framing issues, rather than pre-

fixed conclusions about the state of capitalism or socialism.
Zsuzsa Ferge writes as a Marxist within and about the political
and social history of Hungary.

Dr Ferge has also been influenced by some strands of French
Marxism, particularly the 'social reproduction' analysis of Pierre
Bourdieu and his associates, who write within the broad tradition
with which at least Lukács's early writing is associated. 'Social
reproduction' stresses the importance of ideological and cultural
factors in the functioning and legitimation of a social structure.
Some use 'social reproduction' in a simplified, mechanical way,
underplaying the degree of tension, antagonism and contradiction
that can exist among the components of culture and between
culture and economic forces. But used wisely and empirically –
as it is by Bourdieu and his associates in some studies – the theme
of social reproduction makes the re-examination of the familiar
and the accepted an exercise in the search for the processes of
domination in major social institutions and in cultural attitudes.
This perspective leads Ferge to stress the importance of knowledge as an aspect of social structure and an element in one's class
position. Social stratification is not only about the distribution of
tasks and resources, but it is also about knowledge, the capacity
to deal with cultural, social and political institutions and to
interpret experience. In all this, Ferge writes without the abstracted
prose which mystifies much recent Marxist writings.

As a case-study, *A Society in the Making* has the advantage of
a broad acquaintance with social policy in other nations. Further
it is one of the few useful books for comparative purposes which
is truly a study of social structure and social policy. It is not a
simple recitation of legislation and coverage of numbers and
risks. It imbeds legislation and statistics in economic, social and
political pressures. It is one of the very few broad, informed and
tough-minded accounts of social policy in a socialist country,
stressing consequences rather than intentions.

The long-term contribution of this book of many virtues will,
however, be at the third level of the theory of social policy. Social
policy has suffered from inadequate theory. The debate about
theory occurs largely in the somewhat disguised form of argument

about what should be the objectives of social policy. At times, it seems more anxiety-provoking to present a theoretical perspective than an ideological one.

Richard Titmuss made the field of social policy analysis. It is now time to build on his rich legacy, and this Dr Ferge does very handsomely. She recognizes the virtues of his approach, his attention to detail, process, ideology, and consequence, but is also sensitive to limitations in the Titmuss corpus.

Titmuss believed, as Martin Rein has observed, that moral commitment could override economic exigencies. Will was all that was needed. This vision led him to underestimate the imprint of economic structures and policies and to believe that non-market actions could offset market results. As Ferge demonstrates, economic policy is the basic social policy, determining the division of income and tasks, the security of one group or another. Social policy can alleviate some of the difficulties caused by economic policy, but alleviation is not prevention nor the absence of harm.

Like Lukács, Titmuss was concerned with subjectivity, the way people looked on themselves, how they were influenced by the outlook of others. He sought the moral community of Durkheim and, like Durkheim, tended to sweep the questions of personal autonomy and power into a less than major place. The important issue was to improve the conditions of the poor through the orderly processes of research and electoral politics. One of Ferge's contributions is to see the role of power and participation in social policy.

Dr Ferge's original blending of Lukács, Bourdieu and Titmuss is a significant step towards a new generation of theorizing and policy as well as a distinguished statement in comparative social policy.

S. M. MILLER, *Professor of Sociology and Economics, Boston University*

Acknowledgements

It is almost impossible to acknowledge all the direct and indirect help I received when preparing this book. I would not have undertaken it without the kind and firm request of R. E. Pahl, the editor of this series, and Jillian Norman, my editor at Penguin. My closest collaborator, giving help, criticism and advice in all the phases of the work, was Julia Szalai. The observations of my Hungarian friends and colleagues, Andrea Deák, Iván T. Berend, Mrs G. Gayer and János Illés were invaluable in the revision of the manuscript. I also gained useful experience at the discussions for the Committee on Poverty, Social Welfare and Social Policy of the International Sociological Association, and especially from the critical observations and suggestions kindly offered by Herbert J. Gans, S. M. Miller and Frances Fox Piven. Many other debts are acknowledged in footnotes. Finally I must thank Felicia Pheasant, who revised the manuscript, trying to translate clumsy continental English into real English – an unrewarding task.

Introduction

This account of Hungarian societal policy over the last three decades describes the efforts made to transform Hungarian society, and shows the underlying principles and basic ideals which motivated the transformation, as well as the difficulties and dilemmas encountered in this process.

The concept of *societal policy*, as described in Chapters 1 and 2, is used in a special sense. It encompasses the sphere of *social policy* (the organization of social services or the redistribution of incomes), but also includes systematic social intervention at all points of the cycle of the reproduction of social life, with the aim of changing the structure of society. That is why the term 'structural policy' may also be used instead of the rather awkward term 'societal policy'.

The present study traces the process of social reproduction. Chapters 3 and 4 describe societal policy dealing with the transformation of basic social relations embedded in the social organization of work; Chapters 5 to 7 analyse the relations created or modified through distribution and redistribution; while Chapters 8 and 9 consider some aspects of social policy in relation to consumption and ways of life in general. This rather broad framework stems from the conviction that a coherent and far-reaching societal or structural policy is not conceivable without taking into account the nature of the social forces and social relations it seeks to affect.

Despite this extensive treatment of the concept, some people will find this framework too narrow. Because the subject is so large it would be impossible to undertake a systematic description of all the legal, organizational and historical aspects of the various institutions involved, so I shall confine myself to the most salient points. Some important issues of social policy remain outside my analysis. In fact, since the analysis is focused on the interaction of societal policy and social structure, I shall leave aside those spheres of deliberate social action that do not have a direct impact on basic social relations. Issues which concern the society as a whole, whether in relation to other societies or to nature (such as safeguarding the environment), are therefore left out of the present analysis.

My present field of interest is centred on structural relations, on the static and dynamic aspects of the conditions of the different social classes or strata in Hungarian society. In an earlier work[1] I gave a descriptive analysis of social stratification and of social inequalities in Hungary. In this book I take up the same issue in a more dynamic way, and try to show how far the reorganization of Hungarian society has progressed to date, and to consider how the policy of reorganization could have been more effectively implemented in order to achieve the socialist development of social relations. Once the legitimacy of this framework is accepted, it is clear that different analytical approaches have to be used, on the one hand for societal policy which operates on a level at which the outcome is influenced by the existence of different social groups with varying interests, and on the other hand for policy which intervenes in a sphere where society is much less divided, where there is a closer unity of interests among its groups, as for instance in attitudes to pollution. (I do not imply, however, that in this latter case interests are identical: even in relation to pollution interests vary. For example, those who are adversely affected by anti-pollution measures would be opposed to those trying to implement them.) The two sets of issues raise different types of problems, and I limit myself to one type only. However, I also think that if basic social relations follow a socialist pattern of development, this affects the possibilities of success in other spheres, too. For example, even the protection of the environment might be more successful if the clashes of interest among social groups became less pronounced. Thus I re-situate societal policy in the context of social structure. Without claiming that

1. *Társadalmunk rétegeződése* (The Stratification of Hungarian Society), Közgazdasági és Jogi Kiadó, 1969.

this is the only way of handling the issue, I hope to show that this approach is relevant and valid.

The development of Hungary is the real subject of this book. I do not, however, give a comprehensive picture of the historical background of the Hungarian social and economic scene, because this is available to the English reader from other sources.[2] None the less, I have tried to help the foreign reader, especially the English reader, towards an understanding of Hungarian problems by introducing comparative data and by discussing some issues in an international context. It must be stressed, however, that international cross-references are scarcer and less systematic than one might wish, because of the obvious difficulties of this type of comparative work. Besides technical problems, I also had ethical doubts when handling documents relating to other countries. I am slowly coming to the conviction that the primary duty of an analyst of social policy is to deal with the issues relating to his (or her) own country. In social science there is no neutral act. Even the seemingly most objective international comparison implies a selection and an interpretation which reflect the social values and convictions of the researcher, and the danger of bias then increases greatly. A judicious interpretation of data or facts relating to other countries requires a thorough knowledge of the historical context and of the objective conditions of these countries, the relation of social forces within them, the values and the ethos of their social classes and groups, and the system of priorities that a given situation warrants.

I do not mean that I never try to unravel the logic underlying the theory or practice of social policy in other countries, or that I refrain from pointing out some of their positive or negative aspects. But I am aware of the shortcomings of my knowledge of other countries and also of the difficulty of arriving at an

2. I. T. Berend and Gy. Ránki, *Economic Development in East-Central Europe in the 19th and 20:h Centuries* Columbia University Press, New York, London, 1974; *History of Hungary*, ed. Ervin Pamlényi, Collet's, London and Wellingborough, Corvina, 1973, especially Chapter IX, I. T. Berend and Gy. Ránki, 'The Horthy Regime'

unbiased judgement. In short, I do not think that an outsider is a good judge of the intricacies of another country's social or societal policy – except, obviously, in cases where the problems are clear for all to see.

To make my argument clearer, I shall mention how the Hungarian experience is usually handled by Western critics or analysts. In the course of this book I shall quote some criticisms that Western countries direct at the socio-economic policy of the socialist countries in general, and especially that of Hungary. One group–those with what we may call a 'leftist' approach – maintains that we grant too large a place to economic considerations, thereby introducing the danger of problems akin to those of capitalist societies, including 'consumerism' and excessive social differentiation. The other – conservative – argument criticizes the implementation of Hungarian societal policy for precisely the opposite reason or because it does not pay enough respect to so-called natural social and economic laws and hinders, in particular by excessive egalitarianism, the development of talents or rapid economic development. Both criticisms have some truth in them. But, briefly, the first fails to take into account the history of the country and the objective economic conditions it has inherited, the second fails to appreciate the future and the values which govern the attempts being made to shape our society. Therefore both are one-sided. One of the reasons is obviously political partisanship, which is unavoidable. But another reason may be the lack of the type of analysis attempted in this book, which takes into account the realities of Hungarian society and seeks to interpret them in a comparative perspective.

Part One
Principles and Concepts

Chapter 1

Social Structure and Societal Policy

1.1 The objective of societal policy

Societal policy is deliberate social action, both short-term and long-term. If it neglects the immediate problems for the sake of the distant future, it may easily become inhuman. If it does not strive to do more than solve visible problems without having a coherent image of what the future should be, its results will be fragmentary. And, in the absence of a firm system of priorities, current problems may reproduce themselves in the future, possibly in a more serious form. An effective societal policy presupposes, then, an awareness of the present situation and at least a broad outline of the future.

Clearly, one cannot work out in advance a detailed scheme of this future. Utopias elaborated in minute detail are necessarily naïve: it is only in their everyday experience that people gradually find adequate solutions to the problems emerging under continuously changing conditions. But some general characteristics may be, and have in fact been, worked out by various social scientists. Among these outlines the formulations of Marx, which postulate a new relationship between the individual and society, and a new, less conflict-ridden concept of freedom that helps rather than hinders the self-realization of each individual, are of special relevance for me. 'Only in the community with others has each individual the means of cultivating his gifts in all directions; only in the community, therefore, is personal freedom possible . . . In the real community the individuals obtain their freedom through their association.'[1]

This formulation is, however, on a high level of abstraction: it is couched more in philosophical than in sociological terms. It relates to a future which is still too distant and cannot therefore

1. Marx and Engels, *The German Ideology*, International Publishers, New York, 1947, pp. 74–5.

be considered as a direct goal of current social action. The difficulties involved may be shown if, for instance, one takes a closer look at the goal of 'developing the gifts of each member of the community'. While objective conditions are unequal and frequently bad, the abilities of the individual can often not even be detected, so that they can hardly be 'developed'. Abilities are shaped in constant interaction with the immediate and also the wider environment of the individual. The interaction begins by and large at the time of conception and operates continuously. This, incidentally, is why the slogan of equal educational oppor- tunities is misleading. It implies that equal chances should be given to equal talent. But when the problem of selecting the appropriate educational path arises, at whatever age this may happen, the talents or abilities which can ue detected are already different from what they would have been under different conditions.

I do not mean that broadly formulated, long-range goals do not have any relevance for present-day societal policy. But it seems obvious that the direct objective cannot be anything other than the creation of conditions for the long-term goal – the self-realization of each individual in a new system of social relations.

One of the most important of these conditions seems to be equality, or at least *less inequality*, in people's working con- ditions and conditions of everyday life. This suggests that all a society has to do is to allocate resources in a less differentiated way, in other words to reduce income differences among the various social groups, classes or strata.

Following this logic it seems that the current system of dis- tribution is at the root of the prevailing inequalities and that only a thorough-going change in the distribution can assure social equality. This logic has permeated social action for a long time. In fact, over the last hundred years or so, since the emerg- ence of deliberate and more or less self-contained social policy in Central and Western Europe, the claims and action of social policy have centred on distribution. Such has been the case even with the majority of the radical critics of the *status quo*. This is not a new observation, of course. Marx pointed out that 'vulgar socialism (and from it, in turn, a section of democracy) has taken over from the bourgeois economists the consideration and treatment of distribution as independent of the mode of production and hence the presentation of socialism as turning principally on distribution'.[2]

The relations of distribution are certainly important and the reduction of inequalities inevitably requires their transformation. But it has to be realized that distribution is not an independent, self-determining field of social reality. Social life exists against the background of *social reproduction* and distribution is just one phase of this whole process. Societal policy, if it seeks to be relevant in reducing social inequalities and in contributing to the creation of new social relations has, then, to deal with the whole process.

1.2 Social reproduction

The problem of social reproduction – a favourite topic of nineteenth-century social philosophers and sociologists, but one which was later almost completely abandoned to economists – has recently aroused fresh interest among sociologists. This trend seems to be especially pronounced in France, as witnessed by the works of Bourdieu and Passeron,[3] Althusser and Balibar,[4] Balandier[5] and, more recently, Yves Barel.[6] Barel's book gives a detailed critical view of the various approaches to the problem of biological and social reproduction, together with

2. Karl Marx, *Critique of the Gotha Programme*, International Publishers, New York, 1938, p. 11.

3. Pierre Bourdieu and Jean-Claude Passeron, *La Reproduction*, Éditions de Minuit, Paris, 1970. This book deals mainly with the mechanisms of the transmission of culture and of social positions in general.

4. L. Althusser and E. Balibar, *Lire le Capital*, Maspero, Paris, 1965. Especially Balibar, 'Éléments pour une théorie du passage'.

5. G. Balandier, *Sens et puissance*, Presses Universitaires de France, Paris, 1971. Especially 'Dynamiques sociales'.

6. Y. Barel, *La Reproduction sociale (Systèmes vivants, invariance et changement)*, Éditions Anthropos, Paris, 1973.

the author's own theory, a complex global model of the reproduction of the various 'levels' of social life.

The renewed interest in social reproduction is probably related to current problems of social development, the growing role of economic and social planning (which translates into concrete, measurable terms the guidelines of economic or societal policy) and the difficulties encountered in this field. This is explicitly stated for instance by Barel, whose work was prompted by continued discussions with members of the French 'Commissariat Général du Plan'. The reappearance of the term 'social reproduction' shows a growing awareness of structural forces operating in historically determined social processes and of the complexity of intentional, quasi-intentional and 'non-intentional' processes. In my opinion it represents therefore a more promising approach to the problem of social dynamics than supra-historical functionalism or the behaviourist theory of social change.[7] However, even the most all-encompassing views on social reproduction hesitate to draw certain conclusions. They usually recognize and describe the various 'layers' of social life – from micro- to macro-levels, from natural to 'cultural' levels, from the biological to the social level and so on. What is usually lacking is the analysis of the nature of the relationships between these layers. No explanation is given of how they act upon each other, how changes in one affect the others, how they react to deliberately induced change, whether they react at all, or which are the layers able to trigger off structural change. At the same time, these issues are of the utmost importance for societal policy and planning.

I do not pretend to have answers to all these questions. Nevertheless, the 'model' of social reproduction described below, and directly related to some of Marx's and Lukács's ideas on the ontology of social life may bring us closer to some of the answers.

7. *The Planning of Change*, ed. W. G. Bennis, K. D. Benne and R. Chin, Holt, Rinehart and Winston, London, New York, Sydney, Toronto, 1970, presents a number of studies of a behaviourist orientation.

In the model proposed here the cycle of reproduction encompasses the reproduction of mankind and the production and reproduction of goods and services. All of these processes are taking place at any point in time within a given social structure so that the structure itself and the social relations underlying it are also constantly reproduced. The components may undergo more or less change during the process of reproduction: what is emerging is never the exact repetition of what existed previously. Nevertheless, the amount of change affecting the various components depends on a number of factors. (Thus, for instance, whether the reproduction of goods and services is simple or expanded depends essentially on the technological level of the productive forces already attained and on the nature of the social relations operating them.)

The cycle of the reproduction of goods and services covers the phases of their production and exchange, their distribution and redistribution, their consumption or utilization. The social relations governing and underlying the whole cycle emerge in the phase of production, or, conversely, the actual state and nature of the productive relations regulate the whole cycle. However, these basic 'productive' relations also undergo some alterations during the cycle of reproduction. Though they basically determine how the social product may be distributed, this is never a simple, one-way process: distribution and redistribution may also affect the relations of production in the strict sense. To give just two examples relevant to capitalist conditions: the pressure of the working class, depending on the forms and levels of its consciousness and on the strength of its organizations, may have a more or less significant influence on the distribution of the social product (or the surplus product) even if the nature of the ownership of the means of production (a productive relation itself) remains unchanged, that is, private. Similarly, the utilization of goods is clearly contingent on what is available once the social product has been distributed, but – especially with increasing resources – a wide variety of options is offered in the utilization of goods, affecting more or less crucially the 'original' state of affairs.

In this approach, historically as well as logically, the sphere of production has a crucial role. It is of prime interest *how*, among what social relations and under what technological and social conditions, the goods and services maintaining social life are reproduced. This leads us directly to the category of work and of the *social division of work*. (I use intentionally the expression *'division of work'* instead of 'division of labour'. The latter term usually refers to the technological aspects of work organization, while I emphasize the social contents of the first phase of the cycle of social reproduction.)

This approach may seem self-evident to some, hardly acceptable to others. Its acceptance or rejection is a philosophical rather than a sociological matter, depending on the epistemological and ontological principles one adheres to. This does not preclude a scientific debate on the subject, but one has to be clear about what is being discussed. It may be helpful if I spell out in more detail how I understand the role of work.

1.2.1 Work as a social category

Work as the central category of social existence is one of the main themes of Georg Lukács's great posthumous work, *The Ontology of Social Existence.*[8] His historical analysis gives a clue to the understanding of the link between work and the social structure. It shows how this attribute of man, the ability to work, already contains the germs of a division of work, and how the possibility of dividing work contains from the very beginning the possibilities of oppression, exploitation and alienation. This analysis cannot be reconstructed here in full, but one of the main arguments must be produced, even if in an extremely simplified way.

Lukács sees work, the central ontological category, as the model of all types of social praxis inasmuch as it always has a teleological character. It is not only purposeful, but this pur-

8. György Lukács, *Zur Ontologie des gesellschaftlichen Seins* (On the Ontology of Social Existence), in three volumes. The quotations follow the Hungarian edition, Magvető Kiadó, 1976.

pose is consciously set. Hence the overall importance of awareness and of knowledge in the work process. Even at the stage of the most primitive division of work, there appear two main *teleological aspects of work*. One type is oriented towards the *transformation* of *natural objects* (or natural forces) to make them serve human aims. This teleology and the work oriented by it relates man directly to nature and its objects. The other type of work teleology 'seeks *to exert an impact* on other people's *consciousness*' in order to induce them to act in a posited way.[9] With the evolution of work and the division of work – an extremely long historical process throughout which various forms of activity acquire an increasingly crystallized form owing to the evolution of language, and the possibility of transmitting and accumulating experience and knowledge – the second type of work teleology slowly becomes a separate sphere of action, a separate and largely autonomous complex within the social division of work. The long-lasting separation of 'manual' and 'intellectual' work was one of the consequences of this separation. And, even more crucial, this process also led to the formation of classes. It is the second type of teleology which man has been able to use, spontaneously or in an institutionalized way, as a means whereby one part of society could oppress the other part, to induce it to act in a predefined way. An explanation is hereby offered for the well-established historical connection 'between the systems of class domination and intellectual work'[10] – a connection which, however, has often been challenged: representatives of 'intellectual work' can and often have used their knowledge in the interests of the oppressed.

The ultimate aim and real essence of class domination is always the expropriation of the surplus product, or part of it. But the way in which this expropriation takes place – how far open coercion is used, what the possibilities for further development within the system are – always depends on the organization of the productive community. By this I mean the bond

9. Lukács, op. cit., Vol. II, p. 158.
10. ibid.

between the individual, the means of production and the community.[11]

The form of this bond varies with the evolution of the division of work which, in turn, follows and shapes the means of production. The main trend of socio-economic evolution in Europe has been characterized by various processes during which society has become even more interdependent, or, in Marx's or Lukács's term, more social. The reproduction of social life requires ever increasing co-operation between various parts of society. Within the sphere of production new means and new techniques of production have eliminated practically all previous forms of direct bond between the producer and his tools, creating new, capitalist ownership relations. This process has been accompanied by an intensive fragmentation of work activities, so that in many jobs even the first type of work teleology has been reduced to its lowest level, almost to the level of instinct. At the same time the ever-increasing complexity of social life has required, and a mounting level of productivity has made possible, the introduction of new mediators serving the normal course of reproduction. Again in Lukács's words: 'It sounds like a truism to state that beyond a certain point even economic reproduction would be unable to function without the emergence of non-economic fields of action.'[12] A need to regulate one or other element of the reproduction of social life may reappear again and again, and after a while it may take on a stable, crystallized form. Thus new professions and new institutions emerge which, on the face of it, have no connection with the production of material goods, but are, in fact, required by it and rooted in it. These new institutions and those who work in them fulfil a number of activities which belong to the second

11. The various historical forms of this bond were analysed in detail by F. Tőkei, especially in his book *A társadalmi formák elméletéhez* (On the Theory of Social Formations), Kossuth Kiadó, 1968. One of his works – relevant in this context and dealing with the Asiatic form of production – was published in several languages. (In German: *Zur Frage der Asiatischen Produktionsweise*, H. Luchterhand, Neuwied, Berlin, 1969.)

12. Lukács, op. cit., Vol. II, p. 378.

type of teleology and strengthen, in their turn, the differentiations and cleavages within society.

This brief description of the evolution of work and the social division of work explains why the division of work has a structural relevance and why it can be considered as the most important and most dynamic layer of the reproduction of social life. The approach presented here also offers a way of arriving at an analytical 'model' of the reproduction of social life.

1.2.2 Basic social relations of the division of work

On the basis of Lukács's analysis it becomes possible to examine more closely the web of social relations emerging from the social division of work and regulating it. The relations of domination and subordination – power, in short – originated in the separation of the two work teleologies. Once they emerged, they exerted a continuous influence on the evolution of the division of work, adding new elements to it, for example, by the separation and crystallization of certain functions, or the creation of permanent institutions or specialized agencies taking over these functions (like the state). The private expropriation of the means of production, that is, the emergence of the institution of private ownership at a certain point in history, was also connected with the separation of teleologies. The appearance of this relation changed the nature of the relations of domination somewhat. It offered a new basis for the exercise of power and at the same time offered a new type of legitimacy, especially in case of the expropriation of a part of the social product. A third important relation is more closely connected with the contents of the work performed. The various activities performed within the division of work have always required different types of skill, operating the different work teleologies. With the accumulation of experience, these skills have multiplied and have become increasingly crystallized. Again, specialized institutions have slowly emerged taking over the conservation, development and transmission of codified skills – reinforcing the former splits. Thus a definite pattern for the distribution of knowledge has taken shape.

In short, the social division of work has shaped, and has in turn been shaped by, the relations of power, property and knowledge. These relations have always been interconnected, but their character, their form, the institutions they were embedded in and their relative importance has varied considerably throughout history.

A full historical study is out of the question here. For my purposes it is sufficient to point out that present-day capitalist and socialist societies present different patterns in terms of these relations – with important consequences for social structure and social change.

The ownership of, or control over, the means of production, even if it is considered only an economic category, enables the owners (or controllers) to make the necessary decisions concerning the utilization of these means, to determine, by and large, the organization and conditions of work, and the composition of production. Therefore the owners have an opportunity to shape the structure of present and future needs; and also have a decisive role in the allocation of the resources created by production.[13] The main structural importance of the ownership relation stems, however, from the fact that it is not merely an economic category but is the foundation of power. Ownership gives access to means that are effective in forwarding the owners' particular interests.

If the structure is based on *private* ownership, as it is in contemporary capitalist economies, the particular interests referred to include the maintenance of *this* structure, especially because of the inheritability of property. And by definition, as it

13. This interconnection is recognized by a growing number of social thinkers. Thus we read in an article in *New Society*: 'Owners of wealth contribute to political campaigns ... and receive in return subsidies, tax-breaks and protection against reform. Since the economic system by itself will not distribute wealth more equitably, a political power is needed; but since political power is so intimately an outgrowth of economic power – the vicious circle is seemingly unbreakable. Perhaps this is what Marxists have in mind when they insist that equitable distribution is impossible as long as the means of production are privately owned' (P. Barnes, 'Fair Shares', 21 October 1972).

were, the owners command the resources for realizing this aim. They can exercise great (though for obvious reasons indirect) influence on the 'production' and dissemination of ideas and ideologies legitimizing the given structure. They also influence the operation of the organs of legislation and law enforcement (implying governmental action in the first place). Thus laws will largely operate in favour of the maintenance of the existing order. That is why I tend to agree with John Rex's formulation that despite some changes towards a 'mixed' economy, 'the thrust of the whole system [in Britain] still lies in the fact of industrial ownership lying in private hands; and the central dynamic of the system lies in the defence by the owning class of its interests'.[14] The abolition of private ownership is therefore – as I shall try to show later – of basic structural significance.

Power as a general social relation is viewed here as the relation linking the most important social groups or classes, determining the essential characteristics and, particularly, the dynamics, the direction of change in the given structure. I stress the 'social' aspect of the power relation and, indeed, of all the social relations discussed here, because there is a strong tendency in Western sociology to understand social relations as interpersonal or psychological ones. This restriction is especially marked in cases of power relations.[15]

The workings of power are related to and called into motion by the main social groups who in this process are using the means they command to forward their own interests. Forms of power (as C. W. Mills, among others, pointed out) may vary from direct coercion through indirect, postponed or hidden coercion and unobtrusive manipulation to legal pressure. The concrete form of the exercise of power always depends on the historical context. But power is always an organic component of the social 'fabric', even if it does not show, or is not 'felt' by the participants. Sometimes it is possible to ascertain the orientation of the power relation only indirectly, by analysing the

14. John Rex, 'Power', *New Society*, 5 October 1972.
15. One such approach may be found in R. Dahl, 'The Concept of Power', *Behavioral Science*, No. 2, 1957, pp. 201–15.

structural outcome of its workings, in other words its impact on basic social relations and the consequences generated by the evolution of these relations. For example, it can happen that while the political declarations or the social policy decisions of a country are expressly committed to social change and to the reduction of inequalities, the *ex post facto* statistical and sociological analysis of facts shows a different tendency, with no change or even an increase in inequalities. Thus one must draw one's conclusions about the real balance of power and the interests served by it from these facts. This indirect approach seems to be important for the analysis of the direction of power in both Eastern and Western countries. Unfortunately, this type of analytical balance sheet is rather scarce. An important exception, in England, is furnished by some early writings of Titmuss, and by some recent papers by Peter Townsend, Frank Field and others on the outcome of Labour or Conservative politics.[16] The present book is also, in a way, an analysis of this sort, showing whose interests have been served, or served better than others, by Hungarian societal policy over the last three decades.

It has already been pointed out that the nature of the ownership of the means of production is of crucial importance in the direction taken by the power relation. However, a change in the ownership relation does not at once alter the whole social scene. On the one hand, it is a long way from the abolition of private ownership to a fully developed socialist relation to the means of production, including democratic control over the use of these means. On the other hand, the transformation of the social organization of work, with the inherited separation, fragmentation and hierarchization of jobs, and the related differentiation in allocating various social values, privileges and disadvantages connected with work, does not immediately follow – far from it – the change of the ownership relations.

16. See for example R. Titmuss, *Income Distribution and Social Change*, Allen and Unwin, 1962; P. Townsend, *Sociology and Social Policy*, especially Chapters 20, 21 and 23, Allen Lane, London, 1975; and Frank Field, et al. *To Him Who Hath*, Penguin Books, Harmondsworth, 1977.

The organization of the social division of work has, in many respects, followed the former, capitalist, pattern even under the new socialist conditions. At least, this holds in the Hungarian case, where at the beginning of the socialist transformation all the negative aspects, fragmentation, extreme hierarchization, etc., of this division of work were already fully developed, while the level of economic and technological development still remained relatively low.

The third basic productive relation singled out here is that based on the different levels and types of *knowledge*, a relation that again still retains much of its old asymmetry. The social distribution of knowledge was – as implied in Lukács's description – always interwoven with the social division of work. This is, in fact, one of the most important roots of the historical schism between 'manual' and 'non-manual' work. Knowledge has always played a direct role in power-decisions, though the users of knowledge do not necessarily coincide with the 'knowers' themselves. The exercise of power only presupposes knowing how to use the knowledge of others. In any case, the connection between power and knowledge explains why all former class societies anxiously safeguarded the monopoly of certain types of knowledge. But in contemporary societies – Eastern and Western alike – where science has become a real productive force and where the role of power (and of the state) is increasing to a hitherto unknown degree, the knowledge relation acquires a new importance and, also, a considerable relative autonomy. That is why it is legitimate to treat it, at least, let us repeat, for the purposes of analysis, as a separate basic structural relation.

Under contemporary socialist conditions, ownership relations no longer preclude the transformation of the former distribution of knowledge. The process is, however, long and difficult. The monopoly of knowledge, unlike that of ownership, cannot be abolished by a revolutionary act. The difficulties in the case of knowledge lie partly in the prevailing structure of the division of work, and the interests generated by this division. Another problem is more specifically related to the historically evolved frameworks and methods for the transmission of knowledge. The unequal distribution of knowledge was assured in class societies, and especially under capitalist conditions, in such a refined way that it took a long time under the new conditions to understand its full underlying logic. It seemed at first that a change in the most conspicuous class characteristics (early educational selection, financial barriers in schools, etc.) would transform the system of the transmission of knowledge. It took a long time to realize that this was not the case, and Hungary is still in the process of trying to understand all the implications of the old system and introducing appropriate changes. To give just one example: it is clear that the duality of the school system (which will be described in more detail in Chapter 4) served, among other things, the limited transmission of knowledge connected with the second type of work teleology. The access to the knowledge of how to act upon the consciousness of others was open only to a minority, by and large to those in higher education destined to join or to serve directly the dominant class or groups.

It must be added that the social relevance of knowledge is not confined to its role as a productive relation or a relation built into the division of work. Certain types of knowledge have a major impact outside the social division of work, in the sphere of everyday life, in social contacts, in the utilization of resources, in acquiring and utilizing information and so on. But the distribution of *all* the different types of knowledge followed the same social pattern historically, so that in practice the inequality of the distribution was similar and interrelated for almost all types of knowledge. Thus the *asymmetries* of knowledge operating outside the division of work could not be counterbalanced; instead they reinforced the inequalities originating in the organization of production. Therefore a new, more equal distribution of knowledge is not only a condition and a consequence of changes in the social division of work, but also a condition and a consequence of a more homogeneous general social praxis.

1.2.3 *The social division of work and the social structure*

The three basic relations, ownership, power and knowledge, form a set. Taken together, they determine to a great extent the place that any individual may occupy in the social division of work and the *nature of the work* done by each individual. By this I mean, first, the greater or lesser complexity of the task, the level of skill or knowledge required by it and the level of decision-making (exercise of power) built into it. In fact, the three basic relations define, by and large, on any level of economic and social development, how the two main types of work teleology are 'blended' in any given job, which one is dominant, which one is entirely or partially absent. The notion of the nature of the work also includes aspects of the work connected with its object which inevitably reacts upon the performer (for example, the unpredictability of agriculture or mining, the technologically rational attitudes required in certain types of industrial work, certain behavioural patterns that affect some service workers, etc.). I also include here the level of autonomy and control an individual has over his own social activity and the contents and conditions of the work itself. The autonomy of the individual in his own social activity, and the contents and conditions of the work, in their turn, define the more or less limited opportunity of the individual to choose his work when entering the world of work and his opportunities to re-state, as he goes along, the aims, the object, the means or the pace of the work done.

In this way the system of all the relations linked to each other forms the social division of work. No doubt, on the face of it, this division appears in the form of a vast number of occupations, as a technological arrangement. *But the occupations gain their social significance from this system of relations. This is where their socially determining and differentiating strength comes from.* Otherwise one is never able to explain *why* the often used variable, occupation, has any social (or sociological) relevance at all. The structure of the social division of work with its inherent inequalities and hierarchies is stabilized by the fact that social activities take place within institutions which have their own history, hence their own somewhat autonomous organization and evolution, and their special impact on people, particularly in conserving the outward forms of interpersonal social relations. (Examples are offered by any social institution, from schools to public administration, not to mention the type of residence one inhabits. Since the historical split of 'town' and 'village' this is a factor which greatly influences living conditions and life chances.)

The whole process of socialization – the social milieu one is born into, including, besides the place of residence, the social position and social practices of the closest unit, the family – is another powerful factor of conservation of structural relations. The family transmits – apparently in a spontaneous and natural way – a system of dispositions, 'habitus' to use Bourdieu's word,[17] as well as all kinds of material or symbolic advantages and disadvantages. Thus even if the social position of the individual is not formally defined by birth, this social, economic and cultural inheritance weighs heavily on him and it takes an effort to weaken its consequences.

The inequalities and hierarchies embedded in the division of work are accentuated in the sphere of distribution and redistribution. The distribution of all social rewards, whether they are material or symbolic, follows by and large the same unequal pattern. I have already pointed out that this is not a one-way process. If the relations within the division of work fully determined distribution of rewards, deliberate social intervention in the sphere of distribution would be senseless and useless. This is clearly not the case. Under capitalist conditions the share of incomes between owners and wage-earners, the level of minimum wages or the part allocated to social benefits are all subject to a more or less peaceful 'bargain' among the different social groups. Especially in the last few decades these struggles have often resulted in significant successes for the dominated groups. But social practice also shows that these gains are not

17. See Pierre Bourdieu, *Outline of a Theory of Practice*, Cambridge University Press, 1977, especially pp. 78–87.

stable unless their basis is also changed in the sphere of work. Thus for instance collective bargaining may result in an increase of the minimum wage, but if this increase is not followed by steady endeavours to abolish the 'worst' types of jobs, then the newly acquired standard will not necessarily be maintained. Peter Townsend shows[18] that this has happened quite frequently in England in the last decade. Piven and Cloward have described this pattern for welfare benefits in the United States.[19]

The connection between the organization of work and the distribution of rewards may also take on a different form which does not imply a change in the legal regulations and does not entail formal withdrawals of rights. In Hungary in the fifties, for instance, legal or formal distribution of salaries and wages was more egalitarian than many of the basic relations within the social organization of work. This gap created various tensions, so that with the overt distribution and its formal rules unchanged there appeared a 'covert' distribution or redistribution, working on the margins of legality or even outside it. (This secondary distribution took the form of fringe benefits, reciprocated personal favours, tips, etc.) In this case too, change, or at least flexibility, is needed in the realm of the basic relations of work in order to stabilize a less unequal social distribution of incomes, of knowledge or of any other asset.

The full outcome of the mechanisms of production, distribution and redistribution is expressed by the 'global' social situation[20] both of the individual and of social groups. This situation incorporates, in addition to the set of the relations discussed above, the differential utilization of material and symbolic rewards, yielding different life conditions, differentiated levels and patterns of consumption and varied ways of life or life styles. The global social situation also encompasses the

18. P. Townsend, op. cit.

19. F. F. Piven and R. Cloward, *Regulating the Poor*, Vintage Books, New York, 1972.

20. This term is akin to the one coined by Marcel Mauss, but it is construed in a different way and therefore its meaning is somewhat different.

whole web of social relations, including direct and indirect contacts, with all that they imply in securing information, asserting one's interests and so on. Patterns of consumption, ways of life and social contacts are essentially determined by what one *does* and what one *earns*, but they are also more or less heavily influenced by individual or group interests and by more or less idiosyncratic, more or less socially defined values and ideologies. It must again be stressed that determining forces work both ways within the cycle of production. If, for instance, conditions of everyday life are changed (through distribution or redistribution), new values and attitudes may appear in consumption, new contacts may be formed, hence a new interest may arise in obtaining more information and knowledge, and this may ultimately lead to changes in the work situation. But the basic direction of determining forces starts from the world of work.

That is why it is true that the social groupings, classes or strata which are formed by the way work is organized may also be used in describing the global social situation of individuals or groups, or, to put it more bluntly, that is why occupational groups may be used as explanatory variables in the case of any social phenomenon. In Hungary, detailed studies of various aspects of social differentiation show that the occupational groups which help to highlight structural inequalities are the following:

People at high levels of decision-making (senior administrators, managers)

People at high levels of the knowledge-monopoly (professionals)

People working on lower levels of decision-making (local or organizational administrators)

People performing other subordinated jobs connected with the exercise of the second type of work teleology (office workers, etc.)

People performing jobs involving mainly the first type of teleology (transformation or manipulation of natural objects) at various levels of skill (knowledge) under different conditions, with various contents, i.e.

$$
\left.\begin{array}{l}
- \text{skilled} \\
- \text{semi-skilled} \\
- \text{unskilled}
\end{array}\right\} \text{workers in} \left\{\begin{array}{l}
\text{agriculture,} \\
\text{industry,} \\
\text{transport,} \\
\text{services}
\end{array}\right.
$$

Research done by using the above categories[21] (in a more operational way) has suggested not only that they were important explanatory variables, but also that they justified an even stronger formulation: while social phenomena are certainly shaped by a number of different social, economic, cultural and psychological factors, their most important common denominator is the position occupied in the social division of work: *there is no other social factor which would be of comparable universal relevance.*

If we take into account these elements describing the workings of structural relations, we arrive at the sketch overleaf, which may help to highlight the salient points of the reproduction of social relations.

1.3 Social equality and collective vertical mobility

The basic structural process of socialist evolution requires the gradual lessening of inequalities which have a social basis or social relevance. This is the process often described as the disappearance of classes and strata, or sometimes as the social homogenization of society. The crucial issue is the transformation of the social division of work, and the ability of the present socialist society to transform work itself in the direction described above, in other words to assure the sense and the worth of work by reuniting the two teleologies and lessening the asymmetries of the basic relations.

It must be stressed that this process does not imply the abolition of *all types* of differentiation. Structural policy (societal

21. Especially Zs. Ferge, *Társadalmunk rétegeződése* (The Stratification of Hungarian Society), Közgazdasági és Jogi Kiadó, 1969.

THE REPRODUCTION OF THE SOCIAL STRUCTURE
(based on the analysis of contemporary Hungary)

The cycle has no 'starting point', but at any given time there is an 'input'. This can be understood as consisting, basically, of

— the given social structure
— the given level of development of the means of production, the level of accumulated social experience, the state of man's domination of nature.

A. Basic structural relations formed within the social organization of work

The cycle of the formation of social relations:

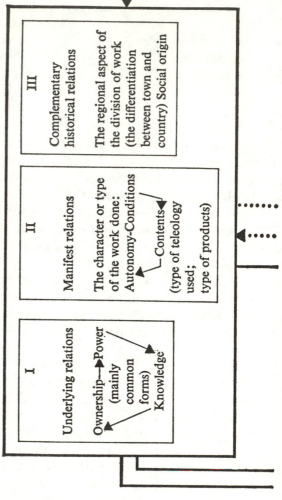

I	II	III
Underlying relations	Manifest relations	Complementary historical relations
Ownership→Power (mainly common forms) Knowledge	The character or type of the work done: Autonomy-Conditions →Contents (type of teleology used; type of products)	The regional aspect of the division of work (the differentiation between town and country) Social origin

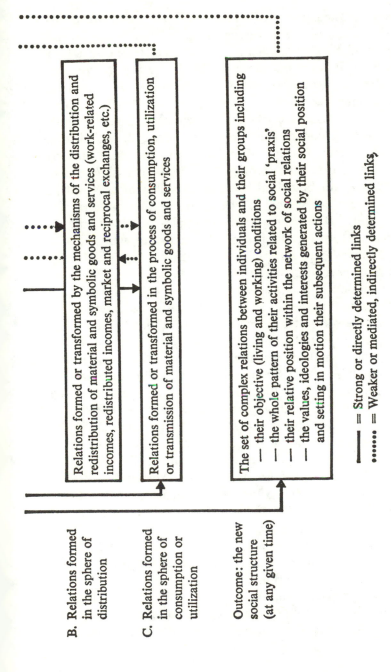

B. Relations formed in the sphere of distribution

Relations formed or transformed by the mechanisms of the distribution and redistribution of material and symbolic goods and services (work-related incomes, redistributed incomes, market and reciprocal exchanges, etc.)

C. Relations formed in the sphere of consumption or utilization

Relations formed or transformed in the process of consumption, utilization or transmission of material and symbolic goods and services

Outcome: the new social structure (at any given time)

The set of complex relations between individuals and their groups including

— their objective (living and working) conditions
— the whole pattern of their activities related to social 'praxis'
— their relative position within the network of social relations
— the values, ideologies and interests generated by their social position and setting in motion their subsequent actions

—— = Strong or directly determined links

•••••• = Weaker or mediated, indirectly determined links,

policy) is interested only in those *differences* which are trans-muted into *inequalities*, implying thereby a *cumulative* and *lasting*, even inheritable handicap in work, in distribution and in life in general. It must be remembered that a far from negli-gible number of these inequalities are not rooted in the struc-tural relations but have a biological or psychological background. In these cases the *causes* usually cannot be abol-ished – though the consequences may be alleviated. (This is one of the main spheres of action of social policy in the strict sense.) In a number of cases the 'biological' origin of a handicap is spurious: there can be a biological difference which is not in itself a handicap but which has become one through the me-diation of work. Illness or age are examples of disadvantages directly related to psychological or physical state, while sex- or race-related handicaps are examples of the type indirectly linked with the psychological or physical state.

The elimination of social inequalities, if effected through the process described above, does not signify the enforcement of uniformity or an impoverishment brought about by the abol-ition of variety in social values. The transformation of the div-ision of work implies essentially *vertical*, not *horizontal* changes. Inequalities and hierarchies must decline or even dis-appear in the long run, but the different kinds of work (implying specialization) will probably persist. This will be one of the bases of variety, the other being the real and many-sided de-velopment of the individual. Thus a 'loss' in inequalities must go together, in this perspective, with a gain in differentiation, with the multiplication of goods, values, tastes and attitudes. But these differences will no longer be the more or less direct outcomes of hierarchized social positions; they should instead be a genuine expression of individual choice. Human society is inconceivable without various historical and social deter-minants – but a socially determined system of inequalities must not be considered the only possibility.

In this perspective, equality is not an end in itself for the socialist society. Nor does Marxism define socialist and commu-nist societies in terms of equality. But in order to approach the basic social goals, equal or similar standards of living are a self-evident *precondition*. Therefore the reduction of basic inequalities becomes a natural and obvious aim, in the present as well as in the foreseeable future, for societal policy carried out in part by social policy as described in Chapter 2 – all the more so because the more distant goals, such as the new relations between the individual and the community or the self-fulfilment of the individual, cannot be formulated as immediate targets of social policy. In other words, the first task is the creation of the conditions for further evolution. This implies that at a given point in history social equality (with a well-defined and historically changing content) or, more realistically, the reduction of existing inequalities may be viewed as an immediate end. Problems arise from this formulation only if it is forgotten that this end is itself only a step towards, or an instrument for, further social evolution. In this case equality may easily become a formally defined term whose implications have become distorted. Instead of helping future development, it then becomes the prime obstacle of evolution, with the forced abolition of all types of variety and differentiation, and therefore of all sources of change. This is, in fact, the major criticism of all types of 'primitive communism', which in Marx's words 'cannot but make want general'.[22] 'This development of productive forces . . . is absolutely necessary as a practical premise: firstly, for the reason that without it only *want* is made general, and with want the struggle for necessities and all the old filthy business would necessarily be reproduced.'

This, clearly, is neither a desirable nor a viable solution. For practical purposes, however, it is fundamental to decide how much and which types of inequality can be abolished at any given point without harming the germs of future evolution; and how much inequality, or which types of it, are tolerable without the risk of their becoming the sources of further, possibly more serious inequalities. In a sense *this* is the basic, the most intricate dilemma of a socialist societal and social policy in the conditions we face. What is more, there does not seem to be a

22. *The German Ideology*, op. cit., p. 24.

clear-cut, theoretical answer to this problem. The practical solutions have to be adapted to the ever-changing social reality,
and have to take into account the current tendencies in the
change of social inequalities.

The most important elements of this process are related to the
absolute and relative positions of the various social classes and
strata as defined by the social division of work. Social evolution
may take on various forms. Social development may mean that
each group acquires advantages, but without a deformation of
the structure. Bourdieu describes, for instance, in contemporary
capitalist societies, compensatory mechanisms which help the
various groups to keep their original relative positions.[23] In
such a case there is an upward shift in the whole structure, but
the *order*, in its double meaning, is maintained. In this case the
objective conditions of all the groups may improve without a
decrease in social inequalities and the tensions they generate.

The requirements of social evolution described here as desirable for a socialist society imply the *absolute* improvement of
the situation of each group accompanied by a *diminution of the
distances between them*. This is an inter-group movement implying a change in the relative positions of the groups. The whole
process may be described in different terms, but the concept of
collective mobility seems to me to be rather well adapted to the
process in question. Social *group mobility*, a term coined by
Sorokin, has various types[24] according to whether inter-group
social distances are growing or decreasing, whether relative
positions remain stable or change. A revolutionary change –
like the one experienced in Hungary in the first years after 1945
– is accompanied by an almost complete reversal of the structure. The lessening (or abolition) of social inequalities in present
Hungarian conditions requires a special type of group mobility.
This implies that on the basis of a general economic, social and

23. Pierre Bourdieu, Luc Boltanski and Monique de Saint-Martin, 'Les
Stratégies de reconversion', *Social Science Information*, October 1973, pp.
112–13.
24. See, in more detail: Zs. Ferge, 'The Relation between School and
Social Structure', *Sociological Review Monograph*, Keele University, 1972.

cultural evolution there should be absolute improvements in the situation of all the relevant groups, but groups which are worst off, which in the past have suffered the effect of the accumulation of disadvantages, should experience a more rapid improvement than the others.

The term 'collective mobility' seems to be useful for several reasons. 'Mobility' in itself refers to the dynamic nature of the process. The adjective 'collective' reflects the collective nature of social aims, the importance of collective interests, the requirement of the simultaneous ascent of the individual *and* the collectivity. Hence it refers to *solidarity* in social relations – a concept which is slowly being rediscovered in our time.[25] At the same time, it is an important homologue to the concept of individual mobility, except that it describes the movement of groups within society instead of the movement of individuals.

Since there are frequent endeavours to evaluate and rank contemporary societies on the basis of the frequency and nature of individual mobility, the concept of collective mobility also serves to show the limitations of this approach. In fact, individual mobility is a double-edged phenomenon. According to the circumstances, it may serve not only the transformation but also the conservation of a given social structure, if, for instance, it continually draws away from the oppressed classes their most gifted members, absorbing them – after a full process of assimilation – in the ruling classes. Individual upward mobility is not necessarily accompanied by downward moves. In contemporary societies, Hungary among them, the main trend is upward individual mobility entailing an increase in the number of members of the higher strata. This type of individual mobility is certainly an important element in maintaining the openness of society, in assuring opportunities for individuals to improve their situation. However, it *does not challenge* the ab-

25. See for example E. J. Hobsbawm, 'Fraternity', *New Society*, 27 November 1975; or Albert Tévoedjré, *For a Contract of Solidarity*, Report of the Secretary General on the World Symposium on the Social Implications of a New International Economic Order, January 1975, International Institute for Labour Studies, Geneva.

solute advantage of some strata over others, and does not imply the decreases of such advantages.

Collective mobility, by contrast, is used to describe a structural process which involves simultaneously an upward shift *and* a transformation of the relations within the given structure. That is why individual mobility data should not be used to judge the orientation or amount of social change, as is explicitly or implicitly done in some cases.[26] This is also why indicators of collective mobility are useful in planning or checking the results of societal policy interventions.

1.4 Societal or structural policy

This structure of social situations or positions may be affected in a number of ways, depending on the point of the cycle of reproduction at which intervention is to occur. But according to the logic outlined above, important and durable structural changes must be started in the sphere of the relations of work. That is why the abolition of private ownership may entail fundamental social consequences.

It has already been pointed out that the new socialist property relations do not immediately alter all the other relations of production. This means that the historically evolved hierarchies still persist, together with a division of work that still means the division of the workers. What then is the real significance of the abolition of private ownership? It is that the interests of private ownership no longer shape the power structure and no longer dominate the evolution of the social structure. It also means that they do not shape the institutions, such as the market, that help (and because of their self-regulating character, help very effectively) to preserve the *status quo,* nor do they shape corresponding liberal individualistic ideologies.

26. This is for example one of the underlying ideas of the bulk of S. M. Lipset's work on social mobility since his *Social Mobility in Industrial Society* (with R. Bendix), University of California Press, 1959. See also: S. M. Lipset, 'Social Mobility and Equal Opportunity', *The Public Interest,* 1972, No. 72.

The theoretical implication of this change is that the absence of the former rigid basis of the social structure and the abolition of the vested interests accompanying it *make the structure more flexible, more open to change.*

One of the characteristics of a socialist society is that it is gradually transforming itself, that it tries to affect its whole structure in an *intentional* way. Its main goal is to serve the interests of the working class through the 'self-abolition' of this class. In this sense it is still a class society, oriented by the long-term historical interests of the former oppressed class. But its class character has to be seen as transitory. Since in the former society the existence of the working class stemmed from its relation to the propertied class, the first condition for its disappearance as a class is the abolition of this relationship. However, this is only a first condition. The other aspects of an industrially advanced (capitalist) class society are changed less easily. The process of transforming the whole division of work shaped by the fixed character of the means of production is long and difficult. All the more so because a thorough-going social reorganization of this type is likely to slow down, at least temporarily, the economic growth and efficiency of the country when economic growth is still absolutely crucial both for social development and for overall political reasons.

It must also be remembered that this is not an automatic process. While mechanisms that are working in an almost self-regulatory way for the *maintenance and conservation* of the given structure come into being relatively easily in any society, there is no precedent for a spontaneous, self-regulatory, mechanism that would run *against* the *status quo*, promoting in a legally approved, institutionalized way *the transformation of the given structure.* We have, then, to face a fairly complex set of dilemmas in societal policy:

● Socialist evolution is based on a more reflexive social praxis than the evolution of former societies, because it is oriented towards deliberately set aims. Thus deliberate intervention and regulation are needed in social affairs. But deliberate intervention is liable to lead to errors being committed. Social reality is extremely complex, so that the knowledge on which intervention is based can hardly be exact. Also, because of the present nature of the structure, there is a variety of different, sometimes opposed interests so that the knowledge relating to social affairs can hardly be entirely objective or unbiased.

• Socialist evolution implies structural change from a more unequal to a less unequal structure of objective conditions, interests and values. The lessening of inequality means that there are not only winners but also losers. The loss may be real as in case of the reduction of fringe benefits. More frequently it is relative; in other words the loss implies the weakening of a monopoly. The abolition of the monopoly of knowledge, for instance, does not mean a real loss, only the loss of a relative advantage. It differs essentially from the elimination of monopolies in, for example, ownership. But even the relative losers may present resistance to change, and may bring about a more overt intervention on the part of central government.

• After three decades of socialist development in Hungary, most of society adheres to the cause of socialism. Overt intervention, especially direct coercion, may harm the already established relative integration of society. It is therefore desirable to diminish the amount of overt and direct intervention. Furthermore, as is well known, the real implementation and stabilization of new achievements requires the inner identification of a majority.

There is, then, a historical paradox involved: durable results have to be based on spontaneous and self-regulatory mechanisms. But institutionalized self-regulatory mechanisms have always been geared towards the maintenance of the structure. The problem is how the conservative character of institutionalized, spontaneous mechanisms can be changed.

One of the solutions seems to be the strengthening of the self-regulatory nature of deliberately established new processes of transformation. Thus the transformation of the social division of work must be started deliberately. Once this is set in motion and accompanied by changes in the distribution of knowledge, decentralized and spontaneous initiatives may – indeed must – occur to carry on this task. The other solution lies in the strengthening of the dynamic, transforming aspects of inherited self-regulatory mechanisms such as the school or the family.

In these processes the role of social awareness and of socialist ideology cannot be over-estimated. But it is also clear that there is a strong dialectic relationship between socialist social consciousness and the objective conditions: consciousness and ideology never operate in a vacuum.

The role of societal or structural policy is, then, to help to create institutional frameworks for this type of evolution. According to the logic of social determinants, it is of the utmost importance in the sphere of production, where it assures tangible and institutional frameworks for the transformation of the social division of work. However, since the most important social inequalities are still generated in the realm of production, it is also in this field that the endeavours of transformation will meet the strongest obstacles. Thus these changes require rather a long period of time. In order to shorten this period and to solve current problems, societal policy, mainly by means of social policy institutions, also has to devise ways of intervening in the other spheres of the cycle of reproduction, especially in distribution and redistribution. Finally, to avoid neglecting the present in the name of the future, societal policy – again through social policy – has also to deal with manifest difficulties, disadvantages and deprivations that are partly or fully independent of the cycle of reproduction. (All the more so because such difficulties or disadvantages, though arising independently of the cycle of reproduction, may have repercussions on the structural relations. An example of such a disadvantage is illness.)

The implementation of societal or structural policy will be marked by tensions and value clashes between short-term and long-term objectives, between social and economic objectives and between groups that are affected more or less favourably by any new measure. All these tensions have an impact on the outcome of deliberate intervention, requiring constant checks and modifications in the orientation or type of measures.

1.5 People and policy-making

In discussing social policy-making in Hungary, I often refer to the responsiveness of government or central decision-making bodies to tensions or to the popular state of mind. In fact, each government needs reliable channels of information transmitting strongly felt popular wishes, although the specific mode of operation varies.

In a social system committed to continuous and planned social change, the information-gathering networks perform an important function in providing feedback information not only about the reactions to past accomplishments, but also about responses to pre-announced steps. Furthermore, a better knowledge of people's needs and expectations helps the central organs to choose among possible alternatives. In order to show how this policy requirement is handled in Hungary, I shall mention some of the most widespread networks.

1. The nationwide network of local (regional or workplace) organs of the Socialist Workers' Party as well as local representatives of voluntary organizations or movements (like trade unions or the youth movement) systematically keep their organizational centres informed about popular responses and wishes. If a particular problem is mentioned with some frequency or persistency, this is a signal to the government that new measures are needed.

2. The second permanent communication channel conveys individual judgements about matters of public interest. The individuals using this channel have a legal right to approach any public authority with their own observations and the authorities are legally obliged to respond to such individual initiatives within a predefined, relatively short period of time. This channel has a fairly large capacity for conveying communications: the number of observations amounts to hundreds of thousands

each year. The matters dealt with range from complaints about small details such as bad street lighting to major issues related, for example, to fundamental educational policies or matters concerning wage claims and working conditions.

Such spontaneous communications as 'letters to the editor' or comments addressed to the radio or TV networks perform similar functions and are fairly popular, although there is no legal measure to guarantee feedback in the case of the issues touched upon in this way.

3. A significant amount of information relevant to social policy originates from social research agencies. Market research institutions and a public opinion research centre constantly test the public opinion about short-term issues and immediate concerns. Social science research institutes of an academic nature gather complex and more general long-range information. The findings of these surveys are usually published, and some of the most important results relevant to policy are presented in a condensed form to the policy-makers most directly concerned.

4. Legislative programmes of considerable scope and significance – such as the family code, the pending school reform or the guidelines for long-term planning – are developed with the contribution of special *ad hoc*, or sometimes standing, committees recruited from groups drawn from various backgrounds. The activities of the various committees result in the application of scientific research findings as well as lay opinions to policy problems.

It may be seen, then, that there is a deliberate attempt in Hungary to gather relevant information, and also to combine the perspectives of different, more or less well-informed, more or less articulate social groups living in the most varied conditions, in order to transcend one-sided (for example exclusively administrative or intellectual) concerns and interests. In this way the knowledge upon which the interventions of societal policy are based may become more adequate, more exact, less subject to erroneous interpretations.

Chapter 2

The Emergence of Social Policy

2.1 Societal policy and social policy

Social policy has emerged historically as a palliative or corrective instrument intended to cope with imminent social problems endangering the *status quo*. In this very general sense one could say that each organized society has had a 'social policy', since each has had to cope with problems. However, social policy as a more or less clearly circumscribed sector of governmental activity did not take shape until the seventeenth or eighteenth century, and only in countries where capitalism was beginning to appear. It was a response to the challenge of a new type of society where the economic sphere and the relations which were apparently economic became separated from all other social and political spheres and relations, where the economic motive became the most clear-cut and most universal motive, where the economic interest began to dominate all other interests, and where the most pervasive economic mechanism, the market, apparently based on individual freedom, no longer assured the livelihood of all the members of a community.

Earlier societies – and Karl Polanyi has probably done most to prove this point[1] – had built-in institutions to avoid mass famine and to assure the survival of their members, even if these institutions could and sometimes did break down, and even if the right to survive hardly ever meant the right of every member of the society to survive equally well. The institutions

1. Karl Polanyi, *The Great Transformation. The Political and Economic Origins of Our Time*, New York, 1944, London, 1945. *Trade and Market in the Early Empires: Economies in History and Theory*, ed. K. Polanyi, C. M. Arensberg and H. W. Pearson, Glencoe, Ill., 1957. *Primitive, Archaic and Modern Economies. Essays of Karl Polanyi*, ed. George Dalton, Doubleday, New York, 1968.

in question were not economic. All of them – the reciprocity based on solidarity in tribal societies or rural communities, the central collection and redistribution of goods in early empires, the paternalistic feeling of obligation to provide for all those who were related by some bond to the lord under feudal con-ditions, or state regulations setting rates of pay or limiting the prices of vital goods (primarily grain) in many pre-capitalist societies – combined economic and other principles, interests and relations. Motives of honour and prestige, considerations of status, religious, traditional or legal obligations, fears of all kinds of punishments were all interwoven, and together they regulated productive as well as other activities. Again in Pol-anyi's words, the economic system proper was enmeshed in the web of all kinds of social relationships. There was no auton-omous economy – and therefore there could not be an auton-omous or independent institution to counteract the harms caused by the economy.

Social policy as we know it corresponds to a new situation. It is a slowly evolving artificial instrument which tries to correct the malfunctioning of the self-regulating economic system which has taken over the domination of society.

Originally, social policy was *not* the *negation* of the capitalist system. On the contrary, it adhered to the basic tenets of the new society – that the economy had 'natural' laws which should not, and indeed could not, be violated, and that man was essen-tially economically motivated and stimulated, either by the fear of want or by the desire of gain. Hence, social policy never sought to interfere with the basic economic arrangements and confined itself to *ex post facto* corrections of the natural out-come (such as income redistribution on a reduced scale). Its interventions were entirely concerned with ensuring that people had the 'right' motivation. Hence the long-prevalent principle of rejecting the 'non-deserving' in favour of the 'deserving' poor – who had the right motivation, but happened to be temporarily unfortunate. The other main principle of social policy, 'less eligibility' – that even poorly paid or heavy jobs should be more attractive than social benefits – can also be explained by the concern not to damage the economy. This underlying logic also helps us to understand why social policy has long been impregnated by the paternalistic and charitable spirit of pre-capitalist redistributive practice. Its benefits could not be seen as rights, because the feeling of security stemming from rights would have threatened the economic motive needed by the market – the fear of want. The cautious concessions based on these considerations yielded only to pressures exercised by an increasingly better organized working class, or by the imminent danger of the system collapsing, as in the case of the world crisis of the 1930s, or again by the threat presented by the birth of socialist societies, first after the Russian Revolution in 1917, later by the emergence of other socialist states after the Second World War.

From its inception to our days, and everywhere where the market is a dominating force, social policy has been torn by this basic conflict. It was created to fill a vacuum, to ensure the individual's right to survive – a right accepted by most societies as a fundamental right and categorically negated by the market logic. And yet social policy could not assume this self-imposed task unconditionally as long as it was reluctant to jeopardize the dominance of the market economy.

2.2 The clash of values in social policy thinking in market economies

This conflict has always marked not only the activities of social policy, but also the theory behind it. Since basic and conflicting social interests are at stake, no consensus is conceivable: the current definitions of the scope, the role or the tasks of social policy depend on the ideological positions and political or social commitments of the authors.

Some may go as far towards conservatism as to reject even the Bismarckian wisdom of appeasing the workers' unrest by 'mixing a few drops of social oil in the recipe of the state',[2] and

2. 'Sie werden genötigt sein dem Staate ein paar Tropfen sozialen Öles im Rezepte beizusetzen, wieviel, weiss ich nicht.' Speech in the Reichstag, 12 June 1882.

deny the necessity of practically any social intervention.[8]

Most social policy thinkers adopt the view which Richard Titmuss called the 'conventional, handbook definition' of social policy.[4] Here the task of social policy is seen as that of correcting the deficiencies of the market and ensuring that those left outside the stream of production are maintained at least on a minimum level of personal and social functioning'.[5]

The spokesmen of the Welfare State usually go somewhat further than the handbook definition in terms of benefit sharing and explicitly adhere to the ideals of equity and even of equality. None the less, the dilemma I have referred to – the necessity of interfering with the market and the impossibility of doing so – also appears in their writings. An argument of T. H. Marshall,[6] reproduced here in an abbreviated form, may highlight the point. Marshall says that the Welfare State believes in equality, therefore its plans must be based on the assumption that every individual is a potential candidate for any post in society. The community is composed of individuals, and the 'Welfare State regards each individual's right to welfare as sacred, and believes in *individual freedom*. Although, of course, like all States, it uses some compulsion, it *must rely on individual choice and motivation for* the fulfilment of its purposes in all their details.'[7] However, individuals differ from each other. In such circumstances the belief in equality is supplemented by the belief that '. . . the Welfare State, as we know

3. In Milton Friedman's view, for instance, practically no state intervention is warranted. If, however, hardships caused for example by poverty need to be alleviated, the ideal solution would be 'private charity directed at helping the less fortunate as an example of the proper use of freedom' (Milton Friedman, *Capitalism and Freedom*, University of Chicago Press, 1962, p. 195).

4. Richard Titmuss, *Commitment to Welfare*, Allen and Unwin, 1968, p. 188.

5. *Social Welfare Institutions*, ed. Mayer N. Zald, John Wiley, New York, 1965, p. 3.

6. T. H. Marshall, 'Social Selection in the Welfare State', in *Class, Citizenship and Social Development*, Doubleday Anchor, New York, 1965, pp. 259–79.

7. ibid., p. 260. Italics added.

it, must necessarily preserve a measure of economic inequality ...' and 'positive action, by improving the physical
conditions in poorer families and by stimulating greater interest
and ambition among apathetic parents, can only be a very slow
process. Family differences will continue to have their influence
as long as the family is the basic cell in the social structure.'[8]
This is a fact that the Welfare State can hardly attempt to alter.
Thus, in the end, while it is true that mechanisms of selection in
education have an influence which is contrary to the basic principles of the Welfare State, and while it is true that, because of
the unequal structure, the ideal of equality which we started with
turns into inequality again, this has to be accepted as inevitable.

The problems of structural economic change are not discussed overtly by some progressive British social politicians.
Yet their demands often reflect how necessary they feel this
change to be. One of the most significant representatives of this
line of thought was Richard Titmuss, who years ago declared
that the main problem for social policy, under the existing
conditions in Britain, was not poverty but inequality. Titmuss
clearly saw that 'in effect, social security' (which is used here
more or less as a synonym for social policy) 'has to be seen as an
agent of structural change: not as a system reflecting and legitimizing the *status quo*.'[9] This viewpoint led him to a critical
evaluation of the mechanisms of British social policy, and to
the analysis of some measures which ultimately produce effects
contrary to the original goals. Thus, for example, it was he who
showed that the prime beneficiaries of the post-1948 legislation,
which practically created the Welfare State, were the middle
class rather than the working class.[10] It was on this basis that he
arrived at the conclusion, which is radically opposed to the
market logic, that social policy benefits must not be accepted as
concessions, but achieved as rights.[11]

8. ibid., p. 272.
9. R. M. Titmuss, *Commitment to Welfare*, op. cit., p. 185.
10. See, among others, R. M. Titmuss, *Income Distribution and Social
Change*, Allen and Unwin, 1962.
11. See, for example, 'Social Policy and Economic Progress', in *Commitment to Welfare*, op. cit., pp. 153–64.

The inherent limitations of the traditional social policy approach and the necessity of structural change are appearing with increasing frequency in the writings of, for example, Richard Cloward and Frances Fox Piven, S.M. Miller and Peter Townsend.[12] This line of thought has recently gained in theoretical clarity and in outspokenness in many Western countries. At some point it is realized by many of those who adopt this view — mainly but not exclusively those who openly accept the Marxist approach — that there is a theoretical and practical incompatibility between the market economy based on private ownership and a real social policy. They thus maintain that effective and lasting solutions to such problems as structural poverty and unemployment require a radical change in present institutions, and first of all in the economic organization of contemporary capitalism.[13]

It is at this point that traditional social policy changes its character, that it becomes more normative than corrective, and that it ceases to confine itself to the non-economic sphere counteracting the economy. In my view this is not a slight shift but a dramatic change and points towards a new type of social policy, rejoining societal or structural policy.

Societal or structural policy, as defined in Chapter 1, is a fairly ambitious concept. It implies the project of deliberately changing the profile of a society, of altering basic social, human relations. This project is oriented by values which express the secular desires of the oppressed as witnessed by a long series of

12. See, for example, Frances Fox Piven and Richard Cloward, *Regulating the Poor. The Functions of Public Welfare*, Random House, New York, 1971; Richard Cloward and F. F. Piven, *Politics of Turmoil*, Pantheon Books, New York, 1975; Peter Townsend, 'The Social Underdevelopment of Britain 1970–1974', in *Sociology and Social Policy*, Allen Lane, 1975; *Poverty, Inequality and Class Structure*, ed. Dorothy Wedderburn, Cambridge University Press, 1974.

13. Ralph Miliband, 'Politics and Poverty', in *Poverty, Inequality and Class Structure*, op. cit.; *Problems in Political Economy: An Urban Perspective*, ed. David M. Gordon, D. C. Heath, Lexington, Mass., 1977; John Westergaard and Henrietta Resler, *Class in a Capitalist Society*, Heinemann Educational Books, 1975.

historical upheavals or revolutions, and which serve the interests of a vast majority. Societal policy also covers a vast field. The basic relations to be transformed by it include economic, cultural and power-related elements alike, and have a direct or indirect bearing on almost all kinds of human bonds, activities and concerns. Societal policy is neither economic nor non-economic; its target is to reintegrate the economic and the social sphere by putting an end to the almost complete hegemony of the economic interest which dominated capitalist society. (This does not necessarily mean that economic policy and societal policy cannot coexist. As long as the reintegration of the economy is still a long-range objective, a separate economic policy may in fact be needed.)

Societal policy is, then, a normative rather than a palliative instrument. It belongs to the social praxis of societies that are explicitly committed to socialist and communist goals – a feature characterizing only present-day socialist societies.

This brief consideration of history suggests that societal policy presupposes the abolition of the domination of the market, while some kind of social policy is a necessary corollary of a market economy. It does not follow, however, that the existence of a broadly conceived societal or structural policy makes all the activities belonging to corrective or palliative social policy unnecessary, or that social policy becomes superfluous after the abolition of the domination of the capitalist market economy. At least, on the basis of Hungarian experience, and under conditions characterizing present-day Hungary, a strong case can be made for the coexistence of these two policies – though a clearly defined societal policy gives a new orientation to social policy.

2.3 The historical background of Hungarian social policy

A historical process somewhat different from that of Western Europe marked the emergence of social policy in Hungary, and it still makes its impact felt on present-day Hungarian social policy thinking.

A rather turbulent history frequently disrupted the pre-industrial charity system, often weakened the feudal principle of *noblesse oblige*, and delayed the appearance of state social policy. Without wanting to go too far back into the past, certain relevant events must be mentioned in order to explain this delay. In the sixteenth and seventeenth centuries Hungary underwent a disastrous Turkish occupation lasting 150 years. The expulsion of the Ottomans, in whose defeat Austria played a major role, was followed by a long struggle to obtain independence from the Habsburg Empire. This again decimated the country and resulted in a compromise in 1711: the formal independence from and factual submission to Austria. The rebel nobility who had carried on the fight for independence was almost entirely replaced by a loyal and monarchist aristocracy (partly of Hungarian but mainly of Austrian origin) chiefly concerned with its own privileges. The new aristocracy not only gave up the autonomy of the country, but became the strongest opponent of the enlightened reformism of Joseph II whenever he tried to interfere with feudal prerogatives – including his attempts at some social policy measures.

The end of the eighteenth and beginning of the nineteenth century were marked by the awakening of national feelings (aroused partly by the Habsburgs' forced Germanization of Hungary) and of the emergence of a politically progressive gentry deeply influenced by the ideas of the French Revolution. The radicalization of the movement and the influence of the revolutions starting with Paris in 1848 resulted in a heroic revolution in Hungary, too. It was again defeated by the joint forces of Austria and Russia and provoked a bloody repression for another ten years. Political independence was still not achieved, but the first revolutionary measures of 1848 abolished the worst institutions of feudalism, beginning with serfdom. The country remained in turmoil until the compromise of 1867, when the Austro-Hungarian Monarchy was formed. It was only then that relatively peaceful conditions opened the way to rapid capitalist development and significant economic growth.

The decades of relative independence and prosperity lasting

from about 1870 to 1914 were favourable to the progressive ideas initiated by the reform movement of the 1830s. Some of the laws enacted in this period were among the most progressive in Europe (for instance the law on public education and the public health service). The workers' movement also became strong enough to force the state at the end of the century to enact some Bismarckian social policy measures (insurance schemes).

However, the new tendencies did not affect the country as a whole. Agriculture – the most important economic branch by far – remained semi-feudal. Serfs were liberated, but only a few obtained land and the majority became landless labourers and hired farm-hands without a stable livelihood. The former ruling class, the landed aristocracy and the nobility, maintained the bulk of their feudal privileges and attitudes. They considered themselves the only historical class called to rule, despised 'business' and looked upon the new capitalists as alien intruders. (In fact, the capital flowing into the country came largely from foreign – German and Jewish – sources. Hard as they tried to become assimilated, members of the capitalist class were never accepted by the aristocracy as social equals.) The growth of industry did not offer a solution to the problem of the landless peasantry. New openings were not numerous enough and many of them were in any case filled by qualified workers coming from abroad – again mostly Germans and Jews. The poor peasants lacked even the necessary education required for skilled factory work and perhaps lacked equally the necessary energy and vitality to try to get there. The danger of starvation provoked instead a massive emigration: out of a population of around 18 million, about two million peasants tried their luck elsewhere, mostly in America before the First World War.

The state's goodwill or ability to compromise were not enough to defeat the resistance to reforms on the part of the altogether conservative ruling classes. The splendid laws were implemented with extreme slowness and none of them were implemented in full before 1945. What is more, the destitute agricultural population – though often in turmoil – was not strong enough or well enough organized to obtain any official social policy support, so that the measures giving some relief to the workers were not extended to them before 1945.

The First World War aggravated social problems and, under the impact of the Russian Revolution, ended in a bourgeois revolution in 1918, which became a proletarian revolution in 1919. During the three months of its existence, the first Hungarian socialist state introduced radically new and extensive social policy measures, carrying out earlier promises to the working class and answering its radical demands. Political defeat ended its social policy, of course: the counter-revolution repealed even its mildest measures.

The next two decades bore the marks of a lost war, of the Versailles treaty and of a revengeful ruling class. The economy was struggling. In contrast to the promising take-off of capitalism at the end of the nineteenth century, the period between the two world wars witnessed rather sluggish growth. Post-war economic hardships and the economic depression of the thirties were followed by a slow recovery. As a result, the per capita national income reached about US $200 in 1938 – a relatively low level compared with Western European countries of the same period. The landed aristocracy revoked the land reform of 1918/19 and the mass squalor of the rural population persisted – now without the possibility of emigration. Against the background of all these tensions, the government allowed the advance of fascism from around the thirties.

During these last decades before the Second World War, the social policy intervention of the state was limited to the most urgent and menacing problems, such as unemployment, massive undernourishment, a substantial lack of housing and of medical care, etc. During the whole period, private charity and voluntary social work played a larger role even in these matters than state social policy. More precisely, the state deliberately used private charity to fill the gaps in a defective state policy.

To give just one example: large-scale and extreme urban poverty was one of the most conspicuous social problems in the twenties and thirties. Government regulations placed the responsibilities on local administration, which proved to be both inefficient and incompetent. The apparent solution, the most highly praised social policy achievement of the regime, was worked out around 1930 by the Franciscan prior of Eger, a small town in the north of the country. This was the 'Norm of Eger', a system of outdoor poor-relief, with strictly defined 'norms', mostly in kind. The costs were divided: the town covered the costs of administering the relief, while the actual means of relief came from donations gathered by lady volunteers.[14]

The workers' movement recovered slowly from the losses inflicted by the 'white terror' of the twenties, but under the political conditions of the thirties it could not go far beyond the traditional claims concerning elementary needs. Some progress was made on the former Bismarckian lines – at least employers with more than twenty workers were legally constrained (as they had not been in the 1890s) to pay their contributions to insurance schemes. Thus, at the time of the outbreak of the Second World War, health insurance, pension and family allowance schemes covered about 25 per cent of the population, though the standards remained low. More precisely, the social benefit system worked with triple standards. There were some means-tested services and relief for the very poor, with almost subhuman standards (though the majority of the rural poor did not qualify even for these services, because ownership of any kind was a disqualification, and they usually owned a hut). The schemes for workers applied standards which were somewhat better than the means-tested ones, but remained far behind those applied to government employees. Private white-collar employees had only private insurance schemes.

On the whole, Hungary's official social policy was characterized before 1945 by institutionalized charity, by an underdeveloped Bismarckism, fragmented and reluctantly applied, and the absence of a clear concept of what social policy should be.

14. Dr Károly Pálos, *Szegénység, szegény gondozás* (Poverty, Caring for the Poor), author's edition, 1934.

2.4 The first achievements and dilemmas after 1945

The end of the Second World War, the liberation of the country from German troops and the revolutionary overthrow of the old regime made possible the profound social transformation of the country. The first years were characterized, as far as social and societal policy are concerned, by momentous practical changes and almost no progress in the elaboration of the theoretical frameworks.

The first revolutionary measures – the long-awaited land reform in 1945, the nationalization of mines, banks and factories in the following years up to 1949 – were not only political acts, but measures of basic structural relevance. They were not considered acts of societal policy but practical applications of a general revolutionary theory. It was assumed that they would open the way to socialism without any further complications.

In this situation, with urgent economic difficulties and the class struggle directed against the positions of the former ruling class, the range of possible alternatives was genuinely narrow. For the Communist Party, intent on carrying through the revolutionary change, the first steps (the distribution of land, nationalization, the first democratic reform of the school system, the realization of earlier demands of workers) appeared obvious. Under the circumstances there was no need, nor was there time among the pressing tasks, to analyse deeply the content of the long-range goals, the precise meaning of the ideal of socialism or communism or the relationship between ends and means, or the long-term, or secondary, unexpected outcomes of the measures which were being implemented. Thus, the need for a general, theoretically based societal policy did not develop. Every accomplishment seemed to be directly relevant to the widest social or structural aims, and the whole socialist system would develop automatically, it was thought, after the first revolutionary steps. This vision was based on a simplified Marxist interpretation of historical evolution, which held that social development inevitably followed change in economic relations, and which saw only one element of economic relations:

property. Hence economic policy and planning did not need to be complemented by societal policy or social planning.

Social policy, on the other hand, was explicit on two levels. The post-war situation was fraught with severe short-term problems. Rapid measures were required to meet the vital needs of the masses and to give relief where it was most needed. Various bodies, such as the National Relief, emerged spontaneously between 1945 and 1948 and secured prompt aid, using state help and self-help alike, but because of the atmosphere in Hungary at the time, they were never thought of as charities. The welfare programme and measures were organized on a national scale by the Ministry of Popular Welfare.

On a level closer to traditional social policy the change was no less radical. The demands of the working class were met as a matter of course much more fully than ever before. The 1948 programme of the Hungarian Workers' Party (unifying Communists and Social Democrats) included among the aims of social policy the reduction of working hours; the granting of paid holidays; the abolition of unemployment; the introduction of social insurance, including insurance schemes for sickness, old age, disablement and accidents; the improvement of health conditions by fighting widespread diseases in particular; the protection of mothers and children; and the improvement of housing conditions by means of slum-clearance and state housing programmes.[15]

As well as its scope, the orientation of traditional social policy changed, too. The multiplicity of standards was abolished and unified clauses were applied to everyone covered by the schemes. Means-tests were almost entirely abolished (and where maintained, their humiliating conditions were changed). The measures were not yet universal, because they were frequently restricted to workers and employees only, but within this area they applied to everyone. The trade unions handled the majority of the programmes, so that the 'charity' connotations were again avoided.

15. *The Minutes of the Unification Congress of the Hungarian Communist Party and the Social Democratic Party*, Szikra, 1948, pp. 351–2.

In this first period the various social policy measures emerged, however, without any consistent, conceptually clarified, large-scale scheme, carried along by the momentum of revolutionary change. It was partly the old demands of the workers' movement, partly the example of the Soviet revolution and partly the egalitarian ideal always strongly present in the post-revolutionary atmosphere which dictated the tasks, made the need for them unquestionable and made them appear as if they presented the only possible solution. This pragmatic approach soon led to false theoretical conclusions and to grave problems. The leaders in policy-making assumed that once they had paid the debts owed the working class – debts contracted in the pre-revolutionary period – social policy would no longer be needed. Belief in the automatic victory of socialism flourished in this sphere, too. It was maintained that with economic growth based on socialist relations of ownership social evolution would soon get rid of all kinds of anomalies and problems, such as delinquency, alcoholism or mental illness, poverty and even economic hardship.

The arbitrary interpretation of the course of social evolution was both cause and consequence of the dictatorial nature of the social leadership of the fifties. The leaders thought themselves infallible in theory and in practice: history was made to conform to their assumptions, and they could not err in their decisions. If, however, things were going wrong, two solutions could be envisaged. Problems could be ignored (that is why social research, including sociology or detailed social statistics were not called for and, indeed, were almost entirely suppressed); alternatively, difficulties could be imputed to the underhand scheming of internal or external agents who had to be fought by any means. The atmosphere of the cold war, of course, helped to prove the necessity of this kind of dictatorial action. (I certainly do not pretend to offer a full explanation of the Rákosi regime at the end of the forties and early fifties, but want only to show the implications it had for social policy.)

Following the logic outlined above both societal and social policy were banned from the official vocabulary from about

1949. (Even the Ministry of Popular Welfare was judged superfluous – because welfare would occur anyway.) Besides pure politics, only the economy seemed to require special central action promoting its development. But arbitrary selection of goals and means characterized this sphere, too. The economic objectives to be attained as well as the instruments serving the objectives were selected on the basis of political considerations. They largely ignored basic economic or social realities such as the economic potential of the country, the spontaneous play of economic and social forces, the various needs and aspirations of the population, the relations between people's objective conditions and their awareness, their motivation and, of course, the need for interaction among the various parts of society, and the need for central responsiveness.

Defective policies soon produced unfavourable phenomena in the economic and the social sphere alike. At the beginning of the fifties, real wages and real incomes began to decrease. The development of social services almost stopped and some of them declined. Social benefits, which at the beginning, in the mid-forties, had covered large numbers of people, remained on the level they had started on, so that their relative level decreased. Some of the unmet needs – especially housing – created increasing tensions. The exclusive reliance upon central planning as an economic regulator, together with the failure to select the right objectives, led to shortages in various production and consumer goods, creating a 'hidden' economy. This, in turn, increased social inequalities, and so led to massive disillusionment. While in the first years the revolutionary *élan* produced significant and, indeed, lasting achievements without a clear conceptual background, the absence of social analysis and reflection was an additional factor hindering social development in these years. All the more so because, despite problems and hardships, economic growth was considerable and would have permitted, or even required at that time, a clearer definition of goals, alternatives and priorities. Yet this work could not start until the end of the fifties.

In the last period – from the end of the fifties and the beginning of the sixties up to the present day – the first, most important task has been to remedy the deficiencies of earlier years–to redress the economy and to fulfil the promises made by social policy and people's expectations of it. As for the theoretical aspects, it is of paramount importance to study the events of the early period and to make explicit certain conclusions. It has become clear that economic goals cannot be fixed, that economic relations cannot be handled at will, and that it is impossible to ignore the social structure in which the economic processes work. It has become manifest that for the success of any intervention knowledge of the real situation is essential, and that even under the conditions of a socialist country like Hungary one cannot take for granted that intentions and outcomes necessarily coincide. It has also been realized that the higher the level of social and economic development, the more numerous are the alternatives for further progress, so that social decision-making has to be based on a thorough analysis of possibilities. These conclusions have gradually been incorporated into the social praxis of the last fifteen years. Thus the study of social reality – by means of social statistics, sociology, public opinion research, etc. – has developed rapidly. Narrowly delimited economic planning has been replaced by socio-economic planning. Closer links have been established between research and planning. One of the most important new developments is a deliberate search for the concrete, specific goals and values of socialism that are valid at this stage of development as well as in the long term, and the analysis of how these goals can be attained, which means the emergence of societal policy.

It is in connection with these new developments that the issue of social policy has again come to the fore. After having fallen into almost total disuse for about fifteen years, the expression made its reappearance in the second half of the sixties. It is not surprising, however, that because previously there was no real continuity and no organic evolution in social policy thinking, the concept is reappearing in a number of different contexts, with as many meanings. The need for social policy is strongly

felt, but the implications of the term depend on who uses it and
for what purpose.

2.5 Approaches to social policy in present-day Hungary

Some economists, very much concerned with the drawbacks of
excessively rigid central planning, are of the opinion that social
policy can be relegated to merely counteracting the deficiencies
of basic economic mechanisms. 'If the regulated market mechanism, as the regulator of incomes ensuring economic efficiency,
can function satisfactorily, then the state's standard of living
policy measures may be largely confined to the regulation of the
minimum wage and the family allowance.'[16] The primary goal
according to this view is maximizing economic efficiency, and
social policy (or standard of living policy) has simply to ensure
that 'no social stratum should fall into worse circumstances
than it had previously occupied'.[17] This line of thought may
over-emphasize the economic aspect. However, even in this approach the market is no longer considered a central category.
The initial assumption is that the economy is based on means of
production publicly owned and that planning has a central role,
while the market is a complementary mechanism. In general,
social intervention is much more widely accepted even in this
view than in the mainstream of Western economic thinking.

In some instances the emphasis on redistribution, the spirit of
charity and Bismarckian paternalism reappear, especially
among those who are dealing with fiscal problems. An essay
written in 1974 states that the main goal of social policy is to
care for the individual as well as possible, to accompany the
citizen from 'birth to death' and deal, among other issues, 'with
the prevention of illness', 'to endeavour to diminish the days of
suffering, to bring comfort to those suffering; ... to assure a
worry-free existence to those who have left work because of
old age or disability, or who suffer from some bodily or mental

16. Dr Béla Csikós-Nagy, *Bevezetés a gazdaságpolitikába* (Introduction
to Economic Policy), Kossuth, 1969, pp. 254–5.
17. ibid.

defect.'[18] True, even this approach recognizes other goals, like the creation of job opportunities, the application of the principle 'to each according to his work', or the general improvement of the standard of living. But the note of charity appears, as well as the old paternalism. The author speaks about care assured by central organs but ignores the rights and the active participation of those to whom this 'care' is offered. The third characteristic of this view is its focus on distribution. 'In socialism, social policy . . . is one of the tools for achieving long-term goals, especially by means of a policy of distribution.'[19] This, in itself, would not cause problems if the policy of distribution were not considered as the only relevant field for central intervention in the realm of social relations.

A third, rather widespread view which has emerged under the present conditions takes an entirely different angle: 'the function of social policy in its wide sense is the gradual elimination, as far as possible, of the factors that differentiate incomes, ways of life and the quality of life independently of the work done ... This social policy is, in fact, an important element of social planning...'[20] Here again, the problem is that differences which depend on work are entirely left outside the scope of social intervention.

We also encounter with increasing frequency terms with rather similar connotations to that of social policy, such as 'income policy', 'policy of consumption', 'standard of living policy'. This last term has become especially widespread. Its meaning is given by István Huszár as follows: 'The regulating principle of our standard of living policy is, on the one hand, that there cannot be any large group or stratum whose standard of living falls or stagnates over a long period. On the other hand it includes the requirement that the rise in the standard of living

18. László Lengyel, 'A gazdaságpolitika és a szociálpolitika összefüggéseiről' (On Relations between Economic and Social Policy), *Közgazdasági Szemle*, 1975, No. 1, p. 64.

19. ibid., p. 65.

20. Kálmán Kulcsár: 'Gazdasági hatékonyság – társadalmi hatékonyság' (Economic Efficiency – Social Efficiency), *Gazdaság*, September 1970, p. 14.

should be perceivable. These two requisites set the lower limit for the rise in the standard of living.'[21] Jávorka uses the same term in an enlarged sense: 'Therefore the task for the standard of living policy is not merely to assure the fullest possible provision, but also the development of a full human life, the conditions for a harmonious relationship between the individual and society.'[22]

Finally, the most all-encompassing view is no longer concerned with social policy in the strict sense, but rather with structural policy – here called social planning. Its goal, as described by A. Hegedüs and M. Márkus, is to assure 'the evolution of social conditions in a way that enables each member of society to develop his personality to the greatest extent possible under given economic conditions, and to fulfil himself in everyday life, including the sphere of work and the activities outside work'.[23] This interpretation stresses the duality of 'economic optimization' and 'humanization'. 'In our opinion the correct amalgamation of goals of optimization and humanization is the basic question for long-range planning. And when we said earlier that it is possible to develop the civilizational model of socialism, we think that this would not be achieved solely, perhaps not even primarily, by the increase of economic efficiency, but only if it offered more to people in terms of the humanization of social relations.'[24]

There is, no doubt, an underlying consensus in the views outlined above: all the authors adhere to the ideal of a socialist society. They realize that today's structure is still at an early

21. István Huszár, *Az életszinvonalpolitikáról* (On the Politics of Standard of Living), lecture given at the session of the 1968 congress of the Hungarian Economic Society.

22. Edit Jávorka, 'The Role of the Trade Unions in the Development and Realization of the Standard of Living Policy', talk given at the session organized by the Trade Unions Research Institute, November 1970, mimeo, p. 15.

23. András Hegedüs and Mária Márkus, 'The Choice of Values and Alternatives in the Long-Range Planning of Distribution and Consumption', *Közgazdasági Szemle*, 1969, p. 1051.

24. ibid.

stage of its post-revolutionary development, and look for the best way to exploit the extensive developmental reserves, the opportunities for further progress. The diversity begins when we look at the different ways they envisage.

On the first level of analysis, there seems to be an essential difference in how the various authors view the relationship between 'economic' and 'social' considerations, or rationalities. One may distjnguish at least three positions.

The *first* orientation – stressing the importance of the regulated market and economic efficiency – restricts somewhat the role of social considerations, and gives outright priority to economic considerations.

A *second* position might be derived from the model described by K. Kulcsár. He regards economic and social considerations as being of roughly equal importance. He realizes that the two might be in conflict with each other especially in the short term. In this case the priority given to short-term economic interests may harm these same economic interests in the long run.

The *third* main position, as expressed for example by the views of Hegedüs and Márkus, holds that although it is impossible to ignore economic rationality and the requirements of economic optimization, these can, and at least in the long run must, be subordinated to a genuinely 'social' aim, the goal of humanization.

This classificatory scheme is, however, rather superficial. A simple juxtaposition of the two rationalities cannot lead to meaningful conclusions. This is a problem which merits a brief discussion. It seems to me that one theoretical difficulty stems from the fact that the two rationalities are of two different types. Economic rationality may be understood as 'goal-rationality' in Weber's term, which in fact is an instrumentally rational, efficient approach to a pre-defined goal – economic development – especially if economy is understood in a restricted sense, as the production and allocation of scarce resources with a view to the maximization of results (total output or profit only). Social rationality, at least in the sense used here, belongs to Weberian 'value rationality', where means are irrelevant in the pursuit of the end, the chosen values. It is clear that the two rationalities cannot be handled in the same way and their results are incommensurable. Whenever one tries to measure them on the same scale, to proceed to mixed socio-economic 'cost-benefit' analyses, the 'common denominator' cannot be anything else but money. One may calculate the monetary costs of social achievements, but the 'value' of the result itself – more culture, more health, more self-esteem, more humanized work, or a more equal distribution of any of these values – cannot be translated into financial terms. On the other hand, the economic result is directly expressed in terms of money, but its human costs cannot be calculated on the same basis, at least not in full. This is true for practically all the social side-effects of economic growth, from the disintegration of sub-cultures to pollution, or from the fragmentation of work and worker to so-called consumerism. The result is an impoverished and lop-sided value-system.

I do not imply that the two rationalities have to be viewed independently. The definition of social goals has to take into account economic possibilities, and when settling economic objectives one has to reckon with social costs. But the equation is not an objective, exact or value-free calculus.

The theoretical difficulty increases if one tries to go beyond the simple juxtaposition of economic and social considerations and tries to define what should be understood by 'economic' and by 'social' goals or interests under present-day Hungarian conditions.

It follows from the argument presented in section 2.1 that if the domination of the self-regulating market is abolished, then the relative autonomy of the economy, which was only apparent, but which served the dominant interests very effectively, necessarily disappears. With this the other basic and useful illusion vanishes, too, namely that the purpose of economic activity (profit maximization) can be unambiguously defined. Under the new conditions of the planned economy it becomes manifest that all the decisions affecting the economy have social components and social motivations.

This does not mean that the economy is already absorbed in the global social sphere. (As long as there are different socio-economic systems, this is not a very realistic perspective anyway.) In Hungarian experience it has already proved harmful and dangerous to ignore the real interrelations within the economic sphere. But a major change has undeniably taken place which should have gradually increasing effect. It seems to me that in Hungary for the time being neither economists nor sociologists are fully aware of the implications of this change. (It is always true that things which are just being born offer few holds to scientific understanding. Marx was right in saying that only the anatomy of man offered a key by which to understand the anatomy of the monkey.) As long as the main issue, the relation of 'economy' and 'society' and the trends of this relation, is not clarified, it is hard to arrive at clear definitions of the economic and the social sphere, or of the place and role of social policy. I do not consider the attempt which follows a final definition of social policy. However, taking into account some of the implications of the changes described, it is possible to impute a new meaning to social policy.

On a very general level, and in a normative perspective, social policy under socialist conditions is called to assert the principle of the unconditional right to survive of every individual, independently of the individual's contribution or achievement. This right is, however, based on the assumption that the individual will feel a reciprocal obligation towards society. This means, as a long-term goal, that – partly by means of the institutions of social policy – the *direct* connection between production and distribution, between performance and reward, between what one gives and what one takes, is severed.

Social policy is, then, an important element and instrument of societal policy. In fact, the equalization of conditions has been shown (in Chapter 1) to be essential in the attainment of long-term structural goals – and social policy may be an important means of equalizing conditions.

Social policy under the conditions of a developed socialist society thus has two major new elements. In contrast to capitalist conditions, it is not a complement, but a negation of the formal economic logic. In contrast to some former societies, it is not only the right to live, but indeed the right to live equally well which it seeks to assure.

For the time being, these are, however, somewhat unrealistic as immediate aims – for a number of reasons discussed later. But they do give an orientation to present-day social policy, charging it with the following tasks:

● To exert the strongest possible influence on the sector of distribution which, apparently at least, still follows a basically economic logic, in other words, on distribution according to work.

● To handle the sector of distribution which is independent of work, in other words, centralized redistribution (detailed in Chapter 7), so as to make more equal the shares of those who do not work and those who do work, and to ensure that within these categories, too, shares become less unequal.

These are its normative tasks, but only the second one appears as an independent activity with more or less independent organizational frames. The first element is built into 'economic' policy.

Besides the normative element, it still has a palliative or corrective function – because social anomalies and problems have proved to be much more tenacious than was supposed in the early fifties. However, even in this field it uses mainly the funds coming from central redistribution.

Thus social policy under socialist conditions is viewed here as a constitutive element of societal policy, deriving its main principles from, and contributing to the objectives of, societal policy.

Part Two

The Transformation of the Basic Relations of the Social Division of Work

Chapter 3

The Social Organization of Work

3.1 The division of work – can it be altered?

In Hungary, the first essential step in the transformation of basic socio-economic relations was the abolition of the private ownership of capital, including landed estates, thereby putting an end to the private appropriation of the surplus product and altering the class structure.

The importance of this step is often questioned. The main challenge comes from conservative or 'managerial' economists.[1] Since Burnham,[2] they have often argued that under the conditions of modern capitalism private ownership has lost its traditional role. They produce two main reasons to support this thesis. They assume firstly that capital always becomes more democratized and that inequalities of wealth are eroded with the diffusion of shareholding and the heavy duties imposed on incomes and inherited wealth. Secondly, traditional owners are replaced in the decision-making process by managers, a practically independent technocratic stratum with a new ethic. Therefore, even if capital owners still exist, they no longer have any real functions. The implication is that the abolition of capital ownership is irrelevant because its nature has already changed.

1. The expression is used and analysed by Michel de Vroey, 'The Corporation and the Labor Process', *Review of Radical Political Economics*, Vol. 7, No. 2, 1975.
2. The most important proponents of the thesis are: A. A. Berle and G. Means, *The Modern Corporation and Private Property*, Macmillan, New York, 1967 (first published 1932); J. M. Burnham, *The Managerial Revolution*, Day, New York, 1941; J. Strachey, *Contemporary Capitalism*, Gollancz, 1956; C. A. R. Crosland, *The Future of Socialism*, Jonathan Cape, 1956; R. Dahrendorf, 'Recent Changes in the Class Structure of European Society', *Daedalus*, Winter 1964; J. K. Galbraith, *Economics and the Public Purpose*, André Deutsch, 1974.

In the last few years there has been a renewal of the debate about the 'managerialist' position in practically all the developed Western countries.[3] It has been demonstrated that inequalities of wealth have remained persistent despite real growth in small-holdings and home ownership. In England, for instance, 10 per cent of the population owns 41 per cent of total personal wealth, according to one estimate,[4] 67 per cent according to another.[5]

Corporate stock ownership is, however, more important than total wealth from the point of view of the control of the cycle of reproduction, and inequalities are even more marked in this case. In the mid-sixties, 62 per cent of corporate stock belonged to the top 1 per cent, 53 per cent to the top 0·5 per cent in the USA,[6] the figures in England being 80 per cent for the top 1

3. See, for example, for the theoretical issues: J. H. Westergaard, 'The Withering Away of Class – A Contemporary Myth', in *Towards Socialism*, ed. P. Anderson and R. Blackburn, Fontana, 1965; J. H. Westergaard and Henrietta Resler, *Class in a Capitalist Society*, Heinemann Educational Books, 1975; R. Miliband, *The State in Capitalist Society*, Basic Books, New York, 1972; R. Miliband, 'Professor Galbraith and American Capitalism: The Managerial Revolution Revisited, *The Socialist Register*, Merlin Press, 1968; Nicos Poulantzas, *Pouvoir politique et classes sociales*, Maspero, Paris, 1971; M. de Vroey, 'The Corporation and the Labor Process' op. cit. Some recent works on wealth distribution: F. Ackerman, H. Birnbaum, et al.: 'Income Distribution in the United States', *Review of Radical Political Economics*, Vol. 3, No. 3, 1971; Pierre Bourdieu, Luc Boltanski and Monique de Saint-Martin, Les Stratégies de reconversion', *Information sur les sciences sociales*, 12(5), 1973; J. D. Smith and S. D. Franklin, 'The Concentration of Personal Wealth, 1922–1969', *American Economic Review*, May 1974; A. B. Atkinson, *Unequal Shares: Wealth in Britain*, Penguin Books, Harmondsworth, rev. edn, 1974; E. Ballerstedt, W. Glatzer, K. U. Mayer and W. Zapf, *Sociologischer Almanach, Handbuch gesellschafts-politischer Daten und Indikatoren für die Bundesrepublik Deutschland*, Herder and Herder, Frankfurt/Main, New York, 1975.
4. Alan Day, 'The Nation's Wealth – Who Owns It?', *Observer*, 20 January 1974 quoted in J. H. Goldthorpe and P. Bevan, *The Study of Social Stratification in Great Britain, 1945–1975*, multigraphed, Oxford, 1975.
5. Atkinson, op. cit., p. 14.
6. J. D. Smith and S. D. Franklin, op. cit.

per cent,[7] and 68 per cent for the top 0·4 per cent.[8] As for the alleged independence of the benevolent technostructure which pursues the interests of the firm against all outsiders and resists even the owners by giving them 'some basic level of earnings' to make them 'quiescent',[9] it may be challenged on several grounds.

The most convincing of the counter-arguments is that neither the distribution of wealth nor that of incomes or benefits suffered a significant change under the managerial rule – and that the 'human concerns' of the technostructure all too readily disappeared in the years of economic recession, as witnessed by the recent rates of unemployment and inflation. This, incidentally, also shows that the belief in the disappearance of the market as a dominant force in a technostructure which 'transcends the market' and only 'uses it as an instrument'[10] is largely unfounded. John Westergaard and Henrietta Resler are, in my view, quite right when they find it odd that the legitimacy of private ownership should be confirmed by its becoming increasingly parasitic, and when they state, after a thoroughgoing analysis of facts and figures, that 'the thesis' of benevolent managerialism turns to dust when one touches it. Profit maximization has not been replaced as the main motor of business by a 'social ethic', by growth maximization, or by a concern merely to 'tick over' and deal with problems as they arise.[11]

But the effect of capitalist ownership transcends the problem of inequalities of wealth or the 'goal' of production, as has already been implied in Chapter 1. The logic of capital as a basic institution permeates, by the intermediary of the market,

7. H. Frankel, *Capitalist Society and Modern Sociology*, Lawrence and Wishart, 1970.

8. A. Glyn and B. Sutcliffe, *British Capitalism and the Profit Squeeze*, Penguin Books, Harmondsworth, 1972.

9. J. K. Galbraith, *Economics and the Public Purpose*, op. cit., p. 110 and passim.

10. ibid., p. 117.

11. J. Westergaard and H. Resler, *Class in a Capitalist Society*, op. cit. p. 170 and the whole chapter on 'Private Business and Managerialism' (pp. 150–70).

practically *all other institutions*, processes and relations of society by means of its two main principles. These are the legitimacy of competition-based individual self-interest at the expense of other types of interests, and the predominance of autonomous economic rationality at the expense of other types of rationality even in fields outside the economy. The obvious exceptions, such as working-class solidarity, are opposed to the given system of institutions. For instance, from Durkheim on,[12] it has frequently been observed that individual competition is an important organizatory force at school and that mechanisms within school are deeply influenced by the fact that knowledge is considered and handled as private property.[13] It is also known that family and marital relations are greatly influenced by economic considerations. One seemingly irrelevant fact is that the duration of housewives' housework follows closely official working hours. Housewives thereby prove unconsciously the economic 'worth' of their work, and its equivalence with the performance of earners.[14]

Hence, the abolition of the private ownership of the means of production which took place in Hungary between 1945 and 1949 was of major historical relevance. It ended the inequality directly connected with capital ownership, and created a new social environment. The absence of capital owners has changed the power and interest structure so that the stakes of individual competition have become much less unequal; hence competition itself has become much less vital. Also, as this book will show, narrowly defined economic interest is much more easily combined with other interests.

Nevertheless, the old mechanisms and patterns of attitudes did not disappear automatically and fully with the elimination of

12. Émile Durkheim, *L'Évolution pédagogique en France*, Presses Universitaires de France, Paris, 1969.

13. See especially Basil Bernstein, 'On the Classification and Framing of Educational Knowledge', in *Class, Codes and Control*, Vol. I, Routledge and Kegan Paul, 1971.

14. Zsuzsa Ferge, 'Les jours de semaine et les dimanches dans la vie des hommes et des femmes', in *Transactions of the Sixth World Congress of Sociology*, Vol. III, ISA, 1970.

private property, because their survival is rooted not only in the relative autonomy of some institutions like school, or in tradition, but also in the continuation of commodity production, in the actual organization of the division of work, etc.

Another aspect of the problem is that the legal expropriation of capital goods does not necessarily and immediately entail the real socialization of the means of production, including democratic control of their utilization. It seems, on the one hand, that the abolition of private ownership is, by now, legitimized in the Weberian sense of the term in socialist countries. The existence of state-owned companies and of co-operatives based on group property is considered natural or normal. In Hungary the stabilization and legitimation of the new institutions took longer in agriculture than in other branches, but the rapid development of co-operatives in the last ten years has practically ended this difficulty. (I might add that even in agriculture the co-operatives were not questioned in the name of big land-ownership but in the name of small-holdings.) This change in attitude is due to certain developments in the last decade. Among them the most important are the following: security of income and regular monthly incomes, improving the formerly precarious situation of peasants; a rapidly rising income level, due partly to increased productivity in agriculture and partly to substantial social benefits; the maintenance of individually cultivated small household plots; and considerably reduced work loads as compared to the traditional unlimited working hours of peasants, All these changes made co-operatives and state farms attractive even when compared to small-holdings.

None the less, although the present forms of ownership are considered a vastly superior alternative to private ownership, they cannot yet be looked upon as fully developed socialist forms. It has been recognized and heavily stressed, especially in the last decade, that the socialist character of the ownership relation is not immediately achieved with the act of expropriation, but requires a process of democratization in the management and control of production and public affairs in general. In other words, the aim is not only the rejection of private ownership, but the development of a sense of 'partnership'. Without this evolution it is only the absence of a former evil which is sensed, creating a kind of 'no-man's land' feeling towards public property. This vacuum leads to the irresponsible handling of common property, to wastages and sometimes to the appropriation of common goods, where even this last act is considered by a sizable majority as a minor irregularity and not as an offence.

The emphasis on the socialist content of property relations has led to different developments in Hungary in the last decade. Various surveys have investigated the current problems of public ownership, such as the passivity of workers on collective forums and their lack of information on collective issues even where they were personally concerned, as in the new regulations on collective labour contracts or the utilization of the firm's benefits. Both their passivity and their lack of information seemed to be related to the absence of real possibilities of participation.[15] It was also pointed out that the different non-material and non-individual forms of incentives that could reinforce the sense of collectivity were frequently malfunctioning because they were handled too rigidly.[16] The political leadership then stressed the importance of change in this respect. János Kádár, secretary general of the Hungarian Socialist Workers' Party, declared at the last Congress of the Party in 1975 that priority should be given to the development of workplace democracy, including the co-opting of workers into the highest forums of management (for example to boards of directors and supervisory committees), and the improvement of the distribution of information on all important issues. In this way the connection between communication of relevant information and effective participation was made clearer. The means of implementing these ideas in social practice are rather varied.

15. *Pest megye munkásai* (The Workers of the County of Pest), Társadalomtudományi Intézet, 1971.

16. Lajos Héthy and Csaba Makó, *A teljesitményelv érvényesitése és az üzemi érdek- és hatalmi viszonyok* (The Implementation of the Principle of Achievement and the Relations of Power and Interests within the Enterprise), Szociológiai Kutató Csoport, 1970.

Administrative intervention or formal control are not very helpful, but a legal framework has to be worked out so as not to hinder the new endeavours. This was offered by the new Code of Work elaborated in 1967, by the centrally devised changes of the collective labour contracts, and also by the different economic regulatory measures that apply to firms. The main points in all these documents are the enlargement of the firm's sphere of autonomy, the creation of forums for public discussion and for the spread of information, and the broadening of the rights of the individual and of trade unions. In fact, in the first Code of Work, elaborated at the beginning of the fifties, the rights of the individual worker were curtailed by the priority given to collective economic interests, with, for instance, restrictions on the free choice of workplaces or job changes. These restrictions were for the most part removed by the 1967 Code, and the rights of the employer to decide about the employee's working conditions, etc., were accordingly limited.

Some comment may be needed on the relevance of the first point, the autonomy of the firm. In fact, the increasing responsibility of the firm serves primarily economic aims. It introduces more flexibility into the structure of production and adapts incentives more adequately to any given situation. However, this growing autonomy does not only have economic implications. Participatory workplace democracy has no sense if no substantial decisions can be taken at the level of the firm. Besides decisions concerning current output, the issues that might be debated and settled at firm level and which are important in a societal perspective are extremely varied. They include the firm's future development and investment policy, its policy in changing or improving the organization of work, the utilization of benefits remaining after taxation, and obviously all decisions concerning the social policy of the enterprise, from the improvement of working conditions to the allocation of social benefits to different goals and to different groups. In this case, then, the interests of economic policy and societal policy coincide on a general level, although they may clash on particular issues. This is why the trade unions' increasing sphere of responsibility and enlarged field of action, granted also by the Code of Work, is important.

The range of problems that can be solved by the firms with the contribution of the workers is, then, quite substantial. Progress, however, is slower than would be desirable. The reasons are manifold and only partially analysed. Attempts to analyse them are made in many ways, among others by means of empirical studies. One of these studies, carried out in two huge ironworks,[17] pointed out, amongst other issues, the management's reluctant or sceptical attitude towards the usefulness of workers' participation, contrasting sharply with the declared willingness of the workers. (In both plants 50 per cent of the workers declared that the efficiency of the management could be improved by listening to workers, while in one plant only 15 per cent and in the other 5 per cent of the managers were of this opinion.) Managers gave their reasons in different terms: a substantial percentage voiced the opinion that if the worker is satisfied with his salary, his interest in the plant's affairs stops there. A similarly large group thought participation irrelevant because under the present socialist conditions no management decision could harm the interests of workers. Two smaller groups of managers declared, on the one hand, that workers already had enough say via the trade unions and, on the other, that participation could be enlarged only if the level of technological and general culture of the workers was also raised. It can hardly be doubted that these reasons are ultimately motivated by the managers' present position of power and the interests generated by this position. In other words, the managers are aware that enlarged participation necessarily entails a change in the power structure at their expense. Changing this attitude depends partly on the pressure exerted by the whole of society towards democratization, partly on the emphasis of central party or government organs on democratization. Giving workers more information and more technological and social

17. Aladárné Mód and Gyula Kozák, 'Az Ozdi Kohászati Üzemek munkásai és az üzemi demokrácia' (The Workers of the Metallurgy Works of Ozd and Enterprise Democracy), *Valóság*, 1975, No. 2.

knowledge is certainly important in making their participation more effective, in proving its usefulness, and in pressing for a change in the outlook and orientation of management.

But again, participation is not a self-sufficient end, although its possible effect on relations within and between groups may be a considerable social gain in itself. Over and above this gain, increased participation has to be directed towards the transformation of the social division of work. This last problem, however, is probably the most difficult of the tasks to be solved. Transforming the present situation implies reducing differentiation not only in conditions, but also in the contents of the work. This requires, among other things, less sharp demarcation lines between the jobs where one or other of the main work teleologies predominates, between manual and nonmanual jobs, or more and less skilled or varied jobs. A change in this direction obviously requires increased participation because of the necessary shifts in power relations, and a less unequal distribution of technologically relevant knowledge and skill. But even if we disregard the possible effects of the interest structure we have to reckon with difficulties stemming from the level of technology.

The actual work tasks are defined by the available technology, or are shaped by it. More precisely, there is a dialectical interrelation between the two fields. Present technical conditions are the outcome of a long process which took place mostly under capitalist conditions. Technological development has thus been motivated mainly by economic or profit interests, disregarding human interests as far as possible. Assembly lines are only one of the most outstanding examples. Even automation seems to enrich jobs only for some, while requiring no skill or creativity from others.

One of the reactions against fragmented and dehumanized work has been, in a number of capitalist countries, the movement towards work humanization and job enrichment programmes. As Zimbalist and others show,[18] the resistance of

18. Andrew Zimbalist, 'The Limits of Work Humanization', *Review of Radical Political Economics*, Summer 1975.

managers or owners to work humanization programmes has not been strong. They might even have initiated programmes themselves because productivity could thereby be increased. Workers were so dissatisfied with the results of technological progress (monotony, job-fragmentation, etc.) that the advantages of modern, highly productive techniques began to be lost. In these cases the relative autonomy conceded to workers represented a new incentive whereby former losses could be compensated for.

The experience gained in capitalist countries is certainly useful for Hungary's purposes, although it is clear by now that such programmes cannot, or should not, be taken over without further thought. In their original setting (in capitalist countries) they usually remain confined to the circle of manual workers. Whenever the programmes try to alter too radically the power balance between workers and managers, their continuation is threatened.[19] Therefore the demarcation line between manual and non-manual workers is not weakened by these experiments, and manual jobs are not enriched spiritually – although this seems to be a key issue in the transformation of the present organization of work.

Hungary's main problem today, however, is relative technical under-development. Technology is still at a relatively low level, so that Hungarian workers are far from being dissatisfied with the disadvantages of new techniques. It has already been pointed out that further economic development is a necessary condition for meeting very pressing social needs, and therefore it is now an important goal. Economic advancement is relatively rapid and easy if technological development follows the *known* patterns of modern Western industry. Workers themselves are usually in favour of such changes, since mechanization, scientific work-organization, etc., usually make their jobs less tiring in terms of physical effort and in working conditions. (I may add that the rapidly increasing working class has been recruited in Hungary largely from former peasants. For them,

19. David Jenkins, 'Democracy in the Workplace: The Human Factories', *The Nation*, 12 January 1974.

even relatively heavy industrial work is a change for the better, if only because this means more sheltered conditions, more human contact, etc.) The interaction of all these factors creates a situation where it is more rational – economically as well as socially – to adopt the available methods of modern technology than to try to create absolutely *new* solutions in a technological vacuum. It is true that Hungary has not adopted the harsh and inhuman aspects of 'scientific management', and that the rhythm and intensity of work are less strained than in developed capitalist countries. (There is no doubt a corresponding decrease in productivity.) But the essential developments, including fragmentation, hierarchization within work tasks according to skill, etc., are inevitably permeating the organization of work.

I do not want to imply that there is only one conceivable line of technological progress. But it seems that once technological development is heavily committed to one particular direction – the one opened up by rising capitalism – then it is practically impossible (at least in the present world situation) to reverse the process, to return to some zero-point and to start afresh on an entirely different road. At the beginning of the socialist evolution in Hungary capitalist industrialization was already at a fairly developed stage, even if not on a par with the advanced Western countries, and so it was not possible to start anew. The problem is obviously not a new one. The historic quarrel between William Morris and Edward Bellamy was motivated mainly by their opposed views on the alternatives to be chosen in this dilemma. And although Morris's utopia is more progressive in terms of individual autonomy, it is altogether unrealistic and therefore questionable in its rejection of modern industry and its achievements,[20] and in assuming the complete reversibility of a social process.

Current ideas about possible ways of reorganizing the div-

20. William Morris, *News from Nowhere*, 1890; Edward Bellamy, *Equality*, 1897; Edward Bellamy, *Looking Backward*, 1888, Signet Books, 1960.

ision of work are as yet not very clear. The main models which are envisaged, even if never spelt out clearly, may be categorized as follows:

● A complete reversal of the present production pattern with a return to a pre-industrial, artisanal world. The advantages in terms of human relations, of work satisfaction and of a saner environment are obvious. Its feasibility is extremely doubtful if only because of the size of the population which has to be provided for.

● The preservation of the present job structure but with alternations so that at some point of his or her life every individual has to take an equitable, or equal, part in the 'worst' jobs. The practical solutions proposed vary, with three main variants:

The 'industrial army' solution, whereby everyone is compelled to begin his or her working life by performing the jobs which are considered worst, so that no one wants to perform them voluntarily.

The rotation pattern, where one performs 'good' and 'bad' jobs alternately throughout one's whole working life.

The parallel pattern, where one is expected to perform 'good' and 'bad' tasks simultaneously.

● The alteration of the present structure by merging 'good' and 'bad' tasks in one job in a flexible way. This solution is not simply a variation on the previous model – although they have the common element of sharing the burden of 'bad' jobs. It is different in that it tries to combine existing elements in new ways.

All these solutions sound rather utopian for the time being, even if we presuppose that considerable technological development will constantly ease and abolish the 'worst' jobs by the use of machines. The main problem is that all of them abolish the present system where 'good' jobs are monopolized, that is they run against the prevailing interest structure. Also, their feasibility is easily challenged on the grounds that while more qualified and gifted people can perform 'bad' jobs, the reverse is certainly not true. However, in the case of the last solution a gradual approach seems to be possible which takes into account the extreme diversity of people's abilities and interests, and the relatively slow change in the distribution of knowledge. This means that the contents of jobs will begin to overlap and that there will be a gradual weakening of the present, clear-cut hierarchy.

To be somewhat more explicit: it is acknowledged and indeed proven that every able-bodied individual is able to do more than simply the most basic, instinctive jobs. If everybody is *trained* to do more than just these jobs, there will be a universal over-training. Under these circumstances, it would be possible to reorganize jobs so that practically *no one* works full time at *the top* of his ability and competence. Everyone will perform jobs which belong to his speciality but are on a somewhat lower level – which could coincide with someone else's 'top' level. The result would be that nobody would remain exclusively and permanently at the bottom of the job hierarchy. The change can be graphically portrayed in the following way:

Present situation:

New situation:

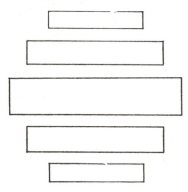

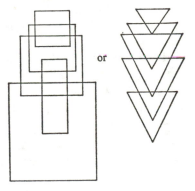

A distinct hierarchy of jobs and people, where everyone is attached to one and only one step, which presumably corresponds to the highest level of his ability and/or qualification

A blurred hierarchy, where jobs combine 'good' and 'bad' elements so that nobody is attached exclusively to the 'best' or 'worst' jobs

This solution may be combined with some elements of the models based on alternation or rotation, for example by working out a pattern of constant improvements in terms of the autonomy, etc., of the jobs.

True, it still runs against the prevailing structure of interests of those at the top. But, after all, socialism is committed to changing the present structure. Nevertheless, it has to be acknowledged that the present evolution in Hungary is very slow in this field. The transformation of the division of work is seen as an absolute necessity on theoretical grounds. There is an increasing awareness of the practical implications of this necessity among politicians as well as social scientists. Some of the changes currently taking place, for instance the reduction of inequalities in the distribution of knowledge or the exercise of power by means of increased participation, are, no doubt, prerequisites for the process in question. But there has been hardly any significant attempt to adapt the technological infrastructure to this type of evolution, and the necessity of economic growth makes it rather difficult to envisage a rapid and appreciable change in this respect. It is easy to see that the solution advocated here slows down economic growth at least for a while, and also that it implies a considerable amount of 'educational waste'. There is no doubt that it is indispensable to reduce the gap between theory and practice in this sphere, but there is uncertainty about how this could and should be done.

There are, however, more marked changes and successes in other spheres of productive relations, especially in the weakening of the primacy of economic interest and the suppression of some of its inhuman consequences. The areas in which former mechanisms have been radically altered are the right to work, working conditions, and the endeavours towards the transformation of the distribution of knowledge.

3.2 The right and obligation to work – unemployment

It is a basic norm in all socialist countries that all those who are of working age and able to work should avail themselves of the right to work. The state guarantees the opportunity to work and the stability of employment, and it is the duty of the individual to utilize the opportunity.

This standpoint is motivated by various ideological principles. One of these is connected with the social importance assigned to work. Work is seen as the most important social activity for the survival and evolution of society as well as for the formation of the individual and of communities. In this sense participation in socially organized work is a socio-economic necessity and a moral obligation. Another element is related to the means of livelihood of the individual: under the new conditions, the only important source of income of the individual must be work. If he does not engage in some remunerative work, he has no livelihood, which is unacceptable for society, or has to live by some form of parasitism, has to acquire semi-legal or illegal sources of income – which is not tolerated.

There is, however, one exception to the general rule: it does not apply unconditionally to women. They need not be independent wage-earners if somebody provides for them. But the above economic and moral considerations apply to both men and women. It is a fundamental tenet that the basis of the real – social and economic – equality or emancipation of women is their participation in the social division of work. Therefore society encourages their earning activity by creating favourable legal conditions, by developing the institutionalized forms of child care and housework and by fighting by all possible means sexual prejudices and traditional conservative attitudes concerning sex-role stereotypes. There was also, at least in the first decades of socialist development in Hungary, strong financial pressure: wages were set in such a way that a family needed at least two earners to maintain a decent standard. In addition, in the ideological climate of the late forties and early fifties it was often seen as somewhat indecent or irregular if women, especially young ones without children, remained at home. The 'push' factors were reinforced by 'pull' factors: the needs of economic reconstruction created practically unlimited working opportunities.

All these factors taken together resulted in a fairly high level of employment. Among those of working age or still working after having attained retirement age, the percentage of men who are not active earners or pensioners has varied for several years between 1 per cent and 2 per cent (the physically handicapped who have never worked or are temporarily unemployed) and the figure is now under 20 per cent for women. (See Table 3/1.)

Table 3/1: The level of employment, 1 January 1976

		Men	Women
Manpower resources (in thousands)			
Men between 14 and 59, women between 14 and 54 years		3,269·3	3,100·9
Active earners above retirement age		109·5	168·1
	Total	3,378·8	3,269·0
Allocation (in percentages)			
Active earners		85·1	68·1
Inactive earners (pensioners)*a*		5·8	9·9
Students		8·2	7·4
Dependants (non-earners)		0·9	14·6
	Total	100·0	100·0

Source: Hungarian Statistical Yearbook, 1975.
a Only those who are temporarily or permanently pensioned before the retirement age for health reasons. One is entitled to the sickness benefit over a limited period (one or two years depending on the illness), but if after this period the person in question is still not fit to take up work he is pensioned regardless of his age, until restored to health.

The combined effect of the different measures promoting female employment has radically altered the male:female ratio among earners. The proportion of women among earners was 26 per cent in 1930, 27 per cent in 1941, 29·2 per cent in 1949,

35·5 per cent in 1960 and 43·9 per cent in 1974.[21] The last figure means that Hungary is now among countries with the highest level of female employment. (According to the ILO data, only two countries, the Soviet Union and Romania, had ratios above 45 per cent at the end of the sixties, and some four or five rank with Hungary, Austria among them.)

If, as in the Marxist conception, work is a right and an obligation at the same time, then *unemployment* is unacceptable on logical as well as on social grounds. There are measures providing for unemployment benefits, worked out originally in 1954 and modified in 1957. In both cases these measures were made necessary by the fact that a number of employees in state administration were released owing to economic considerations. Since their re-engagement could not be assured immediately, unemployment benefits were introduced. These still exist, but according to estimates derived from state budget data, the number of beneficiaries is a couple of hundred people per year. Applicants are scarce because the benefit itself is rather small and because employment opportunities are still so great that hardly anybody qualifies for the benefit on grounds that he cannot find a suitable job.

The rigid rejection of unemployment is frequently debated and criticized in Hungary as well as in other countries. The grounds of the objection are varied:

(a) First, there is the standpoint of *individualist liberalism*, radically objecting to any type of compulsion for the individual. According to this conception the individual has the right to decide for himself whether to work or not to work, to starve or not to starve. Socialist ideology and morality rejects this unlimited individualism. But there are problems in Hungary which can be analysed from this point of view.

The main problem group concerned is the Gipsies. In their case it is hard to reject out of hand the arguments of individualist liberalism. The whole gipsy population probably amounts to no more than 3 per cent of the country's population,

21. Hungarian microcensus, 1973, p. 22.

but a considerable number of them are still following a partially settled way of life, without any stable or even unstable
employment. The extent of the problem is greater than suggested by the percentage ratio of the group, because this population is concentrated in certain areas and because the problems
arising out of their situation affect a great number of people.
The gipsies' 'free' way of life is the result of a long historical
process of exclusion and discrimination. Nevertheless it is now
perceived by them as being of their own creation and choice.
Administrative intervention in favour of rapid integration
would be cruel and not really efficient, especially as the settling
down and the real integration of gipsies is made extremely
difficult by the prejudices still held by the rest of the population.
(And administrative measures cannot eliminate prejudices.)
Therefore the gipsies' present situation is tacitly but not pass-
ively accepted. It is realized that if their social, economic and
cultural disadvantages are left untouched, if no positive action
is taken in their interest, then their disadvantages will constantly
increase and the tensions and social barriers generated by them
will grow stronger. This is obviously opposed to social values
aiming at more equality and solidarity.

Extreme liberalism holds that one has no right to make
people happy against their own wishes. If making people happy
is understood in terms of a forced identification with alien
values and life styles, then the argument is valid. But one has to
realize that present-day 'happiness' can be the source of future
unhappiness. And then the search for indirect ways and means
of altering the present situation is warranted – even if change
means, as is practically always the case, the loss of some values
and nuances. Obviously providing adequate living conditions
does not imply the elimination of all gipsy values and characteristics. On the contrary, from recent experiments conducted in
schools where teaching is done in gipsy language, it seems that
the revival of their language and culture helps, and is helped by,
their fuller integration into the community. Considerable efforts
are therefore being made to promote their integration, especially since 1962, when a decree of the Council of Ministers

laid down certain guidelines for future action and introduced various social policy measures, such as specially favourable terms for loans on construction. Progress is considerable, primarily in the case of male employment. According to a recently published study,[22] about 80 per cent of men between 15 and 60 had a permanent job in 1971. This means that 20 to 25 per cent are still without stable employment, though of course some do have temporary jobs. It follows, then, that individual liberalism has to be accepted in the short run, although the definitive solution cannot be found by relying solely on this principle.

Another, minor point concerns young people who are reluctant for a time to accept a regular job, and prefer to be 'looking around', sometimes supported by parents. In their case the present-day official attitude is rather too rigid. The young in question are seen as irresponsible, and are often admonished. It does, however, seem right to allow the complete transformation of the way of life that occurs with the change from full-time education to employment to take place gradually and also to allow young people to seek more information before choosing a permanent position. Therefore, especially if economic conditions improve and the manpower shortage lessens, more flexibility will have to be introduced in the 'trial and error' process in the search for suitable jobs.

(b) The view that may be termed *radical liberalism* accepts the idea that a compromise has to be worked out between individual interests and more general social interests. Thus it does not argue for an absolute right to unemployment, but a conditional one. The condition in question is specific to the capitalist, more precisely to the Ameriacn labour market, which is called a 'dual labor market' by D. Gordon and other radical economists.[23] In this view the labour market has two sectors.

22. *Beszámoló a magyarországi cigányok helyzetével foglalkozó 1971-ben végzett kutatásról* (Report on the Survey of the Situation of the Gipsies in Hungary, made in 1971), Institute of Sociology of the Hungarian Academy of Sciences, 1976.
23. Michael Reich, David M. Gordon and Richard C. Edwards, 'A Theory of Labour Market Segmentation', *American Economic Review*, May 1973.

The primary one offers good salaries, acceptable working conditions, stability and career opportunities. The second is characterized by the opposite features – low pay, instability and unfair treatment. However, it is in the interests of people engaged in the first sector to maintain the secondary market and – as a corollary – to maintain structural poverty. That is why artificial obstacles are created to hinder the shift from the secondary to the primary sector. Therefore the radical social critic sees it as rational and justified to reject any job with inhuman conditions and to choose unemployment instead. According to him, it is the duty of the society, which incidentally is so wealthy that it can afford the costs involved, to support those for whom it does not create adequate working conditions. This social criticism is directed primarily against centrally devised endeavours to cut down AFDC (Aid For Dependent Children) by introducing employment obligations.[24] Since the AFDC is given mainly to black women without any job qualifications, their only opportunity to work would be in the secondary labour market. In this case unemployment is seen as more in keeping with human dignity than the acceptance of inhuman working conditions.

This type of social criticism – that the choice of unemployment is justified if the job is objectionable on the above grounds – is not voiced in socialist countries. One of the reasons is probably that the construct of the dual labour market is not valid in these countries. Indeed it is probable that it cannot be fully applied anywhere outside the United States. Two conditions seem to be necessary if not sufficient to create a secondary market there, namely the race problem and guild-like trade unions. Both are absent – or present in a much milder form – outside the USA. Besides the absence of these factors, there is a pronounced and in a sense artificial manpower shortage in practically all the socialist countries which also militates against the emergence of a dual labour market. (The artificiality means that the manpower shortage is due to the measures assuring full employment.) The consequences of this shortage are manifold.

24. Frances Fox Piven and Richard Cloward, *Regulating the Poor*, Vintage Books, New York, 1972.

In Hungary, for instance, a high manpower turnover ensues where workers are constantly oriented towards better jobs, so that a whole system of compensatory mechanisms is needed to maintain workers in jobs where the working conditions or the contents of the job are bad and cannot rapidly be altered. (Compensation may be given in the form of advanced retirement age, special bonuses, etc.) The manpower turnover has not always been free from constraints however. Before the introduction of the economic reform in 1967, there were a number of penalties for changing jobs (loss of rights connected with the length of employment, etc.). It is also true – and this is one of the proofs that a more autonomous economic policy can exist alongside a more developed social policy – that since 1967 much more effort has been needed to improve poor working conditions or to establish compensatory mechanisms, and this effort has been made.

None the less, even if the standpoint of radical liberalism is not valid under our conditions, it has some implications that cannot be neglected. The secondary market does not exist in its crude form, that is, in an accumulation of all the negative features of jobs. But it is still true that jobs are extremely varied in many respects. In the future, in order to avoid the former solution which by means of administrative measures transformed the *obligation* to work into *compulsion*, and in order to mitigate the compulsory nature of work, further steps to reduce inequality in the conditions, contents and rewards of work tasks are obviously important.

(c) Finally, there is the *technocratic economist's* view opposing full employment on the grounds of its disincentive effect. In this conception, if the individual is sure to find a job at any time, if unemployment is not threatening, then work discipline will disappear and individual achievement will decrease. Incidentally, this argument may also be used – as was the case in the last decade in Great Britain – against a fair level of unemployment benefits. There are also other more theoretical arguments for the maintenance of a certain level of unemployment, such as the elasticity of the market economy and the avoidance of inflation.[25]

The positive arguments for full employment have been mentioned. But the socialist position *against* unemployment is based on other considerations, too. It is well known that the various occupational groups are not equally threatened by unemployment. It is usually true that the higher the position in the power or knowledge hierarchy, the less the danger of unemployment. If unemployment was a necessary incentive, then one would have to implement measures to assure it for every occupational group, including professions – a claim never voiced by the partisans of unemployment. The fallacy of the argument is thus practically proven – unless one maintains that there is a genetic difference in the work ethics of the different groups. Further, uncertainty and the threat of poverty belong to a punitive logic. They preclude a positive evaluation of work. Even if Hungary has not succeeded up to now in fully elaborating a positive system of work incentives, this does not mean that the negative incentive must be accepted as the only possible solution. Even if unemployment has economic advantages, there is a high social price to pay. The threat of unemployment reinforces individual competition, and competitiveness weakens social solidarity. With unemployment, the emergence of a socially marginal under-class is practically certain: it will be composed of those who, in the absence of adequate assets and chances to succeed, have been forced out of the competition.

For all these reasons, full employment is an organic part of a socialist social system. None the less, a major criticism of socialist countries maintains that they have not eliminated unemployment in reality, but only formally. As Peter Wiles puts it: 'Are the many Soviet workers who do nearly nothing for a full-time wage not really unemployed? Is not this the true equivalent of the dole and, since this practice is so widespread, is the absence of a dole so important?'[26] The situation is similar in other

25. W. J. Baumol, *Welfare Economics and the Theory of the State*, Harvard University Press, Cambridge, Mass., 1969, p. 135.

26. P. J. D. Wiles, 'A Note on Soviet Unemployment by U.S. Definitions', *Soviet Studies*, April 1972.

socialist countries, including Hungary, so that the same criticism applies to them. Peter Wiles's argument is, however, biased, because it neglects some of the basic human consequences of unemployment. It is certainly true that under-employment is a real phenomenon in Hungary and together with 'laziness' exploits the possibilities offered by defective work control and full job security. The causes of these phenomena are varied. Some of them, like inexperienced work-organization, delayed repairs or irregular supply of materials, cannot be seen as necessary corollaries of the present Hungarian system, but real shortcomings which can and must be remedied. Two other factors also leading to under-employment at work belong more organically to the essence of present-day socialist systems. One is a more or less deliberately slowed pace of work as compared to capitalist countries, adapted to the individual's rhythm. The other is the policy of 'job-sharing': in order to avoid real unemployment, society divides some – mostly but not exclusively unskilled manual or office jobs – among more people than absolutely necessary. The two last 'structural' features certainly have many drawbacks in the short term, like the weakening of work discipline, the lowering of productivity and, also, a feeling of lack of self-respect in those whom society does not require to achieve their best. It seems to me, however, that these drawbacks cannot be compared with the harm caused by real unemployment. Job-satisfaction and self-esteem might suffer by our policy in the case of quite large groups, but they are entirely denied to some groups in the case of official unemployment even if there are more or less adequate unemployment benefits. Hungarian policy may imply that salaries, at least in some jobs, are lower than they would be with higher intensity and productivity. But no salient differences are introduced in people's legal situations, in the source of income, even in their working conditions and life style. In this sense the policy of full employment, with all its more or less transitory shortcomings, serves the lessening of social distances between people and helps to avoid socially marginal and rejected groups.

There is also another element in this policy that may have some relevance in a longer-term perspective. The right to work means social justice or equality in the distribution of work *opportunities*. This is certainly contrary to the idea underlying Theobald's guaranteed income concept, where high productivity is supposed to make a growing number of people superfluous.[27] With a generally higher level of knowledge and skills, the same logic may and should generate a socially more just distribution of 'good' work opportunities, that is to say the avoidance of the monopolization of good jobs, as described in the last model of a new organization of work presented in section 3.1.

Let me also add one more point: it is probable that the extent of under-employment at work in the socialist countries is frequently overestimated by onlookers, whether foreigners or not. At the risk of sounding naïve, one must assert that the majority of people in socialist countries work hard and work a great deal, even if they do so for mixed motives. Ironic generalizations are unfair to the vast majority.

On the whole it seems that the rejection of open unemployment even in the short term creates less tension than it helps to avoid, and this seems to be the only socially and economically acceptable solution in the longer perspective for a society that wants to become a real community.

It is, therefore, socio-logically justified for the long-term plan never to question the importance of full employment and job-security, and entirely reasonable that the more flexible economic policy introduced in the last decade should have made provisions for economic mechanisms that indirectly stimulated the enterprises to maintain full employment. Employment security and full employment seem to form a stable feature of the present Hungarian social and economic system.

3.3 Women and work

Equality between the sexes requires more than just political rights – the claim of early feminism – and more than economic

27. Robert Theobald, *The Guaranteed Income: Next Step in Socio-Economic Evolution?*, Anchor Books, New York, 1967.

independence. These are necessary, but not sufficient conditions of full emancipation. Political rights are usually understood as the right to vote and to be elected. But without adequate information gained through personal involvement and participation in social affairs, even the right to vote may miscarry and become an instrument of manipulation, and the right to be elected is certainly illusory. To accede to an elected post means participation in power exercised in the sphere of social affairs, in connection with them, through them. If women do not have an adequate place in all social spheres, their role will always remain marginal in the exercise of power, and they will remain unprepared for many posts of decision-making.

Economic independence can be assured in several ways. One possibility is the citizen's right to share in resources. This is a recurrent idea of different utopias, where usually the only condition for a citizen's right to share is his or her natural obligation to work for the community. In a more theoretical form this is obviously also the basic principle of communism in the Marxist conception.

The universal right to share also occurs in Theobald's[28] 'negative' utopia, in connection with the guaranteed income. But here the citizens are supported mainly as consumers, while the productive efforts of a large segment of the population are not needed any more.

Hungarian society is not yet rich enough to be able to adopt the communist ideal of each citizen's unconditional right to share, relying upon his social conscience to make him fulfil his obligations towards the community. But it already acknowledges – together with a number of other countries – the rig' t in the case of those who, for physical or other reasons, such as age or illness, are unable to engage in work. In the case of women, two such groups are easily discernible: those who have a difficult pregnancy and those who have small babies, especially throughout the period of breast-feeding. In their case, the right to share is based on the biological and psychological aspects of motherhood. The length of this period and the amount of the

28. op. cit.

benefit they could receive obviously depend – as in the case of any social benefit – on the economic resources of society and on its ideological commitment to these rights. In Hungary, this commitment is strong. Pregnant women are legally protected, and the inability to work because of motherhood is now compensated for by twenty weeks' full salary.

More recently attention has been given to an idea which would promote the economic independence of women. This is the redefinition of work so as to cover traditional female activities, child-rearing and housework in general.[29] According to this approach society must acknowledge by means of a mother's wage the economic and social usefulness of the household chores and must pay for them accordingly. It is certainly rather ironic that this solution is in special favour in highly developed societies where housework has already been made quite easy, while those contemporary societies (in the Third World for example) where women still carry out the majority of productive tasks inside and outside the home cannot afford to envisage the idea of 'paying' for housework. It is also somewhat naïve to think that the redefinition of a social phenomenon (work in this case) can alter fundamental economic and social laws that apply to the public sphere and to the labour force working in the social division of work. This means that the 'mother's wage' cannot be transformed by a simple act of redefinition into a genuine wage, but will remain a social benefit -- with its related problems. There are several other practical difficulties connected with this solution, such as the public financing and hence public control of activities taking place in the private sphere. From our point of view the main problem is that the mother's wage, instead of changing women's place in society, legitimizes their present role. It may alter redistribution, but leaves untouched the basic social relations of knowledge, power and participation. By reinforcing the household monopoly of women, it has an adverse effect on the recent trend of changing

29. 'Mothers' Wages, Children's Allowances, Parents' Wages – Analysis and Synthesis of a Social Policy Cluster', in David G. Gil, *Unraveling Social Policy*, Schenkman Publishing Company, Cambridge, Mass., 1973.

the traditional pattern of the division of labour within the family. By confining them to the home, it is a disincentive for women in the free development of their abilities and interests. The right to remain 'only' a mother quickly turns into an obligation. Public opinion, strongly influenced not only by men but by all those women who have already chosen to remain at home, turns against those who try to combine several interests and labels them unloving or unnatural mothers, thus inducing a feeling of guilt in them. That is why I do not share the conviction of D. Gil, who, despite being aware of a number of shortcomings of the mother's wage measure, still thinks that 'the overall ideological thrust of this policy is in the direction of social and economic equality', although it may well be a useful instrument for solving some important problems in the United States.

None the less, it is certainly true for every country that as long as the traditional pattern of the division of work within the family persists and the social institutions taking over family responsibilities (especially child-care institutions) are inadequate in number and quality, the situation of the mother becomes extremely difficult if she has to combine employment and household chores. In this situation a special allocation is warranted to assure adequate care to children and also to alleviate the parents' burden. Hungary introduced this type of grant in 1967 – the so-called child-care grant. Its essential features are the following: it is granted from the end of the twenty weeks' fully paid maternity leave up to the end of the child's third year. Its value corresponds to about 40 to 50 per cent of the average salary of young women, and is permanently kept at this level (that is, it is 'index-linked'). In monetary terms, it was (in 1975) between 800 and 1,000 forints per child per month, depending on the total number of children. At first it could be granted to women who had been in full-time employment for at least twelve months prior to child-birth. Later the right was extended to students, part-time workers, etc. The grant is optional, and the mother retains her post throughout the whole period so that she can go back to work any time she wants. Recently two new elements have been added: the mother on a grant may take care of one or two other babies, or, on the other hand, she can interrupt the grant once a year (that is, she can take up her work for some time and then go back on the grant). The employer is obliged to assure her, any time she wants to go back, a job which, even if not exactly the same, is at least similar in content and conditions and assures a similar remuneration to the one she has done previously. In the last ten years employers have been encouraged to give the same additional benefits in wage increases, etc., to mothers on a grant as to the other employees.

The child-care grant soon became very popular (see Table 3/2).

Table 3/2: Data relating to the child-care grant

Year	Total number of births, in thousands	Percentage of mothers entitled to the grant	Percentage of mothers receiving the grant out of those entitled	Total number of mothers on the grant, at the end of the year, in thousands
1967	148·9	57	72	32
1968	154·4	63	70	92
1970	151·8	74	68	167
1972	153·3	79	73	185
1974	186·3	84	78[a]	229
1975	194·2			265

Source: A gyermekgondozási segély főbb adatai, 1967–1974 (Data Relating to the Child-Care Grant, 1967–74) Central Statistical Office, Budapest, 1975; and Dr E. Szabady, 'Időszerű nèpesedési Pkèrdéseink' (Current Demographic Problems) in Nők-Gazdaság,-Tàrsadalom, Kossuth Könyvkiadó, 1976

[a] for 1973.

One of the signs of this growing popularity is that, while some years ago the grant appealed mainly to mothers with low pay and low skills, now a growing proportion of better trained and better paid mothers use it, too (see Table 3/3).

Table 3/3: Percentage of mothers taking the child-care grant, by educational level

	Primary	Secondary	Higher
1967	77·3	65·3	34·4
1969	71·6	59·9	32·6
1972	76·0	72·5	50·8
1973	81·1	76·4	56·2

Source: As for Table 3/2

However, because of the pull of their vocation and the problems of isolation at home, women with a higher level of training and better jobs take the grant for a shorter period than the others. Thus, for example, the proportion of mothers who use the grant for more than eighteen months is between 18 per cent and 24 per cent for doctors, teachers and engineers, around 50 per cent for skilled workers and 80 per cent for unskilled ones.

Unintended and socially undesirable consequences, such as the slowing-down in the transformation of the household division of labour and the revival of some stereotypes of female roles, could not be avoided entirely, although they were foreseen. That is why there is a search for more ways of minimizing side-effects. The government has now declared that the construction of nurseries must not be slowed down despite the existence of the grant, and it has incorporated this in its five-year plans. Steps are taken to lessen the mother's isolation, to allow her to maintain contacts with the outside world and to acquire some professional training while at home. A further step – still at the discussion stage – is the transformation of the grant into a *parental* right with the possibility of switching roles from time to time. (Fathers are already allowed to receive a grant in the event of the mother's illness or absence.) Certainly habits would change slowly even if the legal position were altered. But because of the norm-shaping force of law, this step would at least stop the revival of the traditional image of the ideal wife and mother.

In general, the child-care grant, in the form in which it was introduced in Hungary, is a compromise between two conflicting aims: the immediate well-being of young children and mothers and the long-term goal of equality between the sexes. It is not really a mothers' wage policy, since its allocation is not universal but related to former employment, and since it is granted only for a three-year period. Rather, it is similar to maternity leave: it is intended not so much to pay for the work done at home as to help the family during the period when the mother cannot engage in a gainful occupation because the small child needs personal care. For maternity leave, however, the reason for the leave is really the biological and psychological aspect of motherhood so that in this case the sex-roles cannot easily be changed. The child-care grant is offered for a long period when it would be desirable to stress not the biological or psychological specificities of motherhood, but the social aspect of parenthood. If development is in this direction – towards promoting the participation of both parents in the education of children as well as in the household chores – then the grant will lose the negative features it has at the moment and might stimulate the employment of women, without any adverse effect either on them or on the children. (Even now this stimulating effect can be seen: since the introduction of the grant the ratio of young women taking up employment before their first child is born has grown very considerably. Table 3/2 shows that many more young mothers are entitled to the grant as compared with 1967.)

The third solution to the problem of economic emancipation is obviously the integration of women into the social division of work, the only solution which can assure full economic, social and political emancipation. That is why this has been the main policy in the last few decades, with the results already mentioned. However, this process can occur in different ways, and the different solutions can be arranged on a hypothetical scale. At one end of the scale there is a situation (characteristic of the early stages of capitalist development) where women are obliged to accept menial and underpaid jobs, inferior positions and the burden stemming from the simultaneous execution of paid work, housework and child care. At the other end a situation is conceivable where men as well as women are able to develop and use to the full their various abilities, sharing in possibilities, responsibilities and obligations in every aspect of life, including work and public affairs as well as family responsibilities. The advance of the cause of women's equality obviously depends on the position a society occupies on this scale and on the developmental tendencies it shows. For the time being no society assures the conditions of this type of self-realization to all its members. The problems stemming from this are of a general order. They affect men as well as women, but for well-known historical and social reasons women are at a relative disadvantage in comparison to men. This was so conspicuous some thirty years ago that special efforts had to be made in favour of women in order to avoid the situation at the wrong end of the scale, that is, to prevent the right to work being transformed into an obligation to earn.

Women-specific social action has developed in several directions. *One* component already mentioned consisted in reversing that traditional process in which biological difference was transformed into social inequality. The direct means used for reversing this process consisted of paid maternity leave and, to a lesser degree, the child-care grant. *The other* component was the institutionalization of a broadening circle of former household duties. This meant and means the steady development of services (usually subsidized canteens, laundries, etc.) and obviously the widening of the network of child-care institutions which were scarce and ill-equipped before the war.

Since primary schools work on a half-day basis, many new day-care centres were created in the schools where meals are provided for the children and where they are supervised during the afternoon. Today these centres receive about a quarter of all children between six and fourteen, with a higher proportion in the younger groups. In the early years after the war standards were not really adequate in nurseries and school day centres, but in the last few years special efforts have been made to improve the care offered there.

Table 3/4: Data on child-care institutions

	Nurseries[a]			Kindergartens[b]			
	1950	1960	1975	1938	1950	1960	1975
Number of institutions	189	816	1,132	1,140	1,773	2,865	4,077
Number of children registered in thousands	7·3	32·0	55·4	112·1	106·0	184·0	329·4
As percentage of the relevant age group	1·4	7·4	10·6	—	23·5	33·7	74·9

Source: 'Statisztikai adatok a nők helyzetéről' (Statistical Data on the Situation of Women), Central Statistical Office, 1975, Hungarian Statistical Yearbook, 1975.

[a] For children under 3 years
[b] For children between 4 and 6 years old

The *third* scheme for improving the situation of women con-sists of endeavours to change old stereotypes and attitudes towards women. The transformation of social reality obviously contributes to this change, but there is certainly a time-lag be-tween actual changes and changes in social and individual con-sciousness. This lag is shown by various data, for example on the household division of labour (still mostly done by women even if they are in employment)[30] or on male and female ideals as described by men and women. A recent survey made by J. Sas[31] showed, for example, that men and women alike felt that the set of character traits important for men were entirely different from those important for women. There was prac-tically a consensus in stating that political understanding, firmness and intelligence were important qualities in men, while thrift, common sense and skill in child-rearing were much more important in women. Direct means of intervention in this field

30. See, for example, *The Use of Time*, ed. A. Szalai et al., Mouton, The Hague, Paris, 1972.
31. Unpublished Ph.D. dissertation, Budapest, 1977.

are non-existent or at least ineffective. Recently, therefore, efforts have been centred on education, especially as analytical studies showed that Hungarian school books were imbued with traditional stereotypes.[32]

The most important factor, however, at least in the long term, is the adequate preparation of women for the various posts within the social division of labour. The first task was to remedy the educational disadvantage of girls, while increasing the level of educational attainment of the whole population. Both aims were carried out successfully. With a considerable enlargement of the educational framework, the relative position of women improved rapidly (see Table 3/5).

Table 3/5: Indices of schooling by sex

Percentage of the population with:

	8 years' schooling completed among those aged 15 years and over		12 years' schooling completed among those aged 18 years and over		Degree or diploma in higher education among those aged 25 years and over	
	M	F	M	F	M	F
1941	16·1	14·1	7·0	1·6	2·8	0·4
1960	34·5	31·3	11·6	6·3	4·5	1·1
1973	59·9	51·7	19·8	15·9	6·9	2·9

Source: Census and microcensus data for the years quoted.

In 1975, 48 per cent of those in secondary schools and in higher education were girls. Still, the level attained in itself does not indicate the presence or absence of special, vocational skills. In this respect the advantage of men persists. Thus for example in grammar-school type secondary schools, which do not offer any direct training or job qualifications, 65 per cent of the students are girls. In technical secondary schools they represent 47 per cent, but they cluster in schools preparing for white-collar and service jobs. Apprenticeship, whether industrial or other

32. Judit Háber and Judit H. Sas, *Tankönyvszagu világ* (The Musty World of School Manuals), Akadémiai Kiadó, forthcoming.

kinds, does not have enough openings for girls, their ratio being under 30 per cent there. The disadvantage of women also persists at the level of higher education. While their overall ratio approaches the magic 50 per cent, they tend to be over-represented in institutions of lower academic prestige, leading to relatively poor jobs, and they tend to be under-represented in branches that prepare for higher-level administrative or managerial decision-making posts. This is certainly not merely a Hungarian phenomenon. On the contrary, in the majority of non-socialist countries girls accede with more difficulty to traditionally 'male' professions. The gap still exists in Hungary despite considerable gains.

Table 3/6: Percentage of women among those with a degree or diploma in higher education

Type of studies	1949	1960	1973
Engineering	1·2	7·1	13·1
Agriculture	4·2	9·8	16·0
Economics	13·9	20·2	38·0
Medicine	17·2	33·7	40·4
Education	49·1	58·1	61·1
Law	0·6	10·4	12·1

Source: Census and microcensus data for the years quoted.

The occupational structure is largely shaped by the educational structure, where women are over-represented in categories of lower skill and lower pay within both manual and non-manual occupations. There are also some other, traditionally evolved and still powerful factors which have an unfavourable impact on the position of women in the world of work. One factor is that women's interest in new, hitherto closed fields, especially modern technology, is developing rather slowly. This is partly due to the differentiated socialization of boys and girls. Another problem is connected with the traditional male–female relation, which used to be that of domination and subordination. This relation is hard to reverse for both parties, and this situation is partly responsible for the slow access of women to positions of leadership. Thus historically shaped attitudes and stereotypes create a major difficulty in the whole process of change, besides the given, initial conditions and the interest-structure generated by them. In recent years more attention has been paid to the 'social psychological' obstacles of change, and renewed efforts have been made to create adequate objective conditions. The results are not negligible. From 1960 to 1970 the number of managers and professionals increased by 18 per cent among men, by 78 per cent among women. For skilled workers, the number of men grew by 29 per cent, the number of women by 42 per cent. The old gaps are slowly closing and this, in itself, acts as an accelerating factor. Once there is a sizable number of women in a given field, it becomes easier to question the old monopolies: new models are created, gradually attracting in their turn new candidates.

The sexual policy of socialist countries is criticized by some Western social scientists mainly on two grounds, as usual both from the 'right' and from the 'left'. Conservative critics often suggest that the policy has gone too far. David Lane for instance mentions that 'there is evidence to suggest that the values of equality of sexes espoused by socialist ideology have created conflict between married partners'.[33] This conflict stems from rivalry and from the desire for women's independence – and is probably due to a misunderstanding of social mechanisms: '... the very continuation of human society requires harmonious relations between the sexes and the apparently universal role of the male in industrial society as giving status to the family group and as having authority in the family is, as Parsons suggests, probably an adaptive mechanism to reduce rivalry'.[34] The facts are correct inasmuch as divorce rates are certainly high in some socialist countries, Hungary in particular. The explanation is none the less doubtful. Divorce may occur not only because women 'aspire to independence', and

33. David Lane, *The End of Inequality ?*, Penguin Books, Harmondsworth, 1971. p. 90.
34, ibid., p. 90.

'engage in rivalry', but also because, having acquired some independence, they can no longer accept a relation which is in fact based on male domination and female subordination. In any case, sexual relations are not the only example of former 'harmonious' relations being disrupted because one of the parties realizes that the 'adaptive mechanism' works at his or her expense and that 'harmony' is maintained by means of domination and exploitation. And it is probably not a mere partisan value judgement if I assume that the real solution of these conflicts, one which may bring with it human progress, lies in the working-out of these conflicts, in order to change the former relations.

Left-wing criticism maintains that not enough has been done and that further progress is jeopardized by the prevailing – still male-dominated – interest structure, served by overprotective positive discrimination (affirmative action). Again, it is certainly true that much remains to be done for sexual equality, a fact of which all socialist countries are aware. There is, however, a difference in the way positive or protective discrimination is viewed.

Overprotection is certainly harmful. But if the historical disadvantages of a group are significant and persistent, some extra advantage is warranted, otherwise the gap cannot be closed. It is true, for instance, that dangerous or dirty work or night work is hazardous and inconvenient not only to women but also to men and therefore both should be 'protected'. However, if all the protective measures adopted up to now in favour of women were to be wiped out while women's disadvantages in the field of vocational training of preparation for the labour market persist, and while the household division of labour is still the traditional one, the withdrawal would be prejudicial to women. It may well be that this type of protection slows the rate of change to a certain extent, but at the same time it makes the change much less painful for the traditionally weaker party.

A case in point is the Hungarian child-care grant. So far I have encountered explicit criticism only in personal discussions at international conferences, but implicit criticism of it is fairly frequent.

Thus Edit Krebs, a leading figure in the trade-union movement in Austria, wrote in this connection: 'In some quarters efforts are being made to get maternity leave extended to three years, but this suggestion is being vigorously opposed by most trade unions, particularly by women's ones, on the grounds that such a measure would in all probability mean the end of suitable employment for skilled or highly qualified women.'[35] I have already mentioned that the Hungarian child-care grant had certain drawbacks for women's emancipation. (That is why it is so important that it should be transformed into a parental right.) But something has been forgotten in the argument above, namely the impact of the *absence* of a child-care grant and nurseries on female employment. In Austria, the proportion of children in institutional care under three years of age is about 1 or 2 per cent. In this case the main solution for a woman after the birth of her child is to leave employment altogether, unless she can afford a paid child-minder or can find an unpaid one. This means that the employers have as little interest in giving responsible or highly qualified jobs to young women as they would if there was a longer maternity leave. The difference between this solution and the child-care grant is that in the second case the woman gets some independent income and retains her employment rights. Thus, she loses much less and she returns to work more easily than in the first case. I may add that in recent discussions with Western critics of the Hungarian child-care grant it has become clear that the main reason for their objections was that under the conditions of a private economy there are no means of forcing the employer to reserve a job for someone over such a long period.

Sexual inequality is one aspect of social inequality and is, therefore, difficult to overcome. There is resistance to change because of the prevailing interest structure and because of

35. Edit Krebs, 'Women Workers and the Trade Unions in Austria: An Interim Report', in *Women Workers and Society*, ILO, Geneva, 1976, p. 195.

traditionally ingrained attitudes and ideas. Progress requires, as elsewhere, deliberate social intervention – but the impact of this intervention reaches directly only the public sphere, for example, when it changes the framework of vocational training or assures the equal rights of the sexes in various fields. Since the role of the private sphere is (probably) greater in this case than in the majority of other social inequalities, and since the private sphere can be affected only or mainly in an indirect way, future progress may not be spectacular. A rigid and mechanical application of the principle of sexual equality could (perhaps) speed up progress. But the price of this forced progress would be paid mainly by those whom it sought to serve, that is, by women, and even among women by the majority who are in the most disadvantaged situation in terms of education, of skill, of income. (This would clearly be the impact of the abolition of many maternity rights or of the abolition of the child-care grant in Hungary.) This makes the issue of sexual equality fairly specific as compared to the other unequal social relations. In the case of a more equal distribution of incomes or wealth, re-distribution clearly works in favour of those who were formerly underprivileged. And even in spheres where there is a price to be paid by the new 'winners' – such as additional efforts required by more equal participation in power – there is no all-round deterioration in the situation of the formerly under-privileged, and the price is only paid by those who also gain.

3.4 Working conditions and terms of employment

It needs no elaborate proof to show that unfavourable, un-healthy or dangerous working conditions affect mainly manual and especially industrial work. The same is true for shift-work.

The improvement of working conditions has been high on Hungary's policy agenda for the last decade or so. In 1964 the percentage of industrial workers exposed to unhealthy con-ditions was 51·4, while in 1970 the overall percentage went down to 35·6, with a somewhat faster pace of decrease for women.[36] Shift-work, more precisely night-shifts, affected about one third of workers in the early sixties, with a somewhat lower ratio in the case of women. This percentage is decreasing fairly slowly: 10·3 per cent of all work periods were night-shifts in 1965, 8·9 per cent in 1974. In this case the efforts to reduce shiftwork were directed mainly at women, especially mothers. Between 1967 and 1971 the number of all women doing night-shifts dropped by 10 per cent, that of mothers by 22 per cent. The issue is, as mentioned already, somewhat controversial: if women were categorically refused the possibility of night-shifts, this would be a disadvantage, lowering their wage and weakening their position in the workforce.[37] If, on the other hand, there were no protective measures whatsoever, the burden of women could become excessive. The actual practice is somewhere in between these extreme positions, but the direction of further change is not quite clear as yet.

One important sign of better working conditions is the decrease of industrial accidents. Before the war and up to the first half of the fifties accident ratios were high, owing to the neglect of security installations as well as accelerated work speed. Since then there has been a steady improvement. The rate of fatal accidents per hundred thousand workers (industry, construction and transport taken together) was 31 in 1938, 45 between 1950 and 1954, 26 in 1960, 19 in 1970 and 15 in 1975. The rate of all accidents per thousand workers was for the above periods, 89, 92, 72, 47 and 39. This is not necessarily a universal trend. According to the data in the Annual Report of HM Chief Factory Inspector there was in Great Britain a constant increase in accident rates in the same period. The rate per thousand

36. *Az állami iparban foglalkoztatott munkások létszámösszetétele, munkakörülményei és bérarányai* (Composition, Working Conditions and Wages of Workers in State Industry), Central Statistical Office, Budapest, 1971; and *Munkaügyi adatgyüjtemény az állami iparban foglalkoztatottakról* (Labour Statistics on Those Employed in the State Industry), Central Statistical Office, Budapest, 1972.

37. See, for example, Anna-Greta Leijon, 'Sexual Inequality in the Labour Market: Some Experiences and Views of the Nordic Countries', in *Women Workers and Society*, op. cit.

employed for example in the manufacturing industry was 22·5 in 1952, 29·8 in 1966 and 35 in 1973.[38] (The two sets are not exactly comparable because of differences in the definitions. On an international scale only fatalities are comparable. In this respect Hungary ranks with countries like Poland, Norway or Italy. Only a few countries, especially Britain and Sweden, show a regularly lower rate, while quite a few, even some technologically more advanced countries (Austria, Switzerland, West Germany), have significantly higher proportions of deaths.)

By now it is clear that the improvement of working conditions is not an automatic corollary of technical development. Some previously prevalent hardships and dangers (for example, excessively hard work) disappear, while new evils are constantly emerging. In Hungary efforts are therefore now concentrated on the following points:

(i) Preventive measures in order to avoid the harmful consequences of unhealthy or dangerous conditions and constant control of these aspects. Responsibility is shared by the ministries, the firms and the trade unions. There are about 200 independently paid safety inspectors in the factories, about as many people responsible for these matters in the ministries, and 120,000 elected representatives of workers throughout the country. The trade unions' right to participate in the making of policy decisions concerning the utilization of work safety funds, the elimination of unsafe processes and installations and so on has proved especially valuable in this field.

(ii) The improvement of workers' education and information about safety at work, and the increase of the management's responsibilities. The importance of adequate preparation is shown by the fact that unskilled workers are more accident-prone than the others, that almost half of the accidents hit inexperienced workers and that quite a high percentage of accidents are due to the non-utilization of the safety installations. (Workers often neglect safety measures because they slow down

38. Dr Hermann Grunwald, 'Problems of Health and Safety at Work', *Marxism Today*, September 1975.

the pace of the work, thus affecting wages.) Workers also have to be given more information about their rights to compensation. The management's responsibility must be and is in fact increasingly stressed in all these respects.

(iii) Stress is also laid in Hungary on compensatory measures. Hourly wages are about 10 per cent higher than average in the case of unhealthy conditions, and 10 to 20 per cent higher in case of night-shifts. These differentials have shown only a slight increase in the last decade. A more substantial increase for shift-work (around 30 per cent) was introduced in 1977. The general welfare measures, work-related benefits as well as facilities such as canteens, medical care, sanitary installations, etc., at the workplace have been continuously and significantly improved. Legally prescribed norms are high in this last respect, so that they are attained in only about 70 per cent of workplaces, especially because there are many old buildings that are hard to modernize. Welfare benefits at the workplace also include prophylactic food and drink, subsidized meals, holiday homes, children's institutions, cultural and sports facilities, etc. Lately firms have been encouraged to contribute more actively to the workers' housing programme. The housing shortage is still so acute that there is a strong demand on the part of workers in this respect, and many enterprises have building facilities that could indeed be mobilized for this aim.

The costs of the firms' welfare and social policy are financed out of their profits: according to new regulations since 1968, a higher percentage of profits remain within the enterprise instead of being centralized in the state budget than in earlier years, and the workers and employees of the enterprise have more discretionary power in the utilization of the welfare funds. However, to avoid haphazard omissions and undue inequalities or imbalances between establishments, a social plan must be prepared by each firm, taking into account suggestions from the state.

According to the new guidelines worked out by the Ministry of Work and the National Council of Trade Unions, the firm's social plan integrates measures aiming at improvements in the working conditions and conditions of everyday life of all the employees. The contents of the plan give an idea of the social policy activities of the firms. The social plans must cover the following points – specifying and adapting them to the concrete conditions of the plant:

● Priority measures favouring women, young people and manual workers;

● The social policy aspects of manpower politics, including wage increases for the lowest-paid workers;

● Programmes of professional training;

● All the measures concerning healthier and safer working conditions;

● Health programme for the place of work;

● Rehabilitation programme for injured employees;

● The development of company welfare benefits – meals, dormitories for commuters, transport facilities for commuters, child-care facilities, holiday programmes, housing programmes, subsidies, grants and aids, study grants, cultural and sports facilities, etc.

On the allocation of welfare benefits the firm has to take into account the social and family conditions of the employee as well as his or her work. (In section 3.5 some of the problems connected with the firm's social policy will be spelt out in more detail.)

There is another sphere of working conditions, namely the terms and legal conditions of employment, which have important implications for societal policy. In Hungary, these regulations are usually laid down centrally, so that there is little variation in these respects among firms. The terms of, or rights connected with, employment are the product of several factors. Unquestioned habits, traditionally acquired rights and newly introduced elements merge. The outcome in Hungary is a less consistent set of regulations than for example in the USA or Great Britain. Dorothy Wedderburn and Christine Craig[39] have shown that in the majority of establishments in manufacturing industry in England separate employment terms applied to different occupational groups, so that manual workers consistently had the least favourable arrangements. Some of the employment terms covered by the English study are differentiated in the same way in Hungary although the differences are usually less marked. In the case of holidays for instance, in Hungary, in 1969, 42 per cent of non-manuals, 38 per cent of manuals had more than nineteen days of paid holidays a year, while in the English survey 38 per cent of the establishments assured fifteen or more days' holiday for manual workers, more than 70 per cent to non-manuals. There is also a differentiation in the length of the period of notice in the case of dismissal, which varies in Hungary between twenty-one days (unskilled workers) and fifty-seven days (non-manuals in the technical professions). The majority of the firms in the English survey had no such schemes for manuals, and only a small number had one for lower non-manuals.

There is a second set of terms in which in Hungary there is practically no differentiation according to occupational criteria, while there was a significant one in the English survey. Thus sick pay schemes (including sick pay provided for more than three months) and pension schemes apply to everybody in employment (whether in industry or elsewhere). Exceptions are only made (that is, more favourable terms are applied) for some illnesses (tuberculosis gives the right to two years of sick pay, other illnesses one year), and for some unhealthy occupations. Clocking-in also belongs to the category which is uniformly applied – if it is introduced at all – though higher managers may form an exception in this case in Hungary too.

39. Dorothy Wedderburn and Christine Craig, 'Relative Deprivation in Work', in D. Wedderburn, ed., *Poverty, Inequality and Class Structure*, Cambridge University Press, 1974, pp. 142–54. For the USA see, for example, A. B. Shostak, *Blue-Collar Life*, Random House, New York, 1969, pp. 67–8.

In most cases there are no separate canteen facilities for manual workers and the staff.

Finally there is one condition, namely working hours, where a deliberate 'bias' was introduced in favour of workers in Hungary. Until the late sixties, Hungarian working hours were longer than in the majority of industrial countries: they remained forty-eight hours a week in practically all occupations (those in unhealthy conditions, etc., excepted). Their reduction was therefore necessary; but the simultaneous introduction of shorter working weeks would have caused difficulties. A gradual reduction was thus devised, giving priority to establishments in industry and construction. Thus the forty-four hour week was attained in industry by the end of 1969, while in the other branches only a minority had this even by the end of 1973. Since then it has spread farther, and by 1976 it had become universal. In any case, state administration was among the last branches to benefit from a shorter working week. This central decision was motivated mainly by the fact that *before* the war state employees formed an extremely privileged group in terms of working hours. Thus the reversal of the former situation had political significance. The percentage of employees on a working week with less than forty-eight hours (mainly forty-four hours) was, on 30 September 1973, 97 per cent in industry, 93 per cent in construction, 32 per cent in agriculture, 37 per cent in transport, 10 per cent in trade and 34 per cent in non-productive branches of the economy (including state administration, health, education and the services). The advantage of industry is slowly disappearing, but the whole process shows a new tendency proving the possibility of reversing established patterns of privilege.

3.5 The social policy of the firm and the division of social policy tasks

The division of funds, responsibilities and tasks among the different agents of social policy is an intricate problem. One aspect with special relevance to the improvement of working conditions is the division of tasks between the state and the firms.

Before the economic reform, the issue was practically never raised. Firms were considered not so much as autonomous responsible units but as mechanical executors of the central plan and subordinated organs of the central budget. They carried out all centrally allocated, productive or social policy tasks without analysing their interrelationships, without questioning the centrally defined priorities and without analysing their rationality. The reform, as has already been mentioned, created more adequate conditions for the development of an efficient economic policy, and also for the evolution of societal and social policy. The increasing relative autonomy of the firm went together with some decentralization not only in the economic field, but also in the sphere of social policy. More funds were left with the firm in order to ensure that it had a deliberate social policy – its main targets being defined by the social plan already mentioned. There is, then, a shift towards decentralization in the sphere of social policy, giving firms greater scope for decision. The process is not unanimously applauded. There are arguments questioning the social policy activity of the firm. Some of them are well-founded, and have to be taken seriously. The debate throws some light on the whole process of deliberate social change and on some of its dilemmas. It may therefore be interesting to review the main arguments for and against the growing role of the company.

(a) *Views supporting a more active policy at the level of the firm*

● It seems that the economic tasks of the firm can be better accomplished if the framework of social policy at the level of the firm is enlarged. It is easier to attract a better-qualified workforce if working conditions are better. Also, if increased production yields more funds for welfare objectives, this represents a supplementary incentive for all the employees, besides individual gains. Since a whole group of people profit from social achievements at company level, this trend is supposed to work against extreme individualism.

● Workplace democracy has more relevance for all those employed at the establishment if the issues decided there directly affect the people's working conditions and quality of life. This is especially true in the early phases of participation, when adequate preparation has not yet been made for debating larger issues.

● The allocation of resources is likely to be socially more just within the firm, because there is on the spot a more informed public and more direct control than is possible within regional units of public administration.

● Priorities can be established on the basis of information elicited directly from those concerned. These will therefore correspond better to people's real needs.

(b) *Views opposed to social policy at firm level*

● The firm is essentially a productive unit. If it has to deal increasingly with social problems, this activity may harm the economic interest.

● Because of the priority of the productive interest, the allocation of social resources within the enterprise is sure to follow a meritocratic pattern, leaving behind all those who are either less 'deserving' or less useful to the firm.

● Firms are varied. Smaller firms in general, and those less able to show a profit (either because of less efficient work or because of their inability to use the advantages of a limited market), will have less funds. Therefore the working conditions and welfare benefits of their workers will deteriorate, at least in a relative sense, independently of their efforts and the quality of their work. This phenomenon is conducive either to greater inequalities among firms or to an unusually large manpower turnover or to both of these.

● If the firm has too much autonomy, its priorities may follow only the immediate needs and wishes of those employed there, disregarding less easily understood long-term interests. Also a 'perfect' democracy at this level practically always favours the interests of those who are more able to present their case and to argue for it. Thus manipulative tendencies might occur.

It is clear that the protagonists and antagonists both have economic arguments as well as social policy ones. It is also true that each of the arguments has some validity. The division of social policy tasks is, therefore, more a pragmatic than a theoretical issue.

The current choice in Hungary is that the tasks of social and societal policy should be divided between the state, the local administration and local welfare agencies and the enterprises (firms, organizations).

This option is based on the thesis that under socialist conditions specifically social (not necessarily economic) interests must permeate all the spheres of social action. The social interest has to be institutionally and explicity protected because earlier experiences prove that otherwise it may be ignored. All the agencies must dispose of funds which can serve typically social aims, otherwise the above requirement will never be met.

It is recognized that all the agencies may function defectively. Their potential shortcomings are, however, different, as are their specific competences. The division of tasks is optimal if it follows the specific competences. At the same time, adequate (public and/or official) control must be built in at every level so as to correct the defects. As for the concrete assignment of tasks, it is currently solved in the following way:

Central administration (the state, in short) is the main agency for establishing the guidelines of societal and social policy, which are laid down in laws and in national socio-economic plans. It regulates directly the level and the distributive principles of some social services or benefits, especially universal ones where a similar level or a similar quality has to be assured everywhere. This holds for universal services such as education or health and for universal benefits (pensions, sick-pay, family allowances, etc.). Some welfare, health and educational institutions which have more than just local functions (universities, hospitals with a practically national catchment area) are also sponsored and administered by central agencies (ministries). Thus, for instance, the funds for the construction of hospitals are directly provided by the state budget. The necessary technical competence (to construct a heart-disease hospital for example) may not always be available at the local level. If enterprises were to join in the regulation or even the allocation of these services and benefits with some discretionary power, they might easily turn against the interests of the beneficiaries. (If, for example, they distribute sick-pay or family allowances from funds which have alternative uses, they will be not so keen to engage people with children or people who are ill.)

Local agencies (public services or welfare agencies such as the Red Cross) are concretely applying the central principles and they administer all kinds of personal services and specific or selective benefits destined for those outside the labour force (for example home care for ill or elderly people). Let me add here that these types of personal social services which take into account individual needs are growing in importance, though they do not take precedence over the solution of more general social problems. The administration and supervision of the institutions with local competence or scope of action also belong to local agencies – schools, outpatients' clinics, etc.

Only the *firms* can deal adequately with the improvement of working conditions and handle the personal problems of the employees. These are, in fact, the main spheres of the firm's social policy, although, as the enterprise social plans show, there are a number of other concerns, too.

The division of tasks between state, local and firm agencies has not always been as clear as this description suggests. As regards the division of tasks and responsibilities between central and local administration, the first two decades after 1945 were characterized by extreme centralization. The first wave of decentralization started in 1968, followed by new regulations and the law on councils (1974), which transferred many formerly central tasks to local councils. It was also at that time that the long-term principles of regional development were worked out and were incorporated in a law. None the less, there is no standstill in this process. There are diverse interests involved. They may oppose not only central and local agencies, but also the administrative authorities at different local levels (settlement, district, department). The issue is too intricate to be discussed here in detail. Only the major dilemma can be spelt out. The regional development programme laid down a twofold aim: (1) to assure the most effective and (economically) rational utilization of local resources and (2) to reduce differences in the quality of life of the inhabitants of the different regions and settlements, to avoid an increase in regional gaps. Clearly, these two aims may be at variance with each other, mainly because natural resources and trained manpower are not evenly distributed. It is also obvious that the practical outcome depends to a large extent on the level at which concrete decisions are made, and on the formal and informal possibilities of influencing the decisions. Since there is not a simple 'best' solution to this dilemma, there are continuous moves and changes in the present arrangements.

The division of tasks between the state administration and the firms raises a problem of a different type, namely that the demarcation lines cannot be clearly and unambiguously defined, so that parallel and overlapping solutions are necessary.

First, there are state tasks that cannot be solved without the contribution of the firm, and vice versa. The avoidance of unemployment or the rehabilitation of the handicapped are state responsibilities. But they have to be carried out by the firms, with adequate state funds, regulations and control, although the firm may not have any economic interest in those tasks. In a more general perspective, the long-term social aim of the transformation of the actual organization of work also belongs to this type of task. On the other hand, job security is a responsibility of the firm, though extra state help may be needed in cases of exceptional risk (for instance in the mines), or where facilities are inadequate at firm level.

Second, there can be overlaps in some services. For example education is mainly a state responsibility, but the firm may be interested in on-the-job training programmes, and in the training of its future manpower. Thus it might offer scholarships, extra holidays, etc., to its future staff during their studies. Often, however, 'strings' are attached to these services. (For example the beneficiary has to commit himself to working at the firm for a number of years after having obtained the qualification.) The differentiated treatment of state and firm beneficiaries of the *same* type may be economically justified but has a socially discriminatory aspect. In the case of such parallel solutions it would therefore be desirable to make the terms of the service offered more universal.

Third, there are urgent and socially justified needs which are not yet adequately covered, and where every effort is welcome, whether it introduces parallelisms or not. Child-care institutions and housing obviously belong to this category, as does the special, selective care offered to those who have special or multiple problems. These may only be temporary tasks for the firm. If, for example, kindergartens (for children from three to six years) become universal and compulsory institutions like schools, then firms will no longer have a responsibility in this connection. But until then, more effort, and even competition between the firm and the state organs, will have salutary effects. None the less, the relative disadvantage of the employees in smaller or poorer firms must be minimized by some means, for example by close co-operation between the firm and the local state authorities. Some such measures are already operating. For example, if the firm has no nursery because it is too small or too poor, it can enter into a contract with the local council: the firm gives a grant to the council, in exchange for which the council will reserve some of the places in its nursery for the children of the firm's employees.

On the whole, then, the shift towards decentralization in general and towards a more significant role for the firm in particular contributes to the development of social policy. However, a twofold control seems necessary. On the one hand, within the company the workers and employees must exercise control so as to prevent partiality or the predominance of the interests of any particular group. On the other hand, state control over the local agencies or establishments must be used to avoid *undue* inequality between settlements or workplaces by means of central priorities or some kind of central intervention.

Here, as elsewhere, the balance is delicate. Elimination of all types of differentiation between settlements or establishments also eliminates incentives for local improvement and initiative, while uncontrolled differentiation is very hard to reverse after a while. That is why the basic principles and the action of the various agencies and authorities of societal and social policy have to be centrally co-ordinated to some extent, and have to be seen as a whole.

Chapter 4

Relations of Knowledge

The future evolution of socialist social relations, including the gradual transformation of the division of work, of power relations and of life in the most general sense, requires fundamental changes in the social distribution of knowledge. The most important social institution which can serve this aim is the school system. Obviously, there are other institutions and agents which transmit knowledge and information. But the knowledge transmitted within the *family* strongly depends on its own culture. The products of the *mass media* are usually 'consumed' in a way defined by the previously acquired, highly differentiated level and structure of knowledge. *Personal relations*, whether chosen on an affective basis or created by social circumstances, are more often than not characterized by social and cultural similarities. Therefore at present none of these agencies can be considered as a major factor of *change*. On the other hand, the role of the workplace in shaping the individual's personality and in carrying information is highly relevant, but – at least in the past – it has rarely worked for a redistribution of knowledge. Work experience and the workplace may and should acquire far greater importance in this sphere in the future. This, however, presupposes a new relationship between work and education, and the transformation of the present educational institutions.

The idea that education plays a decisive role in perfecting the human personality and in raising society to a higher cultural level is clearly not a specifically socialist one. The issue was amply debated by the Greek and Roman philosophers and educators of Antiquity (not to mention those of ancient China). And there has been continued debate on these same points for several centuries, especially since the advent of capitalism. The debate became extremely lively after the Second World War, under the conditions of advanced industrialization and the confrontation of socialist and capitalist systems. One factor motivating this renewed universal interest in education and school was the increased role of high-level scientific and technical knowledge in economic development, which required a large number of trained people. The massive increase in school enrolment raised the issues of educability and of the potential 'reserve of talents'. As Husén observed: 'It is striking to note that most inquiries into the size and utilization of the pool of talent have been inspired by national concerns about the proper use of talent in promoting economic growth and social development in general.'[1] The problems of the school have been considered in recent times increasingly from the point of view of the democratization of education, usually couched in terms of the claims for equal opportunities. Both concerns – the search for talent as well as the search for equality – led in Western capitalist countries to debates over issues that proved to be socially explosive, such as the legitimacy of meritocracy, the optimal amount of social mobility, the opportunities of the underprivileged and of absolutely or relatively deprived social classes and ethnic groups, the relative merits of selective and comprehensive education and, finally, the heredity–environment controversy. The educational debate has always been motivated by different ideological convictions and value systems, but in recent decades both radical and conservative opinions have been expressed more clearly, and the underlying political and social commitments have become more explicit, or at least more transparent.

One clear case in point is the nature–nurture debate. Despite the originally cautious formulations of Jensen,[2] the 'hereditarians' soon found themselves (willingly or unwillingly) the spokesmen of racist and elitist, anti-egalitarian currents,[3] while

1. Torsten Husén, *Talent, Equality and Meritocracy*, Martins Nijhoff, The Hague, 1974, p. 3.
2. Arthur R. Jensen, 'How Much Can We Boost IQ and Scholastic Achievement?', *Harvard Educational Review*, 69, No. 1, 1969, pp. 1–123; and *Genetics and Education*, Methuen, 1972.
3. H. J. Eysenck, 'The Rise of Mediocracy', in *Black Paper Two* (*The Crisis in Education*), Critical Quarterly Society, London, 1970, pp. 34–40; and *The IQ Argument: Race, Intelligence and Education*, Temple Smith, 1971.

their adversaries had to point out not only the uncertain grounds for the scientific proof of the hereditarians but also the social implications of their views, and they had to advance alternative hypotheses. This is the direct aim of books like *Race and Intelligence*,[4] but the same purpose is clearly present in the works of socio-linguists from Bernstein to Labov,[5] the work of UNESCO, and the efforts of biologists and anthropologists.[6]

Another example of a recent radical approach is offered by the debate on school as an instrument of the democratization of society. As new evidence is being gathered on the social composition of schools and on the new hierarchies establishing themselves within the enlarged framework of higher education, optimistic views about rapid democratization are refuted by those who see a relationship between the transmission of culture and the economic and power relations of society. According to this concept voiced with great scientific competence by P. Bourdieu,[7] increased school enrolment does not lead to a change in the social structure and to the diminution of social distance, but only to an upward shift of the whole structure. By means of strategies of 'reconversion' the dominant class succeeds, with the help of its power position, in converting its economic capital into additional cultural capital in order to retain its all-round privileged position. In this process it utilizes school as a legitimizing agency. As a result, the relative positions of the various classes remain by and large unchanged, although their objective situation may have altered. In general, the approach

4. Ken Richardson and David Spears (eds.), *Race and Intelligence. The Fallacies behind the Race–IQ Controversy*, Penguin Books Inc., Baltimore, Maryland, 1972.

5. Basil Bernstein, *Class, Codes and Control*, op. cit; William Labov, 'The Logic of Non-Standard English', in F. Williams (ed.), *Language and Poverty*, Markham Publishing Company, Chicago, 1970.

6. Alexander J. Alland, *Human Diversity*, Columbia University Press, New York, London, 1971.

7. Pierre Bourdieu, Luc Boltanski and Monique de Saint-Martin, 'Les Stratégies de reconversion. Les classes sociales et le système d'enseignement', *Information sur les sciences sociales*, October 1973, pp. 61–114; Pierre Bourdieu and Jean-Claude Passeron, *La Reproduction*, Editions de Minuit, Paris, 1970.

which sees in school not only the agency of cultural transmission, but also a legitimizing agency of the social structure which is dominated by the interests of the ruling class, has gained ground in other countries, too.[8] The social selectivity of the school, its new inner hierarchies and the relatively small gains made by the working class have also been shown by several studies in West Germany, summed up by W. Müller and K. U. Mayer.[9] In Great Britain there is a long tradition of analysis of selectivity, relative social and cultural disadvantages, etc., also recently summed up in a study by J. Goldthorpe and P. Bevan.[10]

In Hungary from 1945 onwards some of the main themes have been quite similar to those mentioned above. Education was seen as a major factor and prerequisite of economic growth, and also as a means of social change, especially as a promoter of individual mobility. From the very beginning, the idea of real cultural democratization was an ideal shared by politicians and educators, and school was seen as an instrument in this process. This means that the idea not only of individual but also of collective mobility gained ground.

The inherited school system was overtly elitist and selective, with structural and financial barriers. The efforts to transform it have met with considerable, sometimes spectacular, successes in the last three decades. However, Hungary encounters obstacles in the process of transformation, sometimes similar to those in Western countries, sometimes specifically connected with Hungarian society. The reasons lie partly in the history of the school, partly in the present conditions. Separate analysis of these two factors may help us to understand the current situation.

8. Samuel Bowles, 'Unequal Education or the Reproduction of the Social Division of Labour', *Review of Radical Political Economics*, Vol. 3, No. 3, 1971, University of Michigan, Ann Arbor.

9. Walter Müller and Karl Ulrich Mayer, *Social Stratification and Stratification Research in the Federal Republic of Germany, 1945–1975*, mimeo, 1975.

10. John H. Goldthorpe and Philippa Bevan, *The Study of Social Stratification in Great Britain, 1945–1975*, mimeo, 1975.

4.1 The inherited school system

4.1.1 *The dual school structure*

A number of analytical studies dealing with the European school system agree on its dual character. Some observe this duality at the post-primary level where one path leads after a short period of specialized training to the world of manual work, while the other leads to higher learning. According to another view the duality begins before the formal separation of children: already at the primary level two more or less distinct groups are formed on the basis of their 'affinity' to school and their ability to cope with the school's requirements. They are destined respectively for the 'primary-and-vocational' or the 'secondary-and-higher' itineraries, that is, to use the French expression, for the *'primaire-professionnel'* and the *'secondaire-supérieur'* channels.[11] A deeper scrutiny uncovers the historical roots behind this duality. According to this approach, the present-day European school system is the combination of two historically evolved institutions. The first goes back to medieval universities. This is a system which grew 'from the top downwards'. As Roger Gal put it: '... a peculiar phenomenon explaining many of the deficiencies and difficulties of our present educational system is that the construction of the school system was begun at the top, with higher education. The lower floors were adapted to the upper ones already in existence.'[12] These schools were not primarily places of professional training: only a few 'professions' existed at that stage, and the exercise of a profession was incompatible with high social rank. For the majority of the students the pursuit of knowledge, although various social and religious motives were often involved, was undertaken simply for its own sake (which was, incidentally, a very important factor in the development of theoretical thinking). The prerequisites of university studies, including financial

11. Christian Baudelot and Roger Establet, *L'École capitaliste en France*, Maspero, Paris, 1971.
12. Roger Gal, *Histoire de l'éducation*, Presses Universitaires de France, Paris, 1969.

facilities as well as the knowledge of Latin, together with the university's basically non-utilitarian character, made it an essentially elite institution. The nature of universities changed only with the advance of capitalism, when professions requiring higher studies multiplied. Even then, and up to the second half of the twentieth century, the university remained socially a more or less closed institution, reserved for a small minority of the population.

The absence of systematic general education obliged the universities to form their own preparatory institutions if they wanted to maintain acceptable standards. This process began with the creation in France of so-called colleges during the fourteenth and fifteenth centuries, and continued with the creation of schools preparing for Latin studies, teaching mainly Latin and its grammar. Thus the contents and character of the higher levels of education determined those of the lower levels.

The second institution is much more recent. It was created by the rising capitalist system, and was designed, especially at the beginning, to cater for the children of the lower classes. Unlike the first system, it developed from the bottom upwards in several respects. Its main original function was to prepare the future labour force for the new industrial conditions, and also to 'stamp out immorality and poverty of the lower classes'.[13] Thus it set out to enable the children of the poorest segments of society to understand a minimum amount of information and to teach them discipline and respect for authority. Ariès quotes an English source from the sixteenth century: 'We have a great number of poor people in our parish who are not able to keep their children at grammar. But we are desirous to have them taught the principles of Christian Religion and to write, read and cast accounts, and so put them forth to prentice.'[14] Let me add that the creation of schools destined especially for the poor, and considered as a means of solving the poverty problem, was mainly, in this explicit form, an English phenomenon.

13. Philippe Ariès, *Centuries of Childhood* (English translation), Vintage Books, New York, 1962, p. 304.
14. ibid., p. 303.

But the same idea was applied on the continent in the creation of the earliest laws and regulations prescribing the implementation of compulsory schooling at the end of the eighteenth century.

Another factor operating in the same direction, especially in the towns of Central and Eastern Europe, was the need of the urban bourgeoisie, including the members of the guilds, to give their children an adequate education. (The difference in emphasis between developments in England and on the continent is largely related to the differences in the evolution of their capitalist systems.) The education desired was mainly practical. The bourgeoisie wanted their children to have moral education and some of the basic skills needed in the exercise of a craft. These urban schools have a long history, but they remained somewhat scattered and loosely organized until the education systems converged.

The length of time children were obliged to spend at school steadily increased. The earliest laws – which could never be fully implemented – prescribed some three to six years. In Hungary (then part of the Habsburg Empire) the Ratio Educationis of 1777 planned a school of two cycles of three years each, but the majority of children, if they went to school at all, did not stay more than three years (and many stayed less) even eighty years later. The system of primary schools was not fully established until the last thirty years of the nineteenth century: at that time the majority of European countries enacted their educational laws introducing general compulsory elementary schooling. The length of general compulsory education was then about six to eight years, and primary schools began to be complemented by different vocational or finishing schools. Until the mid twentieth century this general and vocational cycle could take up to twelve years to complete, if we consider all its ramifications, like the technical secondary schools.

Thus, the gap between the two historically distinct systems lessened. However, they did not really merge. Even at the lowest levels there are traces of the original duality in the form of private or semi-private schools. In our day this is most conspicuous in the case of the English prep schools. At the post-primary level, until the recent development of comprehensive schools, the traditional grammar schools and the various vocational courses or short finishing cycles co-existed, and only the grammar-school type gave access to the institutions of higher education. The social composition of the two types of institution differed radically, and even if the elementary level became comprehensive in its organization, the probable future of the children really marked them already at this level.

Thus, the social distribution of knowledge did not become much less unequal despite an increasing average level. The situation does not seem to change much even in those countries where for one or two decades deliberate efforts have been made to abolish the duality, as with the introduction of comprehensive secondary schools or the efforts to eliminate 'dead-end' courses. The reasons for this situation are to be sought in the class structure and the interest-structure generated by it, as shown for example by Bourdieu. But it is important to ask *how* school can function in this way, despite the democratic convictions of the majority of the teachers (at least in some countries like France), despite the elimination of most of the financial or formal barriers and despite the now almost total absence of open or organizational selection.

4.1.2 *Types of knowledge*

It seems to me that one of the most efficient yet hidden tools maintaining the duality of the educational system is related to the traditionally evolved *contents* of the two component systems.[15] The way knowledge functions in a given society may be classified in various ways, and in fact different classificatory schemes have been proposed, for example by Scheler,[16]

15. I deal with these issues in more detail in a book, *Social Determinisms in the School System and Educational Knowledge*, Akadémiai Kiadó, 1976 (in Hungarian).

16. Max Scheler, *Die Wissenformen und die Gesellschaft*, Der Neue Geist Verlag, Leipzig, 1926.

Machlup[17] and Lukács.[18] The underlying rationale of the classificatory schemes also varies. In the case of Machlup for example, the main dimension is the subjective interpretation given to knowledge by the knower, while Lukács's approach is epistemological and is concerned with 'objectivization' and the problems of the creation of new knowledge. I am concerned here with the *social application* of knowledge, how and in what spheres we need and use knowledge, and how we acquire the necessary elements of knowledge. Obviously, the accumulation of human experience not only produces more knowledge, but also leads to differentiations, new classifications of this increased knowledge.

One of these differentiations is related to the relevance of knowledge. Besides the well-known problems of obsolescence, which make some information irrelevant (at least in its original sense), my main concern here is with social differentiation in relevance. In a society where there is a more or less clear class differentiation, where the social structure is hierarchically articulated, we may speak of relevance not only in a global historical sense, but also from the point of view of classes and strata. The social structure determines the whole praxis of a group including the elements of knowledge it is likely to use. The individual may question and pass beyond these social boundaries, but a whole-scale social reorganization or reallocation is impossible without a radical change in the basic structure.

Another distinction is related to the spheres or functions of the utilization of knowledge. There is a set of elements of knowledge, such as skills or know-how, which are used in various jobs. This set includes all those abilities that enable the individual to participate *in the social division of work*. In this sense, then, the unskilled worker also has some 'vocational' knowledge. A second set is composed of all kinds of knowledge

17. Fritz Machlup, *The Production and Distribution of Knowledge in the United States*, Princeton University Press, 1972.
18. György Lukács, *Az esztétikum sajátosságai* (Aesthetics), Magvető Kiadó, abridged version, 1969.

and information that are used in everyday life – outside work and outside the 'festive' sphere discussed below. At least two subgroups are to be distinguished here: *everyday practical knowledge*, used in handling objects, and *everyday social knowledge*, used in social communication and in the handling and understanding of social relations. The last type to be defined here, the ability to understand and to enjoy creations of the arts or science, the ability to act without external economic and social constraints, is what we may call *'festive' knowledge*, to imply more positive overtones of play and rejoicing. The boundaries between these sets are not rigid. Thus elements of everyday knowledge (from cooking to child-rearing) are constantly becoming 'vocational' knowledge too. In addition in the most privileged situations vocational knowledge and festive knowledge merge. In short, the whole system of categories of knowledge is the result of a long historical development, which is still going on, constantly reorganizing the whole pattern.

Again, from another perspective we may distinguish between two types of knowledge following Lukács's suggestion about the differentiation of work teleologies. In this sense one type of knowledge is used in the manipulation of natural objects, the other type allows some people to exercise influence over the consciousness of others.

All these types of knowledge are differentiated, containing qualitatively different sub-types and quantitatively different levels. These different levels seem – and in a sense are – consecutive stages on a continuous scale. None the less, in practically every case we find socially determined sub-sets which, throughout history, have been driven so far apart that the continuity has disappeared. The clearest case in point relates to the inner differentiation of festive knowledge.

Festive knowledge began to be separated from everyday knowledge at a fairly early stage of human history, although their respective autonomy was for a long time limited. They remained interwoven in many situations – as witnessed for instance by the artistic decoration of peasant instruments or utensils, where the user and the decorator were generally one and the same person. But the separation continued to increase. Soon the knowledge required for the full understanding and enjoyment of various cultural products became the monopoly of the most privileged social classes. This process became very pronounced – in Europe at least – in the eighteenth century. Cultural monopoly, like all monopolies, acquired an additional significance over and above its objective importance. Thus, this so-called 'high culture' became not only a simple concomitant but also a symbol of 'high' social position.

High culture was confronted, on the one hand, by a kind of 'universal' or 'mass' culture. By this I mean (departing from many other definitions) the more or less common core of festive and even everyday knowledge. The criterion for defining what is 'mass culture' is that it may be understood and enjoyed by practically everybody in a society, at any given time (many newspaper items, many mass media programmes, games, sports, some works of fiction, etc.). On the other hand a kind of 'low culture' emerged, too. This last is no longer a more or less autonomous product of a section or a class, such as folk-lore; nor is it a festive expression of the special circumstances in which the people in question live, as was the youth culture of the sixties. It is, instead, a culture which is *forced* on those excluded from the knowledge monopoly and deprived of the means of creating their own festive expressions. It is, then, a festive knowledge which is intended to fill the vacuum created by the absence of an autonomous subculture and the lack of preparation for 'high culture', perhaps also for many elements of 'mass culture'. The emergence and the social role of this culture directed from above is admirably described by Hoggart.[19] Throughout this process of cultural differentiation, creation and reception both undergo a process of polarization, as described by Lukács: 'the centralized production of the pleasurable, where pseudo-aesthetic elements and themes grow in a more or less conscious competition with true art, forces art into an unhealthy esotericism and particularism'.[20]

19. Richard Hoggart, *The Uses of Literacy*, Chatto and Windus, 1957.
20. Lukács, op. cit., p. 578.

This description is not an aristocratic over-valuation of high culture, nor a way of despising 'low culture'. I tend to agree with H. Gans, who wrote: 'the evaluation of any taste culture [his main categories of taste culture being high culture, upper middle culture, low culture and quasi-folk low culture] must also take its taste public into account . . . and to the extent that all taste cultures reflect the characteristics and standards of their public, they are equal in value'.[21] The tastes of these taste publics are, of course, strongly influenced by their circumstances, which are economically, socially and culturally unequal. Therefore to establish the existence of 'high' and 'low' culture (which is often empirically verified) is not a socially biased aesthetic judgement. If it contains elements of judgement, then it judges and condemns the social conditions under which elements of human culture – the historical heredity of all mankind – can be monopolized by some so as to exclude the majority in an institutionalized way from the possibility of gaining access to or enjoying this culture.

My contention is that the dual character of the school and the existence of the different types of knowledge described above are strongly interrelated. It is almost a tautology to affirm that the contents of the two school systems were different. If they were designed for different social classes – a fact recognized by all the specialists like Roger Gal or Torsten Husén – and if it is true that relevant knowledge varies from class to class, then the contents of the two curricula *had* to be radically different.

If we take Lukács's two categories of work teleology, then the first, elite, system was reserved almost exclusively for elements of knowledge connected with the second type of teleology, preparing its clientele to deal with and to influence others. Again, it is a truism to say that this knowledge had to be kept from those who were destined to be influenced, and had to be made inaccessible to them by all means available. The inclusion in the elite system of knowledge connected with the handling of objects (the first type of Lukács's teleologies) came

21. Herbert J. Gans, *Popular Culture and High Culture*, Basic Books, New York, 1974, p. 128.

much later, when the elite system began to deal with technical knowledge.

In terms of the other classification of types of knowledge described above (vocational skill, everyday knowledge and festive knowledge), the elite system stressed, especially at the beginning, the transmission of festive knowledge, of everyday knowledge belonging to the everyday activities of the higher classes, and some types of vocational knowledge connected especially with the second work teleology (church vocations, government). All other vocational or professional skills became an integral part of the elite curriculum only when science itself became a productive force, so that the monopolization of science also became one of the interests of the privileged class. This did not occur before the end of the seventeenth century and really gained ground only in the nineteenth. Even then, we may observe two peculiarities of the new institutions of higher vocational learning. One is that the acceptance of these new schools as 'social equals' was rather slow. It probably took longest in England, where Colleges of Technology have been transformed into Universities only in the last decade or so. It seems, also, that when this upgrading of the colleges takes place, the proportion of students with middle-class origins begins to increase, that of students with working-class origins begins to decline within the colleges.[22] The other interesting feature of the new vocational institutions is that they unobtrusively merge purely 'object-oriented' skills with the elements of knowledge serving to influence or dominate or handle others. This holds not only for the medical profession, but also for engineering for instance.

The universities were not the only – perhaps not even the main – agencies transmitting the knowledge necessary for the ruling classes. The family has always retained a fundamental role in transmitting everyday and festive knowledge. But in addition, either because some elements of everyday and festive

22. M. Couper and C. Harris, 'CAT to University: The Changing Student Intake, *Educational Research* 12, 1970. Referred to in Goldthorpe and Bevan, op. cit., p. 38.

knowledge began to require more systematic preparation or because the family began to lose some of its hold on children,
special institutions were created. These were, for instance, in
early times the education in chivalry, later on institutions like
the *Académies* in France, and more recently the English public
schools, which were practically always boarding schools, transmitting much more than traditional educational knowledge.

As for the other system, the popular or folk school, its curriculum was defined by its original function. At the beginning,
it covered mainly the handling of symbols (reading, writing,
elementary arithmetic) which allowed its clientele to understand the intentions of those who wanted to influence or dominate them (who exercised the second type of work teleology).
The curriculum included rudiments of religious and moral
learning, serving the same aim of teaching pupils to accept
orders and the given order. In this sense these last elements
belonged to the everyday knowledge that was relevant for the
oppressed classes in the opinion of the ruling class. Later on,
vocational training was more extensively introduced in this type
of school, for manual or lower-grade white-collar jobs. Except
for the most modern types of secondary vocational schools that
approach the grammar-school curriculum (and are really transitory types), the vocational training which began in the second
half of the nineteenth century and which often took place at the
workplace shared one characteristic with the curriculum of the
elementary schools: the teaching of festive knowledge was practically absent. 'High culture' was denied these children, and
'low' culture did not require any preparation. The modern
training in skills was also more cut off from everyday knowledge than in any earlier form of transmission of vocational
knowledge. As long as vocational training was carried out by
the guilds, they dealt with the 'whole person', placing emphasis
on moral principles and on all aspects of everyday behaviour
too. The new industrial apprenticeship taking shape from the
second half of the nineteenth century concentrated on skill (possibly defined quite narrowly so as to fit the interests of the
employer), and the time spent in schools retained something of

the character of the original Sunday schools. Here the underlying aim was not so much to increase understanding in everyday or festive knowledge, as to rehearse the rules of behaviour
already drilled into the children, and to prove by the narrow,
dull and boring character of the material taught the uselessness
of knowledge in general. It is certainly true that in the last
decades progressive tendencies have broadened this curriculum
somewhat. Everyday knowledge (civic instruction for instance)
has been enriched, and elements of high-level festive knowledge
have made at least a sporadic appearance. These endeavours,
however, appearing in a number of European countries especially from the sixties on, have not proved particularly
efficient up to now.

What in fact seems to have happened in the last decades in
France, in England and in Hungary as well is that the structural
reorganization, even the move towards comprehensive schools,
has not been accompanied by a re-thinking of the implications
of the historical duality of the curricula. Thus the educational
instruments for the maintenance of social duality have practically been built into the formally unified school. School has
retained from the elite system the implicit belief that every child
enters school endowed with a high level of everyday culture. It
builds on this culture (assuming linguistic, communicational
abilities, a set of aspirations, etc.), and does not transmit it.
Children who do not catch up quickly with their peers only lag
behind, with an increasing gap. Another divisive element is the
teaching of high-level festive knowledge. This teaching again
builds on similar assumptions about the children's backgrounds, so that the knowledge that is transmitted becomes in-
comprehensible and irrelevant for a child coming from a milieu
which has been already driven away from this culture. A third
divisive element is the retention of socially obsolete components
of the most exclusive layer of 'high culture'. The most conspicuous example of this strategy is the survival of the dominant role of Latin until the most recent times, in Hungary until
around 1950, in France until even more recently. These
artificial obstacles have a particular function: by demands that

can only seem irrelevant for all those who come from a background where the indirect relevance of the irrelevant is far from obvious, they prove the irrelevance of any type of higher learning for this very large group, and also their unfitness for it. The combination of these obstacles continues, then, to deny those who should not 'know' access to those institutions which specialize in teaching pupils to influence or dominate others.

Finally, the most interesting and specifically European aspect of educational class strategies is the specific 'structurization' of the different types of knowledge. Each of them is hierarchized, and the different levels of those hierarchies have become interconnected in predefined patterns. Through the elite system it became a rule that high-level professional knowledge could not be conceived of without everyday and festive knowledge of a similarly high level. Even the stereotypical exceptions like the absent-minded professor who ranks high in everything but everyday knowledge, or the brute genius who is highly creative in his craft but otherwise ignorant and who cannot even 'behave', prove that the *rule* is the interconnection. However, high-level festive and everyday knowledge usually gives access to positions which rank high in the social division of work, even without any specific skills, because historical tradition legitimates the tacit assumption that high levels in those spheres can easily be converted into some high-level 'professional' knowledge. (This explains the long-lasting prestige of an Oxford degree in 'Greats'.) This last factor makes it almost impossible (again, in Europe) to acquire really high-level professional knowledge without high-level general preparation, or to get one's professional knowledge 'officially' accepted if it was acquired by hard work, in non-traditional ways. (This is the typical problem of the self-made man.) The long traditions of school not only legitimate these elements, but make them appear as natural, obvious and unquestionable. With their help, the way is paved to a social selection which is practically invisible. In short, they help to maintain the social duality of the school system even if the formal structure no longer shows the dual origins. And the final result is the persistence of the socially determined unequal distribution of all types of knowledge.

4.2 The transformation of the inherited school system in Hungary

Before the war the Hungarian school system operated with an openly dual character. After four years of elementary schooling (where the duality was maintained by means of private schools, selective denominational schools and the absence or great flexibility of regional 'catchment' areas) three itineraries could be followed: two more years at the 'folk-school', leading only to industrial apprenticeship, though these extra years were not compulsory for apprentices; four (or six) years at a 'bourgeois' school, frequented mainly by children of the petty bourgeoisie and preparing for lower white-collar jobs; or eight years at a grammar school, giving access to the universities. The transitional types – commercial or technical secondaries with an eight-year cycle but not qualifying pupils for university entrance – also began to make their appearance in the thirties. The majority of children remained in the elementary school, 18 per cent went to the 'bourgeois' schools and 7 per cent to the grammar schools. No more than about 1 to 2 per cent acceded to higher education. Social selection was so effective that at the secondary as well as at the higher level only 5 per cent of the students were children of workers or peasants. Schools – especially elementary schools – were overcrowded, the number of teachers was insufficient (the teacher–pupil ratio in elementary schools was 1:42), and in 93 per cent of the 4,000 elementary schools there were no separate classes, just a mixed group of children with one teacher.[23]

In the first years after the war the most salient features of this system were transformed.

Organizational aspects

First the conspicuous organizational aspects of elitism and selec-

23. *Mai iskolarendszerünk fejlődése* (The Evolution of Our Present-Day School System), Tankönyvkiadó, 1972, and statistical data.

tivity were abolished. These steps included the creation of the eight-year comprehensive general school, unifying all three former school types for ten- to fourteen-year-olds; the nationalization of schools, since 70 per cent of elementaries were denominational before the war (a pre-capitalist arrangement); and the elimination of financial barriers by making education free at all levels. Also pre-primary education became an almost universal and organic part of the educational system.

The secondary level (from fourteen to eighteen) was gradually reorganized. The *grammar school* (*gimnazium*) was retained as the main preparatory institution for higher education, but its elite character was changed. The number of students nearly tripled from 1938 to 1970, and various organizational, pedagogic or sometimes even administrative measures assured a high level of individual social mobility. The proportion of children of manual workers, which was about 4 per cent before the war, varies at present between 40 and 50 per cent according to the strength of the efforts specifically deployed to this effect. The network of *technical secondary schools* (industrial, commercial, administrative, etc.) was gradually built up. In 1975–6, 51 per cent of all four-year secondary school students attended these institutions (the proportion was only 30 per cent in 1960). Technical secondary schools give access to higher education with certain restrictions (the continuation of studies is easier in a branch akin to that of the secondary school), and give an almost complete vocational training. They are socially rather heterogeneous: about 60 per cent of their students have working-class or peasant backgrounds. The third form of education at this level is the *vocational training* of skilled workers. These schools, in their present form, are fairly new. Industrial apprenticeship before the war was loosely organized, the formal schooling at a low level, and apprentices were subordinated to their employers with almost no restrictions on the latter. Now the completion of eight years at primary school is required for vocational training. The vocational training lasts two to three years. By and large half of this time is spent in the classroom and half in the workshop. In the first year the practical training is usually carried out in the school workshops, where the interests of production do not interfere with teaching. Vocational schools acquired the status of secondary schools in 1969, when various new methods were introduced to assure the access to institutions of higher education for those completing a vocational school course.

The process of transformation has been going on at the level of higher education almost continuously since 1945. The number of students has multiplied by about eight. The composition of the student population follows social and economic needs more realistically than it did before the war, when the two largest faculties were Law and the Humanities. There are efforts to find organizational solutions to bridge the gap between mostly theoretical studies and practical work. Social democratization is also assured, as in the case of the grammar schools, so that the proportion of children of manual workers has been maintained at between 40 and 50 per cent, as against less than 4 per cent before the war.

Certain complementary organizational aspects also merit some attention. Free education is complemented by a system of scholarships. This is universal in vocational training in the first two years (while in the third year salaries are introduced), sporadic in other secondary schools (6 per cent get scholarships) and almost universal in higher education (82 per cent benefit from it). Also, a network of dormitories gives access to schools to children from rural areas (available for 1 per cent of students at the primary level, for 18 per cent in vocational schools, 20 per cent in other secondaries and 47 per cent in higher education). Especially at the primary and secondary level these 'homes' are considered as important means of general and also of compensatory education. Another new element is the opening-up of possibilities of abandoning the rigid itineraries of the old system – linked to the interrelatedness of the different types of knowledge. Especially in the first decade after the war there was great scope for pupils to accede to higher levels without formal credentials, with the help of short preparatory courses. This option was reintroduced around 1970, although less extensively.

Table 4/1: Changes in school enrolment

	Kinder-gartens (3 to 5 years)	Primary schools (6 to 15 years)	Secondary (grammar and modern) schools (14 to 18 years)	Voca-tional schools	Higher education

A. Total enrolment (full-time, evening and correspondence courses), in thousands

1938	112·4[a]	1,075·8	91·8	67·8	13·2
1950/51	106·4	1,279·3	107·9	56·8	32·5
1970/71	227·3	1,137·3	347·2	223·2	80·5
1974/5	315·6	1,039·5	374·6	174·9	103·4

B. Proportion of the total student population on full-time (day) courses (%) within total enrolment

1950/51	100·0	91·5	88·7	100·0	81·6
1970/71	100·0	98·3	67·2	100·0	70·0
1974/5	100·0	95·4	56·0	100·0	61·0

C. Proportion of the total student population on full-time (day) courses within the respective age-cohorts (%)

1938	23·6	78·8	7·4	—	appr. 1
1950/51	23·5	96·1	16·2	12·8	—
1970/71	57·7	98·4	30·3	38·2	4·1
1974/5	71·8	97·2	33·7	32·3	5·5

D. Children of whom at least one parent is a manual worker

1938	—	—	4·0	—	3·5
1950	—	—	59·0	—	48·5
1970	—	78·9	52·8	81·8	37·1

E. Proportion of female students (%)

1938	—	—	34·7	16·3	14·5
1950	—	—	—	16·9	23·8
1970	—	—	54·2	24·6	42·8
1974	—	—	58·6	28·6	47·2

Sources: Statistical data of the Ministry of Education, and census data.
[a] The majority of kindergartens operated at that time on a half-day basis.

Evening classes of all types, organized on a massive scale and helped by reduced working hours, also belong to this system. A last feature to be mentioned is the constant concern with career opportunities for girls, assuring them by now a nearly equal status in education. (See section 3.3.)

Table 4/1 gives a comprehensive picture of some of the quantitative and organizational aspects of change.

Content of education

The reform of the content of education was no less radical than the organizational transformation, but it was less well conceptualized or less consistently thought out. The first changes affected the manifest ideological aspects of the former 'everyday' and 'festive' components of the curriculum through the whole range from openly fascist, racist and chauvinist elements to the moral justification of the capitalist class-system.

The question of relevance also came to the fore, but only in its crudest forms. Thus the dominance of Latin was the most conspicuous problem in this connection, and it was therefore abolished almost too thoroughly. I should add at this point that in periods of revolutionary change the issue of irrelevance and that of the inaccessibility of knowledge are often confused. The aim is the abolition of privilege, but the process of abolition is different with each privilege. For ascribed privileges (rank by birth) or capital ownership the elimination of the monopoly implies the abolition of the *institution*. By simplifying the same logic, one can rapidly arrive at the claim for the abolition of power in general (this is the anarchical tendency in any revolutionary movement), and a demand for the total rejection of knowledge, which I would term the ideology of the reversed cultural revolution. It is not easy to recognize the bias in this logic, especially when applied to knowledge which was often used in a concealed and 'unjust' way by the former rulers. The short-cut is the rejection of *all* types of knowledge with the label 'class culture', while the long way is to make accessible or – to use Bernstein's word – permeable as much of it as possible. In the process of transformation of the Hungarian school, both elements were present. Rejection occurred more frequently in the first years after 1945, not only in the case of Latin, but also with a considerable decrease in educational standards, especially in subjects which had been least accessible under the former conditions. The long way – the way of achieving universal appropriation of knowledge – was worked out slowly in a number of fields. These methods endeavoured mainly to destroy the systematic unity within the different types of knowledge, to prove that 'high culture' was not synonymous with an elite culture and to prove that there was no necessary interconnection between similar levels of the different types of knowledge. One achievement of this logic was the introduction in schools of the composer Kodály's method of teaching music. This method was worked out by Kodály as early as the thirties but was not officially recognized. It was introduced in primary schools in 1948 and in kindergartens in 1957. The results showed conclusively that with adequate teaching the music that was considered before as elite culture could be transformed into an organic part of the festive culture of every individual, and could be enjoyed by everybody. Endeavours were also made to enrich the contents of everyday and festive knowledge in all the schools (including primary and vocational schools), and to incorporate into the curriculum new elements which might be necessary in the course of everyday life.

However, some inconsistencies can easily be pointed out both in the organizational reform and in the change of the content of school education. They are by and large related to the dilemmas currently facing those concerned with the further transformation of the school system and of the relations of knowledge in general. Obviously, I shall deal in what follows only with dilemmas that are connected with the social aspects of education.

4.3 Dilemmas of change in the educational system

1. One crucial problem is connected with the relation between the social division of work and the school system. Several conceptions exist here. There is a highly individualist current,

sometimes with liberal, sometimes with utopian connotations. It stresses the autonomy of education and the individual's right to free choice. The right to learn can be considered an elementary personal freedom, or a condition of further social change which allows the individual to reveal all his natural abilities. The almost inevitable economic and social consequences of the policy of free choice are usually ignored. The economic consequence is the discrepancy between supply and demand on the labour market, meaning that, if only individual inclinations are followed, then shortages in some fields and overproduction in others are practically inevitable. (At least this is the case if the division of work is not fundamentally reorganized.) With economic recession in some of the most advanced countries it is overproduction which seems now to be coming to the fore, in the form of the employment of many highly trained, mainly young professionals[24] – although the less well trained are still much more exposed to unemployment. But even without visible over-training problems constantly arise in this field, such as the frustration of those who cannot find a job that corresponds fully to their qualifications; the economic insecurity of some; or a distorted wage system more or less heavily influenced by imbalances of supply and demand.

Another consequence is the economic loss due to over-training: skills that are learned but never used are certainly forgotten. This is clearly a loss which a society may or may not be able or willing to afford. One may suggest that this loss is not inevitable: people who value knowledge will use it even if there is no external pressure or motivation to do so. This assumption, however, ignores the fact that the autotelic valuation and enjoyment of knowledge is, in a sense, a luxury. And this luxury is possible only for those whose more or less elementary needs are fulfilled reasonably easily. Unfortunately, this group is now a minority in all contemporary societies. Therefore a general 'overtraining' which does not take into account the present or future requirements of the social division of work serves only to

24. Marzio Barbagli, *Disoccupazione intellettuale e sistema scolastico in Italia*, Il Mulino, 1974.

hide social determinisms without changing them. In this sense, it is not real individual freedom which is assured by this strategy, but only the illusion of freedom.

The other – technocratic – current seeks fully to subordinate the educational system to the needs of the economy, by direct or indirect intervention. Minor imbalances between supply and demand occur even in this case because forecasts can never be exact. A more important drawback of this solution is that it almost certainly slows down progress. Technical development proceeds with unforeseeable irregularities, and a smoothly planned development in terms of manpower cannot easily cope with technological leaps and bounds. The most adverse social effect is that a technocratic approach considers economy of education all-important and tries to adjust training to more or less well-foreseen needs in production. It therefore hinders the efforts for a more equal distribution of all types of knowledge. It maintains the hierarchy in vocational knowledge because of economic needs and pays no attention to other types of knowledge because they are not directly profitable. Thus the old patterns of unequal distribution of knowledge are maintained and little is done to develop the abilities of all or to overcome the former social differentiation in cultural matters. A strictly technocratic orientation is also opposed to policies of democratization, like, for example, compensatory education, because the least expensive way of forming a professional elite is to build on family advantages. Finally, as an outcome of all these negative features, an educational system dictated by technocratic options certainly hinders the transformation of the social division of work.

Hungary, as well as the other socialist countries, recognizes the bonds between school and work but seeks to reject both extremes, the rigidly technocratic approach as well as unlimited individualism. However, partly because of limited economic resources and partly because of the given interest structure, there is a tendency towards more intervention of the technocratic type than is probably necessary. The most visible result, which is – or at least was, before the rise of youth unemployment in Western countries – the most frequently criticized, is the limitation of places in higher education, excluding, at least temporarily, a certain number of candidates. Selection is based on the school results obtained in secondary school and on an entrance examination. It is undeniable that this system of selection carries the danger of misjudging ability and also of denying individual aspirations. Some of the indirect consequences of the technocratic bias are less conspicuous but perhaps more important. One is the neglect of ways to improve the transmission of everyday and festive knowledge. This is especially true for the vocational schools where this type of teaching had no tradition in the dual system. Another indirect effect is to encourage the early choice of a profession which is a condition of success in the university entrance examination. The overvaluation of vocational subjects at the expense of other types of knowledge is spreading from industrial training to other schools. Even at an earlier stage, the difficulty of going on to higher levels of education discourages all those who cannot afford to 'waste' four years in the grammar school and this group is composed mainly of the children of manual workers. Therefore they readily opt out of these schools.

2. A second set of problems is connected with educational selection in general, and the relation between 'meritocratic' and 'social' selection. The open social selection of the traditional school system has been abolished. However, for the reasons already mentioned – the given social structure and the structure of interests related to it – it is still true that some social advantages are transformed into educational advantage and vice versa. One of the ways in which this happens is to be seen in the fact that changes in the structuring of educational knowledge have not been consistent. Thus, Kodály's method remained unique for a very long time: it was not followed in other spheres of knowledge. Everyday and festive knowledge were not given enough weight in vocational training. The problem of relevance was not thoroughly considered. In short, social and cultural disadvantages have not been consistently overcome. Therefore children's achievement – at least the achievement measured by

the assessment of the school – varies greatly according to social background, and the gap between groups of different social origin does not diminish over the eight years spent at primary school.[25] Another – connected – educational factor is the practice of streaming, which appeared unobtrusively in Hungarian schools towards the sixties, first in grammar schools, and later, if only sporadically, in the primary schools, too. This is directly related to the problems of access to higher education. With limited resources at their disposal, schools had to concentrate their efforts on those children who were likely candidates for higher education. Because of the variations in achievement discussed above, this group consisted mainly of children who gained high marks because they had an inherited cultural advantage, and also of the so-called gifted children of workers and peasants (who could overcome their disadvantages). In order to give them adequate preparation, they were regrouped, frequently unintentionally, in separate classes. This procedure yielded symptoms and consequences of streaming which are widespread and often analysed in England.[26] Selection at the secondary level also produced the effect known as reverberation on primary schools. The explanation lies partly in limited resources, and partly in the fact that the secondary stage is directly connected to the primary level. (The choice of a secondary school is free from any constraints and does not depend on school results, but still the suggestions made by the primary school are decisive in orienting the desires of parents and children.) Thus, even if selection according to social origin has diminished it still operates.

Concern with individual social mobility has helped to motivate the search for the gifted children of manual workers, but the methods used to help these children have not always been

25. On concrete data about streaming in Hungary: S. Ferge, 'The Relations between School and Social Structure', *Sociological Review Monograph*, Keele University, 1972.
26. For example Julienne Ford, *Social Class and the Comprehensive School*, Routledge and Kegan Paul, 1969, and David H. Hargreaves, *Social Relations in a Secondary School*, Routledge and Kegan Paul, 1967.

successful. Help usually comes too late, at the end of the primary school or even in the secondary stage. But the main problem is – in terms of the usual social policy dichotomy – that almost all the compensatory strategies used in Hungary are *selective* and not *universal*. Instead of the creation of adequate frameworks and educational methods from which every individual could profit, various selective solutions are applied – with advantages and disadvantages which are well known.

One of these methods is singling out, within a class community, the 'disadvantaged' children, and quite openly giving them help or special treatment. This method may – and often does – improve results at school but it lowers the self-respect of the children involved. Another strategy appears mainly at the level of university entrance. Each institute of higher education demands a certain standard, which may vary from one institute to the next, which means a pre-defined number of points. (This overall score is made up of secondary school results and the results obtained in the entrance examination.) If the student is considered as coming from a 'disadvantaged' background, especially if he or she comes from a worker or peasant family, the standard may be lowered in his case (by no more than 5 to 10 per cent). The underlying rationale is that to a certain extent poor results are to be imputed to poor conditions, and not to a lack of ability. Thus two different results may be considered as equivalent if the original conditions differ. The logic is certainly valid. The measures themselves have been entirely justified for a long time on social as well as on historical grounds. Nowadays, however, they are questioned for several reasons. Those who are favoured by positive discrimination complain because of the humiliating aspect of the procedure, and those who are 'negatively' discriminated against are often hurt and discouraged. The conviction is therefore spreading that social and cultural disadvantages should be compensated for much earlier than at the university entrance stage, and by means of universal methods. This implies continued efforts to overcome initial 'disadvantages' unobtrusively and with less discrimination. A number of current experiments – special compensatory education at pre-primary level, no marks in the first and fifth forms, the introduction of modern maths, etc. – point in this direction.

It is nevertheless true, despite all the difficulties, that the combined effects of an altered structure, new methods and positive discrimination favouring children of manual workers has helped to overcome the worst problems of strong social selection and low individual mobility. Approximately 40 per cent (and often more) of the students at secondary and higher levels come from this background, and this figure is significantly higher than in capitalist countries. As Husén wrote in 1974: 'The papers prepared for the OECD Policy Conference on Educational Growth in 1970 cited surveys which showed that in spite of a massive expansion in enrolment the imbalances in participation with regard to social classes, sex and ethnicity were very much the same as they had been some ten years earlier,'[27] that is the proportion of students from working-class backgrounds did not exceed 25 per cent even in the best cases (5 per cent in West Germany and the Netherlands, 8 to 10 per cent in France or Austria, 25 per cent in Great Britain and Norway).[28] More recent data (gathered by Guy Neave) show similar trends – that the gains in the seventies, in terms of working-class students in higher education, have been less than spectacular. In France for instance, the proportion of working-class university students was 10·5 per cent in 1967/8 and 11·8 per cent in 1973/4.[29] I do not want to minimize the role of social determinism in educational selection in Hungary. Even if the overall ratio is acceptable, it does not mean equal representation of all the social groups and it varies a great deal according to the prestige and standing of the different professions (it is high in pedagogy, low in medicine, etc.). But there is another aspect to this problem: if we continue to concentrate our efforts on a high rate of individual mobility, this will necessarily diminish the resources that

27. Husén, op. cit., p. 102.
28. Frank Parkin, *Class Inequality and the Social Order*, Praeger, New York, Washington, 1971, p. 110.
29. Guy Neave, *Patterns of Equality*, NFER Publishing Co., 1976, p. 79.

may be mobilized to promote collective mobility. I have already pointed out that, although the two types of mobility are interconnected, a special emphasis must be put on collective (upward) mobility, which obviously implies a less unequal distribution of all kinds and types of knowledge.

In this sense, Hungary's concern with the selection of the best candidates raises several problems: how to weaken further the impact of social factors in educational selection; how to give free expression to all the talents that are produced by a better and larger secondary school without creating an excess of supply in highly educated people; how to avoid damaging the chances of the children of the better-off strata if positive discrimination in favour of workers' children is successful, how to avoid the (relative) exclusion of workers' children if only scholarly merit is considered, and – most importantly – how to make the requirements of a meritocratic selection compatible with those of collective mobility in a general sense. We do not have any all-round practical solutions at hand. These questions are, however, perceived with increasing awareness, which is an important step in the search for solutions.

In many respects, then, Hungary's achievements since the war have been quite considerable in an international perspective. We have attained an average, or somewhat better than average, level in comparison with fairly developed capitalist countries in pre-primary enrolment and in primary and secondary enrolment, in the student–teacher ratio, in the training of teachers, and in making the curriculum up-to-date and relevant. We lag behind in enrolment in higher education, but up to now this has been a deliberate decision aiming to avoid a surplus of professionals. In other fields, such as the elimination of regional differences, or of the lasting trends in social selection, change is slower than desirable. Partly because of the lack of adequate funds, there are also permanent problems in the quality of school buildings, in the remuneration of teachers, in the expansion of school services (canteens, day care for small children). There are, on the other hand, aspects where the results obtained are outstanding, and these are usually connected with the specific values and aims of a socialist society. Among these we may mention the unusually high rate of 'multi-step' individual mobility; the efforts aimed at ending the traditional systematic patterning of socially revelant knowledge; the new system of vocational schools which has begun to develop a new relationship between academic and manual training or learning; and finally the relatively open character of the school system where dead-ends are gradually being abolished and elements of permanent education are increasing, in the form of various special courses, and of evening and correspondence courses at secondary and higher levels. Nevertheless, the problems I have mentioned (and others not dealt with here) make it clear to everyone working in, or with, education that even partly satisfactory solutions require a series of educational reforms in curriculum content and in the organization of the school structure as well as in teaching methods. A reform is now in preparation, along the lines I have discussed. However it is also clear that the immediate interests of the economy cannot be overlooked. This pressure – together with what I have already said about the problems of transforming the main organizational lines of the social division of work – makes it probable that changes will not be rapid or spectacular, even if adequate educational conditions are assured.

Part Three

The Sphere of Distribution

Chapter 5

The Main Trends of Income Distribution

5.1 Economic background

Personal incomes depend ultimately upon the level of the national product (gross or net) and on its primary distribution between accumulation (including investments, the increase in stocks and the amortization of capital or fixed assets) and current consumption. It is only the second part that can be distributed by different mechanisms among the population. Economic, social and political forces and interests are at work in the phase both of primary and of secondary distribution. Traditional social policy was interested only in some of the aspects of the second distributional phase. However, the final outcome, the level and the distribution of the incomes of the population, is the result of the *whole* process. Therefore my analysis must cover the totality of the utilization of the national product.

The evolution of the Eastern European socialist countries, as is well known, was characterized after the war by accelerated accumulation and industrialization. Per capita gross domestic product (GDP) was around US $150 to 300 a year. A rapid increase in this level seemed possible only by severe limitation of current consumption. Between the two world wars in Hungary, only about 5 to 6 per cent of the GDP, for instance, was invested yearly, with an accordingly low growth-rate.[1] From 1948 until the end of the sixties the rate of accumulation in Hungary increased gradually from 15 per cent to 20 per cent and then to 25 per cent. Thus, with a great effort the growth-

---

1. According to A. Eckstein, the yearly increase of the per capita national product hardly attained 0·8 per cent and *gross* capital formation remained under 10 per cent of the net national product. (See A. Eckstein, *Hungarian National Income and Capital Formation 1900–1950*, Income and Wealth Series, Vol. 5.)

rate in fact accelerated, surpassing that of developed capitalist countries. Hungary's growth-rate was, incidentally, relatively low compared with the other socialist countries. None the less in Hungary too there was a rapid evolution, and the gap between the growth-rate of current consumption and that of accumulation increased more than in the developed capitalist countries. Later, from around the mid-fifties, the rate of growth of the socialist countries slowed down and the gap between consumption and accumulation lessened.

In the mid-sixties, East European socialist countries were grouped around the middle of the world scale of economic levels. Their per capita GDP was usually between US $600 and US $800, except in the German Democratic Republic where it exceeded 1,000 dollars in 1965. This level was still lower than that of the USA, Canada, the UK and Sweden before the war, was similar to the 1937 level of Switzerland, the Netherlands and Belgium and to the 1955 level of Austria and Finland. I must add that Hungary surpassed, to a greater or lesser degree, those capitalist countries that were on a par with her before the war, such as Greece or Portugal.[2]

These basic facts point to the greatest difficulty facing Hungary, namely, that distributable incomes are still on a relatively low level. The strain was especially great in the first years after the Second World War, bringing some additional difficulties that are still making their impact felt. It is also clear that intervention in the distributive mechanisms only (the target of traditional social policies) could not solve adequately the basic problems stemming from the low level of economic development.

5.2 Specific characteristics of income distribution in the socialist countries

(a) The first point to mention is a result of the abolition of private ownership entailing the disappearance of incomes con-

2. *UN Statistical Yearbooks* and computations of E. Ehrlich from the Hungarian National Planning Board.

nected with *capital*, a type of income distributed in a practically uncontrollably unequal way. True, incomes from assets do not amount to more than 4 to 13 per cent of all final incomes in Western European countries[3] and about 6 to 7 per cent in the USA. But this sum is unusually highly concentrated – for example, one third accrued to the group with over $100,000 of taxable incomes in the USA in 1966, which made up less than one thousandth of all tax payers. (See Table 5/1.)

Table 5/1: Distribution of different types of incomes in the United States, 1966

Size of taxable income	Number of tax returns in 1,000s	Total income, all types	Of which, capitalist[a]	Percentage distribution of incomes		Capitalist income as % of total income
		in thousands of millions of US $		Total	Capitalist	
Under $20,000	68,230	401·1	12·5	83·9	38·0	3·1
$20–50,000	1,644	48·0	7·0	10·1	21·3	14·6
$50–100,000	218	15·4	4·4	3·2	13·4	28·6
Over $100,000	53	13·5	9·0	2·8	27·3	66·7
Total	70,145	478·0	32·9	100·0	100·0	6·9

Source: Internal Revenue Service, *Statistics of Income, 1966,* Individual income tax returns, quoted in F. Ackerman et al., 'Income Distribution in the United States', *Review of Radical Political Economics,* Summer, 1971, p. 27–8.

[a] 'Capitalist income' includes dividends and capital gains.

3. *Incomes in Postwar Europe. A Study of Policies, Growth and Distribution,* UN, Chapter 6, p. 12.

The long-term trend in capital incomes is not quite uniform. It seems that the proportion of capital income is slowly decreasing in most capitalist countries. For example, according to Kravis, capital income represented around 20 per cent of all personal income in the twenties as against the current figure of 7 per cent[4] (obviously there was no comparable drop in the absolute value of capital incomes). In Western Europe, however, since about the fifties, the percentage has remained practically constant and in some cases an increase may even be observed (in France or in the UK). According to Hughes, for instance, personal property incomes multiplied in the UK by 2.34 from 1955 to 1965, while in the same period earned incomes increased by only 1.84.[5]

(b) The transformation of the relations of ownership also changed the whole system of distribution by abolishing the domination of the market and increasing the role of central redistribution.[6]

Unfortunately, comparative statistical data to support this thesis are rather scarce. A UN study relating to the mid-sixties, *Incomes in Postwar Europe*,[7] was the only one available to me which related the value of social benefits to the total net personal income of the population. There were two sets of figures (percentage ratios) for nine advanced capitalist countries, one for the mid-fifties, and another for the mid-sixties. For the six socialist countries only one set was available, relating to the beginning of the sixties. The range was from 11 to 22 per cent in the first case (capitalist countries in the mid-fifties), from 17 to 26 per cent in the second (the same countries in the mid-sixties) and from 18 per cent to 30 per cent in the third (socialist countries in the early sixties).

4. I. Kravis, *The Structure of Income*, University of Pennsylvania Press, 1962.

5. J Hughes, 'Why the Gap between Rich and Poor is Widening', *New Statesman*, 1968, No. 8.

6. See Chapters 2 and 7 for a more comprehensive discussion of this problem.

7. See note 3 above.

This suggests that the socialist countries used non-market allocation more extensively even at a lower economic level than did capitalist ones. Moreover the role of redistributive incomes has grown steadily ever since the sixties. The percentage of social benefits (social welfare incomes) in the total income of the population of Hungary was 17·4 per cent in 1960, 22·8 per cent in 1970 and 27·3 per cent in 1975.[8] According to long-term plans, this tendency is to continue, reaching about 30–34 per cent in 1985.

In a Manchester Liberal view the rapidly increasing importance of social benefits would certainly be seen as a sign of the 'inefficiency' of socialist countries. However, this type of liberalism is no longer a dominant trend in political and economic thinking in capitalist countries. For about the last forty years there has been a growing consensus that government intervention is likely to be salutary in counteracting the malfunctioning of the free market. Some specialists (even those free from any radical inclination) go so far as to suggest that growing government intervention in income maintenance and the allocation of public goods is a necessary corollary of economic growth, independently of the political order. For example, '. . . the need for a highly organized form of income protection increases as a society becomes industrialized and urbanized and that need is independent of the nature of the socioeconomic order.'[9] None the less statistics quoted from the UN survey do not fully sustain this contention. The alleged 'independence' is far from complete. It also seems doubtful that the implied 'necessity' evolves spontaneously. Detailed historical analyses show that in capitalist countries internal struggle, class tensions and conflicts are a crucial factor in bringing about this 'necessity'. Furthermore, the international scene can hardly be neglected: it is probably true that the experience of socialist

8. *Hungarian Statistical Yearbook*, 1974, CSO p. 367, and *A lakosság jövedelme és fogyasztása 1960–1975* (Income and Consumption of the Population 1960–75), Central Statistical Office, Budapest, 1976.

9. G. V. Rimlinger, *Welfare Policy and Industrialization in Europe, America and Russia*, John Wiley, New York, 1971. p. 334.

Countries (first at the beginning of the twenties, and later after the end of the Second World War) had a significant part to play in changing corresponding attitudes and practices in Western countries.

I do not deny that a higher economic level creates more scope for social intervention. But the facts about developed capitalist countries before the Second World War, and those about relatively underdeveloped socialist countries after the war, show first that good opportunities are not necessarily exploited in this way and second that limited possibilities do not preclude social action in this sphere.

(c) The third point worth mentioning – one that is connected with the first two characteristics – is a radical reduction of the inequality of income distribution as compared to the pre-war situation. The fundamental change between the pre-war and post-war situations in Hungary is summarized by the figures in Table 5/2.

Table 5/2: The shares of income in quintiles, before the war and in 1962

Quintiles	1930/31[a]	1962
Top quintile	59	36
Second ⎫ Third ⎬ quintile Fourth ⎭	35	57
Lowest quintile	6	7
Total	100	100

[a] A. Schmidt, *A személyi jövedelemelosztás a szocializmusban* (Distribution of Personal Incomes in Socialism), Közgazdasági és Jogi Kiadó, 1964, p. 88.

This change means that at present the inequality of income distribution is smaller in Hungary than in the majority of capitalist or non-socialist countries. Since this is one of the most controversial issues, I shall dwell upon it at somewhat greater length. There is a widespread belief among social scientists in capitalist countries that the wage and income distribution of the socialist countries is not less but more unequal than that of capitalist countries. There are two favourite arguments to support this point. One uses individual examples obtained in a more or less reliable, scattered and haphazard way. In this way maximum incomes or wages in the socialist countries are estimated to be thirty to forty times greater than the minimum by R. Aron, thirty times greater by Bottomore, three hundred times greater by Mehnert.[10]

The other method is to use available statistics. but to question their reliability on the grounds that they – unlike comparable ones in Western countries – do not take into account 'grey' or 'black' incomes, such as second jobs, tips or fringe benefits. It was on these grounds that Peter Wiles 'corrected' the Hungarian income-distribution statistics,[11] affirming that after the correction there was hardly any difference between the two sets of countries.

I have no doubt whatsoever that Hungarian income statistics are not entirely reliable. Besides the usual systematic under-reporting, some kinds of income, especially fringe benefits and some benefits in kind which are socially rather unequally distributed, are rarely included in the figures. (Later I shall deal more extensively with this second problem.) However, it seems to me that biases of the same type exist practically everywhere, and the official statistics never take them into account. Still, sometimes there are estimates concerning these omissions. Frankel, for instance, quotes the *Economist* of 27 August 1966,[12] according to which the proportion of fringe benefits to

10. R. Aron, *La lutte de classes*, Gallimard, Paris, 1964, pp. 130–31; (for Bottomore and Mehnert) D. Lane, *The End of Inequality?*, Penguin Books, Harmondsworth, 1971, p. 74.

11. Unpublished manuscript, prepared for a conference on income-distribution, held in December 1971, organized jointly by LSE and Essex University.

12. H. Frankel, *Capitalist Society and Modern Sociology*, Lawrence and Wishart, 1971.

salaries in England was 11 per cent at a yearly salary of £1,000, 19 per cent at £3,500 and 31 per cent at £7,000. J. A. Pechman made some calculations for the United States for 1966 about unreported and under-reported incomes. After his corrections, the share of the lowest quintile would drop from 4·1 to 3·2, that of the top 5 per cent would climb from the official 15·8 to 19·1 per cent – even without fringe benefits.[13] A fairly recent OECD study[14] makes some estimates about the under-reporting of some selected income categories. The study concludes: 'Since investment and self employment income are subject to more under-reporting than wages and salaries and transfer income, and since the former categories of income are disproportionately received by the upper deciles, inequality will tend to be underestimated everywhere. (The most under-reported income categories are practically non-existent in the socialist countries.) Much has been written recently on tax avoidance and tax abuses in England, which again imply a more or less significant under-reporting of high incomes.[15] It would seem, on the whole that income statistics for the socialist countries are no more uncertain or biased than in other countries. And it seems especially unwarranted to 'correct' them arbitrarily, assuming that they are the only ones in need of correction.

International comparisons remain difficult, however, even if we leave aside the reliability of statistics and accept them at their face-value. There are several biasing factors with different, sometimes contrary effects. It seems, for instance, that the value of home consumption of agricultural products is omitted from the income statistics of capitalist countries. If this were included, it would probably reduce slightly the inequality of the whole distribution. Income tax also plays a much larger role in some capitalist countries than in others, and than in socialist countries in general. Thus only after-tax income distribution

13. L. L. Upton and N. Lyons, *Basic Facts: Distribution of Personal Income and Wealth in the U.S.*, Cambridge Institute, May 1972.

14. Malcolm Sawyer, *Income Distribution in OECD Countries*, July 1976.

15. Frank Field, Molly Meacher and Chris Pond, *To Him Who Hath*. op, cit. especially pp. 155–69.

figures should be compared – and that is a condition that can hardly be fulfilled: until recent years, few systematic and comparative studies were made on after-tax income distribution. The OECD study refers to attempts to fill this gap at least for some countries, and arrives at the conclusion that income tax does not significantly affect the original inequality of the distribution of incomes.

A less technical detail concerns the interpretation of the significance of income differences. Here the price structure has also to be taken into account and it is usually acknowledged that the price system of socialist countries (again in Wiles's words) is more 'anti-rich' than in capitalist countries. One has to conclude that income statistics are never exact and never entirely comparable between countries. They seem, however, to offer a more solid basis than idle speculation or haphazard impressions. Thus, despite all their shortcomings, it is worth analysing them more closely.

As for the long-term tendency in income distribution, there seems to be a decrease in inequality as we move from countries with pre-capitalist economies and a low economic level, often with colonial ties, to economically more developed capitalist countries. The first category is characterized by extremes of wealth and poverty, by a high concentration of assets, by a lack of work opportunities with correspondingly low wages, and by feeble central intervention in income distribution. These characteristics also held for the Hungary of the 1930s, a slowly developing capitalist country with strong feudal features. Without attributing any mythical quality to figures, it seems that under these conditions the share of the top-income quintile was well above 50 per cent (56 per cent in India in 1949/50, 56 per cent in Puerto Rico in 1948, 58 per cent in Hungary in 1930).[16]

The developmental tendencies of the advanced capitalist

16. S. Kuznets, 'Economic Growth and Income Inequality', *American Economic Review*, March 1955, pp. 1–28; and A. Schmidt, *Distribution of Personal Incomes under Socialism* (in Hungarian), Közgazdasági és Jogi Kiadó, 1964

countries do not present a uniform picture with respect to trends in income inequality. Variations among them are significant. The figures available for the longest period are those for the United States. Here inequality of income distribution grew from 1919 to 1930, then gradually decreased until the war, and has remained at practically the same level since the war. According to UN data for the decade between 1950 and 1960, there were two countries where income inequality was growing (Finland and France), while it remained constant or decreased in the others. The OECD study referred to above presents time-series for some selected countries, concluding that 'in the 1950s there has been some movement towards greater equality almost everywhere. In the 1960s and early 1970s the same trend continued in the majority of the countries under scrutiny, but in the Federal Republic of Germany, in the United Kingdom and in the USA either there was no clear overall trend or there was a marginal move away from equality.'

All this evidence, then, seems to support the well-known hypothesis about the correlation between economic growth and the decrease in the inequality of incomes. A recent and unusually exhaustive endeavour to substantiate it was made by F. Paukert.[17] Starting from, and completing, the work of I. Adelman and C. Taft Morris, he analysed fifty-six countries at different levels of economic development. The data (presented in Table 5/3 in a concise form) by and large support the assumption, with the important exception of the last two lines, which I have added to Paukert's table.

Thus data referring to socialist countries do not fit Paukert's hypothesis. The last two countries would belong to the group with GDP of $501 to 1,000, but their inequality indices remain far below those of even the most developed countries. And, after all, there is really nothing astonishing in that. The absence of incomes from capital and entrepeneurship, a controlled wage-scale, full employment and a relatively well-developed system of social benefits make it practically inevitable that there should be less income inequality in the socialist

17. Felix Paukert, 'Income Distribution at Different Levels of Development: A Survey of Evidence', *International Labour Review*, 1973. No. 2–3.

Table 5/3: Indices characterizing the income distribution in
countries of different levels of economic development
(based on incomes per household)

Gross Domestic Product (GDP) per head in US $ around 1965	Number of countries in the group	Lowest 20%	Highest 20%	Top 5%	Some of the countries belonging to the group
Below 100	9	7·0	50·5	29·1	Burma, India
101–200	8	5·3	56·5	24·9	Tunisia, Pakistan
201–300	11	4·8	57·7	32·0	Brazil, Peru
301–500	9	4·5	57·4	30·0	Chile, Lebanon
501–1,000	6	5·1	50·1	25·4	Argentina, Greece, Japan
1,001–2,000	10	4·7	46·6	20·9	UK, Federal Republic of Germany, France, Italy, Austria
2,001 and over	3	5·0	42·7	16·4	USA, Sweden, Denmark
Hungary, 1967 (GDP: 600)		6·4	36·2	11·8	
Czechoslovakia, 1965 (GDP: 900)		6·3	34·4		

Sources: Except the last two lines of the table: Felix Paukert: 'Income
Distribution at Different Levels of Development: A Survey of Evidence',
International Labour Review, August–September 1973, Vol. 108, Nos.
2–3. For Hungary: *A lakossági jövedelmek szinvonala és szóródása*
(Level and Dispersion of the Incomes of the Population), Central
Statistical Office, Budapest, 1972. Data in this case refer to 1967. For
Czechoslovakia: P. Machonin a kollektiv, *Československa spolecnost.
Epocha 1969*, p. 297. Data refer to 1965.

countries. The contrary would certainly be considerably more surprising.

It still remains to be seen whether this difference between socialist and advanced capitalist countries can be considered as significant. The answer is not simple. In fact, despite all the changes in Hungary, the lowest decile still gets five times less than the average, and the top decile twice as much. This means that tenfold or even greater differences occur. It is clear, then, that we cannot speak about the 'end of inequality'. (I have already stated that this was not, in fact, the immediate aim of socialist countries.) In the light of these facts the difference between the two sets of countries seems only quantitative, and not a substantial one. However, we might also take a different view. It is well known that even in those non-socialist countries where constant efforts are made to this effect, it is extremely hard to reduce the share of the top groups even by as little as 2 or 3 per cent. It is also known that even these gains may easily be lost if political or economic conditions take an unfavourable turn. Now, in this light a lasting 10 per cent reduction in the share of the top group is in no way negligible, but indicates structural changes as well as changes in the 'ethos' of the population. Again, one must obviously not over-estimate the figures relating to one point in time. It is essential to know how the actual distribution is brought about and what its dynamic tendencies are. In the following section I shall analyse the Hungarian situation with these problems in mind.

5.3 The wage system

The central control of wages and salaries follows new norms and new principles introduced immediately after the war. The scope of action was enlarged and ensured by successive nationalizations so that the policy has been functioning fully since about the end of the forties.

The main goals of central control have remained practically unchanged through this period. It was necessary to eliminate the blatant injustices of the pre-war system which favoured those close to the centres of power and which was directed against manual workers in general and especially against those who had fewest assets, such as unskilled workers, young people, women and workers in agriculture. Central administration also had to assure that the minimum wage level did not fall too far behind the average, because otherwise the problem of 'the working poor' could not have been eased, given the relatively low wage fund. This means that a strong tendency towards the levelling of wages has always been present. But this has created a series of problems connected with the lack of incentives, the impossibility of rewarding work of above average quality, of stimulating further learning or taking over responsible jobs, etc. Moreover, those groups who experienced a relative loss as compared to the pre-war situation felt injured. This feeling of injury also characterizes some people, mainly among managers or professionals, who compare their absolute or relative situation to that of their Western counterparts who undeniably fare better.

The absence of wage incentives, combined with full employment, slowed down the increase in productivity and, hence, the improvement of the economic situation. Thus, on the whole, a dual process has over the last thirty years characterized the evolution of the wage system or the distribution of wages according to achievement. The first trend consisted of efforts towards a relatively level wage-system leading, from time to time, to the limitation of high incomes and to higher than average increases of low wages, in order to maintain the income level of large, usually unskilled masses. The other trend meant a search for more work incentives, for instruments that would favour creative and productive work and also the acquisition of skills contributing to a higher degree of productivity. The second trend necessarily led to a more pronounced differentiation of wages.

The two tendencies were not always equally strong. The 'equalizing' tendencies were predominant immediately after the war. The control of wages followed the stabilization of prices in 1946, at a time when the total amount of goods available for consumption attained only about 40 or 45 per cent of the 1938 level. The conversion rates for manual workers' wages were fixed at 50 per cent, those for non-manuals at 35 per cent of the 1938 level.[18]

Table 5/4: Wages and salaries of certain occupational groups, before and after the Second World War

	Monthly wage		Comparison of wages (average wage of industrial workers=1)		Rate of increase between 1938 and 1957
	1938 in Pengős	1957 in Forints	1938	1957	
Manual workers Workers in manufacture, national average	96	1,480	1·0	1·0	15·4
Non-manual workers Head of department in a ministry	877	3,979	9·1	2·7	4·5
University professor	758	3,900	7·9	2·6	5·1
District attorney	550	2,213	5·7	1·5	4·0
District judge	528	2,340	5·5	1·6	4·4
Administrator in a ministry	470	2,286	4·9	1·5	4·9
Doctor of medicine	382	2,200	4·0	1·5	5·8
Grammar school teacher	372	1,634	3·9	1·1	4·4
Engineer, technician	300	2,351	3·1	1·6	7·8
County administrator	294	1,695	3·1	1·1	5·8
Primary school teacher	228	1,350	2·4	0·9	5·9

Source: Unpublished computations of Dr János Sötér of the Ministry of Finance, based on available statistical and budget data.

18. Dr Béla Csikós-Nagy, *Magyar gazdaságpolitika* (Hungarian Economic Policy), Közgazdasági és Jogi Kiadó. 1971.

The former range of wages was lessened within both groups – but particularly within the group of non-manuals. In the case of salaries in public administration for instance, the pre-war range with maximum salaries seventeen times the minimum was reduced so that maximum salaries were only five times the minimum towards the mid-fifties. There was one major inherited problem, that of incomes in agriculture, which could not be handled at this time because of scarce resources. The gap between agricultural and other incomes was not bridged until the end of the sixties. Table 5/4 illustrates the changes at an early period of socialist development. It shows that despite an overall levelling some differences, presumed to be necessary and rational, were maintained, such as differences according to responsibility and skill. Some hierarchical differences were also retained – although it is hard to know whether at that time this was motivated by unquestioned traditions or by a new interest structure. Certain political preferences affecting especially the working class are not shown in the table. They assured preferential treatment of some of the previously worst-paid groups, like the miners, and a relative loss for groups which belonged to the former so-called workers' aristocracy.

Criticisms directed against too strong a levelling of wages started in the early fifties. A report of the Central Statistical Office in 1954 stated that, though the regulations introduced in the years after the Liberation in 1945 corrected many of the pre-war injustices, 'they did not solve some important problems. The wage system does not stimulate increases in the level of skill. It has hardly any incentives for good quality production work, for economizing with materials, etc.' It also mentioned that in a number of branches of industry the highest wage was only twice as much as the lowest, which did not give scope for a meaningful differentiation.[19]

19. 'The Functioning of the Principles of the Socialist Wage System in Industry', Central Statistical Office, August 1954, in *Adatok és adalékok a népgazdaság fejlődésének tanulmányozásához* (Facts and Information for the Study of the Evolution of the National Economy), Central Statistical Office. Budapest, 1957, pp. 127–8.

Renewed criticisms and, more importantly, some malfunctioning of the economy led to *ad hoc* corrections from the
beginning of the fifties. Wage supplements appeared in different
fields – for example, for the knowledge of foreign languages if
this was required at the workplace, or for the acquisition of
scientific degrees. More or less publicly, different fringe benefits
were also introduced, especially for managers. A third solution
was the wage correction introduced in one or other of the occupation groups (teachers, etc.) if they proved to be lagging too
far behind. Alongside *ad hoc* increases, the lowest wages were
also increased. Interestingly enough, despite renewed criticism
of too much 'equality', the dispersion of wages continued to
decrease throughout the fifties and the sixties. This may be ex-

Table 5/5: Indices of the dispersion of wages among workers
and other employees 1950–70

Year	The proportion of the wage fund accruing to		The average wage of the top decile as a percentage of that of the bottom decile	Inequality ratio[a]
	the top 20%	the bottom 20%		
1950	—	—	—	2·00
1952	34·7	10·7	4·27	—
1955	33·1	10·9	3·98	1·89
1960	31·6	11·4	3·58	1·78
1964	31·3	11·6	3·47	1·76
1966	31·9	12·1	3·37	1·79
1968	32·2	12·1	3·29	1·83
1970	—	—	—	1·84

[a] The inequality ratio – worked out by Ö. Éltető and E. Frigyes – shows
the relation of the average wages above the arithmetical mean to the
average wages below the mean.[20]

20. Ö Éltető and E. Frigyes, 'New Income Inequality Measures as
Efficient Tools for Causal Analysis and Planning', *Econometrica*, Vol. 36
No. 2, 1968.

plained by several factors. It is probably true that with a higher standard of living and a higher average wage level (from 1960 to 1970 real wages more than doubled) the absolute difference between low and high wages grew so that there was less pressure towards additional increases in the high wage brackets. Another factor was that the proportion of low-paid unskilled workers diminished with technological development. There was probably also a third factor, namely that variations occurred in the 'middle-range' fields: rather more differentiation was introduced among those doing a similar job, without affecting the top and the bottom of the overall dispersion. The diminution of wage-differentiation is characterized by the figures in Table 5/5.

None of these measures, then, significantly affected the wage distribution, which retained its relatively level character, or the differences between the occupational groups, or the rigidity of wage-control.

The reform of economic management introduced towards the end of the sixties created the conditions for a thorough reconsideration of the wage-system. It was only then that questions of theoretical relevance concerning the wage-system began to be formulated. The 'distribution according to work' was always an accepted norm and requirement, but it was never made clear which components or characteristics of work ought to be taken into account for the purpose of differentiation. This is an important point because the work which is accomplished cannot be measured on the basis of individual output or achievement, as these are usually incommensurable. On the other hand, the operation of market forces has been almost entirely suppressed, so that one cannot argue that wage-rates formed on the labour market reflect the 'value' of the achievement. (This is never true. But if the labour market is in full swing, one may impute an economic meaning to salaries and wages and assume that they render comparable the incommensurable.) If outputs are not commensurable, and if there are no self-regulatory mechanisms, the differentiation of wages has to be based on the intrinsic characteristics of either the worker or the job. And once the relevant characteristics are agreed, it is still necessary to define what their relative weight should be and how much difference in wages each of them should necessitate.

The debates about these points are not over in Hungary. Economists are still engaged in a discussion centring on the meaning of the principle of distribution according to work, the scope and forms of adequate work incentives and also the role of the labour market under Hungarian conditions.[21] Up to now, there have been no endeavours to introduce a system of scores in the determination of wages as in the Netherlands or in the German Democratic Republic. But the regulations introduced in 1970 spelt out the criteria of wage-differentiation more explicitly and more systematically than those previously in force.

The regulations applied since 1970 may be briefly summarized. In the case of manual workers, the centrally prescribed elements were the minimum and maximum wage level (ranging then from 4 to 16 forints per hour), and the two factors of differentiation within these limits, namely the level of skill and the working conditions including the physical effort required by the job. Five levels of skill and four degrees of working conditions were defined, yielding a total of twenty categories. The decisions affecting the other components of wages, including the tariffs in each category, were decentralized, in other words left to the discretion of the ministries or firms. As for the non-manual workers, the range of wages was increased in their case, too, and factors of differentiation were defined. These included the level of qualification, the number of years in employment, 'rank' in the structure, the number of subordinates and – in some cases – the size of the enterprise. Professional skill and rank were separated so that expertise could be highly rewarded without a high managerial post.

Another new element of this system of control was the intro-

21. For example Gábor Révész, 'Ösztönzés, munkaszerinti elosztás, keresetszabályozás' (Incentives, Distribution according to Work, Regulation of Wages), *Közgazdasági Szemle*, 1973, No. 11.

duction of participation in the share of profits at company level. (The category corresponding to profit under capitalist conditions is called 'benefit' or 'gain' in a socialist economy. I use the term 'profit' here in order to make the point clearer.) Before the reform, the work of the company was measured on the basis of centrally defined indicators obtained from global plans and profits were not considered as income-regulating factors. The reform gave more autonomy and responsibility to the firms, made production more flexible and measured the success of the firm less by formal indicators and more by the profits directly connected with economic efficiency. That is why and how profit-sharing could be implemented as one of the incentives.

The new system, however, raises serious theoretical problems which are still being debated. One of them is related to differentiation between companies. Even if profits only reflected the quality of the firm's work, large wage differences might occur between firms. But in practice the profits are not simply a reflection of the company's work. They also depend on the trends of the business cycle, especially that of foreign countries, because they affect the various firms more or less directly and more or less favourably. Also, the nature of the initial equipment (for example the modernity of machinery) has an effect on economic results, although under the former economic regulations the firm had practically no say in the development of its equipment. Large income differences, stemming from differences in profits between firms, whether due to 'merit' or to 'chance', but specially in the latter case, might create tensions and/or an unwarranted manpower fluctuation. If, however, the proportion of the income from profit is reduced too greatly within the total income, then its stimulating effect becomes negligible.

It has now been decided that profits may make up around 10 per cent of wages, and the decentralized profit-sharing system has been complemented by so-called central wage-increase preferences. These extra increases (in basic wages), financed by the central budget, are given to firms which have limited possibilities of exploiting the market forces, or which were initially at a lower-than-average wage level, or again were handicapped by their outdated equipment. The firms favoured by central preferences belong mainly to heavy industry.

The other main dilemma of the profit-sharing system is related to the relative importance of the 'fixed' and the 'moving' components of the wage in the case of individuals and the distribution of profits *within* the enterprise. Profit introduces an element of risk into the wage system, and risk means uncertainty. If the proportion of profit within the wage is too large, then unfavourable results for the enterprise may endanger the secure existence of those who work there, particularly the poorly paid categories, and disproportionately large incomes may occur in the case of success. It is hard also to know what is the role of each individual in the creation of profit (a problem connected with the impossibility of measuring individual achievement), although the difficulties are not exactly the same for wages as for profits. By and large there is, however, a consensus that management decisions play a major part in the formation of profits. The regulations therefore specified that managers in the most responsible positions had the right to a larger than average share, but they were also the only ones who could be penalized by a wage reduction in the case of failure. (Obviously, they can never be made financially responsible for all losses because they do not have any private means. But this is a very far-reaching problem.)

These dilemmas have made their impact felt throughout the whole period since 1968. The part of profit within the total income from employment amounted, on a national average, to less than 10 per cent, but this ratio varied over periods of time and among different groups of the workforce. During the first year there were endeavours towards open and marked differences in distribution. (Bonuses and premiums were offered to managers before 1968 as well, but the principles of their distribution were not clearly laid down.) It was in 1968 that the overall proportion of income from profits was at its highest and distribution of profit was more influenced by 'rank' than in later years. This differentiation was based on a rather rigid categorization of the whole personnel, with a marked variation in their relative shares. The first category – top managers – could get up to 80 per cent of their salary in the form of profits, the second – middle management – up to 50 per cent, and the third – other employees – up to 15 per cent. The majority of employees strongly opposed this categorization, especially because of the labels it attached to people. Differentiation itself was by and large accepted, as shown by sociological studies which made inquiries about acceptable or 'just' wage differentials.[22] These categories were abolished in 1970, entailing a radical reduction in the differentiation of the distribution of profits. Managers' incomes were greatly reduced as a consequence in 1971. In that year they suffered an absolute loss as compared to the previous year. After 1971 there was again a slow increase in the amount and in the differential distribution of profits, but the 1968 level was not approached. On the whole, between 1968 and 1975 the wage level of management increased at a much slower pace than that of other groups. (See Table 5/6.)

The relatively rapid increase in workers' wages was due less to the new system of profit-sharing than to steady efforts to increase the lowest wages and to give priority to groups which lagged behind the majority (women, workers in heavy industry, etc.). With the spread of skills and an increased level of schooling there occurred a shortage of manpower willing to accept unfavourable conditions or exhausting jobs. So 'market forces' also acted in favour of wage increases for these groups.

The tendencies characterizing the evolution of wage-differentials in the productive sector of firms have, by and large, been similar in other branches. The average level of wages and

22. Studies on the just wage, the *'iustum praetium'*, were first undertaken by A. Sarapata in Poland around 1960. The method has since been applied several times in Hungary, too, and the original findings – that the factual and the 'just' wages were highly correlated – have usually been corroborated. One study was done among employees in the retail trade, and the other one in two factories. The first study is now under analysis; the second yielded a study: M. Csákó, L. Kende and P. Lederer, *Opinions about the Prestige Order of Occupations in Two Hungarian Factories* (unpublished).

Table 5/6: Incomes in firms in the socialist sector

Year	Top manage-ment	Middle manage-ment	Other workers and employees	Total (all levels)	Ratio of	
					top	middle level
	average monthly incomes (forints)				to workers and employees	
	(A) Monthly wage				**(A) Wages**	
1968	4,503	3,016	1,829	1,915	2·5	1·6
1970	4,897	3,298	2,033	2,129	2·4	1·6
1971	4,797	3,021	2,094	2,228	2·3	1·4
1973	5,156	3,341	2,286	2,416	2·3	1·5
1975	5,695	3,740	2,688	2,828	2·1	1·4
	(B) Ratio of total monthly income (wage and profit share) to the monthly wage				**(B) Total monthly income**	
1968	1·31	1·19	1·08	1·09	3·0	1·8
1970	1·27	1·14	1·06	1·08	2·9	1·7
1971	1·21	1·12	1·06	1·07	2·6	1·5
1973	1·25	1·12	1·06	1·08	2·6	1·5
1975	1·26	1·13	1·07	1·08	2·5	1·5
	(C) Time series of the total monthly income 1968 = 100					
1968	100	100	100	100		
1970	105	105	109	110		
1971	100	95	113	114		
1973	109	104	123	128		
1975	121	117	146	147		

Source: Foglalkoztatottsági és kereseti arányok (Employment and Wages), Central Statistical Office, Budapest, 1970, 1972, 1975, 1977.

Table 5/7: Wages and salaries in various branches of the national economy, full-time workers and employees, 1973[a]

Branch	Proportion of all workers %	Average monthly wage	Total income from work	Ratio of total monthly income to the monthly wage
		Forints		
Industry, mining	35	2,524	2,699	1·07
Construction	8	2,718	2,912	1·07
Agriculture, forestry	22	2,388	2,565	1·07
Transport, communication	7	2,620	2,796	1·07
Trade	9	2,254	2,456	1·09
Personal services	3	2,276	2,466	1·08
Health education	9	2,408	2,630	1.09
Public administration	7	2,852	3,178	1·11
Total	100	2,512	2,703	1·08

Source: Foglalkoztatottsági és kereseti arányok, 1973 (Employment and Wages, 1973), Central Statistical Office, Budapest, 1975.
[a] The proportion of part-time workers including pensioners with a reduced working time was 6·5 per cent in 1973.

salaries is fairly similar in the various branches. The lowest averages are found in trade, services and agriculture: besides the relatively low level of schooling, the high proportion of women in trade and services is responsible for the low average. The average is highest in public administration, where the level of education is highest. The difference between these extremes is, however, no more than 25 per cent, even if we take into account that bonuses are somewhat more important in public administration than elsewhere.

The distribution of wages and salaries is also fairly similar

Table 5/8: Monthly average wages and salaries (total incomes from work) by occupational group

	1962	1967	1967 in % of 1962
	monthly average forints		
Managers, senior administrators, professionals	2,686	3,129	116·5
Skilled non-manuals	1,840	2,217	120·5
Office workers	1,481	1,687	113·9
Total non-manual	1,950	2,280	116·9
Skilled workers	1,888	2,196	116·3
Semi-skilled workers	1,531	1,799	117·5
Unskilled workers	1,212	1,429	117·9
Total manual outside agriculture	1,563	1,844	118·0
Manual workers in agriculture	1,183	1,662	140·5
Average	1,655	1,964	118·7

Source: A keresetek szóródása és szerepe a munkás-alkalmazotti háztartások jövedelmében (The Distribution of Wages and Their Impact on the Total Income of Workers' and Employees' Households), Central Statistical Office, Budapest, 1971, p. 147–9.

within the various branches. This means, in terms of broad occupational groups, that the group with the highest average level gets about twice as much as the worst-off group. Unfortunately, wage statistics covering *all* the occupational groups are not available for the last few years. None the less, the data derived from the national income surveys for 1962 and 1967 give an idea of the distribution of wages and salaries. The absolute levels have increased since 1967 by about 30 per cent, but the relative differences between the groups were not deeply affected. (The impact of economic reform can be seen in the data presented in Table 5/6.)

The broad occupational groups do not give a full account of the wage differentials, since there is a fairly considerable dispersion within each group. On the whole, however, the minimum and maximum levels – under 800 and over 5,000 forints respectively in 1967 – occurred rather rarely, in 1·7 and 0·3 per cent of all earners, while 75 per cent of earners received between 2,000 and 4,000 forints. This concentration did not change radically in subsequent years. In 1974, the lowest wage was somewhere below 1,000 forints, with 1·1 per cent of earners at this level, and another 1 per cent belonged to the highest wage group earning over 7,000 forints. Out of this group, only 0·1 per cent had a monthly income over 10,000 forints (roughly US $500), and 78·9 per cent of all employees earned between 1,500 and 4,000 forints.[23]

The distribution of wages and salaries shows a tendency that might be judged favourably by the standards I have applied throughout this book to social phenomena. Differentiation according to skill and the hierarchical rank are certainly not levelled, but they do not seem to be exaggerated either; they are certainly less marked than in the majority of non-socialist countries, and they tend towards less inequality, at least in relative terms. This does not mean that the wage system has no shortcomings. The main points that need attention and further corrective steps are the following:

● There is confusion about the role that should be played by the differentiation of wages or salaries between those who perform similar tasks. According to the various economic theories about individual work incentives, this type of wage-differentiation should have a strong stimulative effect. In reality, however, it is in this area that resistance to differentiation is probably at its highest, at least among workers. Whenever a group of workers has the opportunity to fix the respective share of remuneration of its members, the workers will, more likely than not, opt either for equal or similar shares of any given extra amount of money, or for a distribution that follows the existing wage-pattern, or again for including among the criteria of distribution considerations that have nothing to do with achievement (for example, social conditions). If the rules of differentiation are settled outside the group (for example by the management) then

23. *Foglalkoztatottság és kereseti arányok, 1974* (Employment and Wages, 1974), Central Statistical Office, Budapest.

tensions are likely to occur within the group. Thus it remains to be studied what type of differentiation is accepted within a more or less homogeneous group, and what is the impact of any given strategy of differentiation on the economic achievement and on the attitude and atmosphere of the group.

● There are occupational groups which cannot profit directly from the economic progress of the productive sector and which have no direct access to central decision-making. Consequently, they are likely to lag behind the average wage increases. The so-called automatic wage increase, following a centrally defined rate, applies to them, but they do not benefit directly from other gains, being in 'non-profit' institutions. The two most important of such groups are those working in the educational system and the health service (at all levels of skill). For them, occasional extra wage increases from central funds are granted when the gap between their wages and those of other workers generates palpable tension. (This was the case in 1972, and again in 1977. In both cases there was an extra 20 to 30 per cent increase of the average wage.) The difficulty is that it is hard to institutionalize the extra increase, because the factors of improvement of the other groups are varied and their full impact cannot be foreseen, less still planned in advance.

● Further, there is still a wage-difference between the sexes. Legal discrimination was abolished long since, for the most part in 1949, and – as was shown earlier – many steps were taken to assure an equal start for women within the social division of work. Nevertheless, the average wage for men is still about 30 per cent higher than that for women. Of this some 20 per cent might be accounted for by the fact that women still lag behind in length of schooling, skill acquisition and access to top positions. These are, partly at least, objective factors which, once made explicit, may be (and mostly are) handled rationally. The remaining 10 per cent is harder to explain and to reduce. This is due mainly to prejudices and traditions which are difficult to unravel and to handle, such as, for example, the relatively low wage level of branches which are feminized, such as the textile industry, the retail trade or teaching. In the case of women, however, at least the aims are clear: there is no doubt that the existing differences are not deliberate and that they should be eliminated. The position in this sphere is therefore constantly under observation. If progress is stagnating, efforts are revived, for instance by means of a Party decision, refocusing attention on the issue. (This was the case for instance in 1970.)

● The relation between age and wage represents a much more controversial issue although the problem is certainly not a new one. Already in the twenties the Lynds had observed, quoting A. Epstein, that '. . . economic superannuation . . . stands like a spectre before the industrial worker . . . Meanwhile among the business class of Middletown . . . advancing age still appears to mean increasing or stable earning power and social prestige.'[24] The universal pension scheme solved the worst problems in this respect. But it is still true that ageing affects blue-collar and white-collar workers unequally, and its effect is most unfavourable in the case of groups with least skill, whether blue or white collar.

As far as I have been able to ascertain, this problem is practically universal though international comparative data are scarce.[25] In Hungary it seems to be somewhat attenuated compared, for example, with France or England (on the basis of data from the mid-sixties for France and Hungary, from 1970 for England). Upper white-collar workers have a less steep upward gradient in Hungary than in France or England. The

24. R. S. and H. M. Lynd, *Middletown*, Harcourt, Brace and World, New York, 1956, p. 35 (first published in 1929).
25. Sources: for Hungary: *A keresetek szóródása és szerepe a munkás-alkalmazotti háztartások jövedelmében* (The Distribution of Wages and Their Impact on the Total Income of Workers and Employees' Households), Central Statistical Office, Budapest, 1971; for France: Data of the INSEE; for England: Data from the *New Earnings Survey* of April 1970, quoted by J. Westergaard and H. Resler, *Class in a Capitalist Society*, op. cit., pp. 80–84.

lower skilled groups face a somewhat smaller loss than in France, but are affected rather more than in England. Despite some improvements, the biological process of ageing still has social consequences which are advantageous if other conditions are favourable, but which represent a more or less serious disadvantage otherwise.

No doubt this phenomenon has rational causes: the individual's output probably declines with age more considerably, and certainly more visibly, in the case of jobs requiring physical effort than in non-manual jobs. Structural social causes are, however, probably more important here. Groups which have more impact on the social mechanisms of distribution also have a more advantageous income trend. There have been some endeavours to correct further the unfavourable consequences of ageing in general, and in the case of manual workers in particular. The efforts are most visible in relation to pensions. All salaried people have a right to choose, for instance, the most favourable period out of the last years of their active life as a basis for setting the pension level (which is wage-related). There is also an informal tendency to increase as much as possible the earnings of those who are close to retirement. But the economic (or socio-economic) basis of the problem is not eliminated by these efforts and is likely to be quite persistent.

This is, however, only one aspect of the age problem. The other is the reconciliation of two contradictory requirements. The first requirement is the norm of 'equal pay for equal work'. This can entail equal or even higher wages for younger people. Their achievement may be higher not only because they are more fit, but also because they may have acquired during their more recent training more modern, more productive methods both in manual and non-manual jobs. The second requirement is the necessity to assure a continuous improvement for everybody. In a society where a dynamic change takes place, each individual must profit from the general development – otherwise people have the impression of a relative deterioration, with all its unfavourable consequences. (A special survey of family budget statistics[26] showed, for instance, by comparing the real change in income level and the subjective evaluation of this change, that the families asked interpreted a small increase – less than 12 per cent for five years, 5 per cent for one year – as stagnation, and an increase of less than 10 per cent for five years or less than 3 per cent for one year as deterioration.) This social norm favours a wage-system where ageing is accompanied by a steady improvement.

These two often contradictory requirements probably cannot be reconciled without deliberately introducing non-economic considerations into the wage system, by means of some form of age-supplement. This is in fact done in the case of white-collar employees, although it is not clear whether the factor taken into account in defining the salary, namely that of 'years spent in employment', has an economic or a social significance. More precisely, it is handled as if it were an economic factor operating only with some groups. If this were not the case, if the length of service were considered a social factor, the same supplement ought already to have been introduced everywhere. However, this policy is hard to generalize – and not only because of the present interest structure. It calls for a thorough reappraisal of the nature of the wage system, and the role of economic and non-economic factors in shaping it.

It is true that even now it is a mixed economic *and* social category. Redistributive considerations are amply built into it already (for example with the minimum wage), while for instance some of the sex-related wage differences are due to another type of 'social content' in the wage. Men often get a higher wage than women in the same position because they are seen as heads of families. Another social element in wages consists of sex-related differences in earnings which are due simply to historical and other stereotypes working at the expense of women.

The long-term problem then is the following. It has already been stated that economic considerations have to be gradually

26. *Vélemények és tények* (Opinions and Facts), Central Statistical Office, Budapest, 1966.

reinserted into the social sphere. For the time being, and in the case of distribution, the 'economic' principle is being weakened by central redistribution. The growing role of central redistribution is not contested. There is, on the contrary, a general consensus about its importance. The question is whether in the long run the economic consideration will fade away by being relegated to the background through a gradual but significant increase of central redistribution, or whether the economic principle (achievement motivation through economic incentives) can be weakened in itself.

5.4 The main trends in incomes

The aims and methods of Hungarian incomes policy have gradually taken shape over the last three decades. Immediately after the war, as I mentioned above, the consumption fund of the population dropped to about half the level of the pre-war period. This meant a rather low average standard of living despite a radical reduction in income inequalities. The pre-war level of real income was attained around 1949. At that time the structural foundations of a new incomes policy – nationalization, land-reform, the organizational framework of central planning, etc. – were laid down. However, subsequent economic and political difficulties hindered the full exploitation of these opportunities. This situation was gravest at the beginning of the fifties. Forced industrialization, the atmosphere of the cold war and a neglect of the needs of the population led to measures that significantly lowered the level of real incomes of all employees. The situation of peasants, mostly small-holders at that time, was less directly affected by the central income regulations, so that they suffered less from the rapid, real losses. But a whole cluster of measures contributed to maintain their incomes on a relatively low level in the interests of rapid industrialization. The measures included a low price level for agricultural products, a comparatively high level for products bought mainly by the peasantry, agricultural means of production included, and a very strict tax policy that forced the peasants to give over to the central funds a large part of their products in kind. These measures were gradually altered from the mid-fifties. From then on, the incomes of the peasants grew rapidly. In the last years of the sixties the absolute level of agricultural incomes by and large reached that of workers. Later, especially in those peasant families where one or two members engaged in regular employment outside agriculture, their income level even surpassed that of workers. (See Table 5/9.)

The most important factors behind the increase of incomes were the growth of wages, the growth of the rate of employment and the expanding scope and level of social benefits. The

Table 5/9: The evolution of real incomes

Year	Per capita personal real income of the population belonging to households of	
	workers and employees	peasants
	(a) 1950=100	
1949	97	89
1950	100	100
1952	85	95
1953	89	106
1954	112	108
1955	118	116
1959	164	132
1960	168	131
1965	198	161
1970	263	220
1971	273	245
	(b) Yearly average rate of change	
1950–53	−4·0	+1·8
1953–9	+10·7	+3·6
1959–65	+3·2	+3·4
1965–71	+5·5	+7·2
1971–4	+4·8	

(see graph)

Source: Hungarian Statistical Yearbooks for the years quoted.

wage increase continued from 1953 on, while the rise of the employment rate was more important in the first half, the increase of social benefits in the second half of the period under scrutiny.

The continuous though not entirely regular rise of the income level was accompanied by the slow diminution of differentiation in the distribution of incomes. The three main factors of this trend have been the levelling of wages already described; the spread of agricultural co-operatives which assured, after some years of extreme difficulties, a secure income for those working in agriculture, and which have to a certain extent diminished the former discrepancies between poor and rich peasants; and, again, the growing role of social benefits, which, as will be seen in detail in Chapter 7, have usually been less unequally distributed than work-related incomes. Changes in the composition of incomes highlight some of these tendencies. (See Table 5/10.)

Table 5/10: The composition of total incomes of the population

Year	Total incomes, nominal value, in thousands of millions of forints	Percentage of this which represents:					
		Wages	Agricultural incomes from		Social benefits		Other income[a]
			co-op-eratives	others	in cash	in kind	
1960	118·5	50·0	1·7	24·8	7·0	11·4	5·1
1965	146·0	51·4	5·8	17·2	8·6	12·3	4·7
1970	221·7	49·9	8·0	14·0	10·4	12·4	5·3
1973	263·4	49·5	7·3	13·0	12·5	12·8	4·9
1975	311·5	49·8	7·3	11·0	14·5	12·8	4·6

Source: A lakosság jövedelme és fogyasztása 1960–1973 (Incomes and Consumption of the Population, 1960–73), Central Statistical Office, Budapest, 1975, and computations based on the data.

[a] This category includes the income of the self-employed, interest from savings deposits, etc.

The decrease in income inequality was probably characteristic of the whole period if we judge on the basis of those
factors the evolution of which is known (for example wages,
etc.). The exact figures are only available from the beginning of
the sixties. (The first income survey in 1959 covered only those
in employment; the second, in 1962, was extended to cover the
whole population.) The decreasing trend, however, changed
somewhat at the turn of the seventies. At that time, owing to
new opportunities for earning high incomes, offered by the
economic reform, and also to a relative slowing-down of the
gains in family allowances, there was a slight rise in inequality.
The level of inequality was, however, still lower than ten years
before.

Table 5/11: Deciles of per capita personal income (percentage
distribution of the whole population according to
the per capita income level)[a]

Income deciles	1959	1962	1962	1967	1972
	Only the house-holds of work-ers and employees		Total population		
Lowest (1st) decile	4·0	4·1	3·6	4·1	4·0
2nd decile	5·5	6·0	5·6	6·0	5·9
3rd to 8th decile	54·9	56·9	56·0	57·0	56·4
9th decile	14·6	14·0	14·1	14·0	14·0
Top (10th) decile	21·0	19·0	20·7	18·9	19·7
(Total)	100·0	100·0	100·0	100·0	100·0
Top 5%	11·5	10·9	12·1	10·8	11·6
Inequality ratio	2·11	1·91	2·09	1·92	1·96

Sources: Jövedelemeloszlás Magyarországon 1962-ben (Income Distribution in Hungary in 1962), 1967; *A lakossági jövedelmek szinvonala és
szóródása, 1967* (Level of Dispersion and the Incomes of the Population,
1967), 1970; *A családi jövedelmek szinvonala és szóródása 1972-ben* (The
Level and Dispersion of Family Incomes in 1972), 1975; all published
by the Central Statistical Office, Budapest.

Note on page 192

The incomes policy of the last decades, especially of the last two, may be considered as efficient, since the main tendencies by and large conform to socialist aims. I do not want to imply that everything that has happened was deliberately planned in exactly this way. Probably the main aim of the deliberate steps taken has been income-security. The relevant policy measures

---

[a] The distribution of incomes is portrayed by means of different data. Hungarian income statistics use three basic measures: income per household, income per capita and income per consumer unit. For international comparative purposes only the incomes per household can be used because usually these are the only ones available for other countries. It is clear, however, that the standard of living of a family depends not only on the amount of income accruing to its members, but also on the number and the socio-demographic characteristics (sex, age, earning ability) of those living in the household. Per capita incomes take into account the number of the household members (by dividing the amount of the pooled incomes of the household by this number). The income per consumer unit reflects the composition of the household too. In this case the members of the family are converted into equivalent units by means of an adult equivalent scale based on family budget data. The conversion rates are the following:

Children from 0 to 3 years	0·4 units
Children from 4 to 6 years	0·5 units
Children from 6 to 10 years, if at school	0·6 units
Children from 6 to 13 years, if not at school, and dependants over working age	0·7 units
Children from 11 to 13 years, if at school, and pensioners	0·8 units
All others	1·0 units

This scale is then combined with a so-called economy scale by adding 0·4 units to the sum derived from the adult economy scale, for each family. This means that a one-person household represents 1·4 c.u., two adults total 2·4 consumer units, that is 1·2 on average, etc. The income per consumer unit is a useful index when groups of different demographic composition are compared. (The idea of the economy scale was derived from: J. Hajnal and A. M. Henderson, 'The Economic Position of the Family', in *Papers of the Royal Commission on Population*, Vol. V, HMSO, London, 1950.)

include the assurance of job-security and the rejection of unemployment; a system of social benefits insuring against so-called risks (although the concepts and vocabulary of the social services have changed in this area so that they no longer use the concept of risk); finally, a change in the payment system in agriculture was also introduced. In traditional agriculture income followed the cycle of production, that is, it was spasmodic. Peasants used to get a sizable sum of money once a year. With a relatively low standard of living, with many deferred needs, etc., this meant comparative well-being for a while and uncertainty or strained circumstances for long months. Even after the creation of co-operatives, this question could not be solved for some time because the co-operatives did not have sufficient current assets. This was one of the gravest complaints of peasants (and one of the main attractions of fixed-income work) until the beginning of the sixties. That is why the co-operatives introduced – sometimes with substantial state help – the system of advance monthly payments, assuring a secure income throughout the year, and a larger sum after the yearly settlement. The prices policy must be mentioned here, since this is another way in which central regulations are aiming at stability and security. (For further details, see Chapter 8.)

Another characteristic of the incomes policy measures was the gradual elimination of conspicuous, status-bound aspects of remuneration. Salaries and wages are being replaced more and more by the uniform concept of a wage. There may still be a difference in the instalments of payments to manuals and non-manuals, but it is less conspicuous: there are no more weekly wages, and monthly payment is spreading. The income-tax policy also has similar implications. Wages and salaries are not taxed directly except for the compulsory pension contribution, which is progressive (10 per cent in the highest income bracket). Instead of direct taxation, wages are centrally regulated so as to assure the desired differentiation. The underlying rationale is that progressive income tax can never entirely avoid overtones of an additional hierarchy based on the differentiated contribution of citizens to the 'maintenance of the government'.

This does not mean the rejection of all types of income tax: it is retained where central regulations are ineffective, as in the case of artisans or small shopkeepers. Indeed, with tendencies of decentralization the necessity of income tax has come to the fore and is debated in various circles.

The generally favourable income trends do not preclude the existence of unsolved problems and lasting difficulties. These are related partly to the still strained economic situation, and partly to the contradictions of short-term economic and social aims under the present circumstances. Some of them will be treated separately in what follows.

Chapter 6

Aspects of Income Distribution

6.1 High incomes

Around the 1950s, even with a system of fairly unequal income distribution, 'high' incomes did not represent very substantial purchasing power. At a low economic level, with prices that penalized luxury items, and amidst general scarcity, one could hardly begin to accumulate a fortune even if one received five times the average income. Since then, the average income level has trebled. Thus, even though the relative distance between lowest and highest incomes has lessened, the *absolute* difference has grown considerably. At present high incomes in Hungary, a monthly 10,000 or 15,000 forints on average for a household in the top decile or top 5 per cent, would not be considered high in rich capitalist countries. (Because of the differences in price systems, the purchasing power of these sums cannot be compared on the basis of average conversion rates. A list of prices is given in Table 6/1. If we apply the official

Table 6/1: Average consumer price of some important selected consumer goods or services, 1972

Food	Forints
Pork fat (per kilo)	20
Pork (first-quality, boneless) (per kilo)	39
Beef, on the bone (per kilo)	30
Edible oil (per litre)	21·60
Sugar (per kilo)	9·60
Bread, white (per kilo)	3
Wheat, white (per kilo)	4·60
Rice (per kilo)	16
Milk (per kilo)	3·60
Butter (per kilo)	50
Cheese (per kilo)	40
Eggs (per dozen)	20·40

Potatoes (per kilo)	3·40–4
Onions (per kilo)	4·50–5·30
Apples (per kilo)	5·90–7·20
Lemons (per kilo)	19
Wine (per litre)	18·10
Beer (per litre)	7–8·60
Cigarettes – a packet of 20 (the most popular brands)	2·80–4·40

Manufactured goods

Cotton, per metre (80 cm. wide)	29·80
Wool, per metre (140 cm. wide)	283–424
Men's shirt	75–293
Men's shoes, leather (one pair)	268
Women's shoes, leather (one pair)	200
Washing machine	1,700
TV set	5,800–6,500
Coal (per hundredweight)	26·10–44·90
Toilet soap (per kilo)	27·60
Toothpaste (50-gramme tube)	2·50–3·50
Daily newspaper	0·80

Services

Gas (per cubic metre)	1·41
Electricity (per kWh)	8·87
Tram ticket in Budapest[a]	1
TV licence (one month)	50
Haircut	4·60
Monthly rent, urban average per household[b]	250

Source: Hungarian Statistical Yearbook, 1972.
[a] In Hungary, bus and tram fares are uniform, irrespective of distance.
[b] Family budget data for 1974.

conversion rates, 15,000 forints would correspond to about US $750.) Still, under present conditions in Hungary, such incomes make accessible not only a very comfortable everyday life (comfortable by any contemporary standards), but also the acquisition of important assets (such as a holiday home). This means that Hungary is confronted with a twofold problem. One is the opportunity to acquire unearned incomes by means of such assets; this runs against the basic tenets of a socialist society. The second is the growing gap in inherited wealth, which runs against the efforts to reduce inequalities at birth.

As to the first point: it is true that capitalist goods, shares, etc., cannot be bought and private money lending (at usurious rates of interest) is illegal. The two accepted forms of unearned income – interest from state banks and state organized gambling – offer limited scope. Still, in recent years new possibilities of gain have cropped up in the form of exploitation of either the housing shortage or the growing demand for building sites or small plots. A small number of people began to engage in real-estate speculation and, even though this could be done only on a tiny scale, acquired comparatively large unearned incomes. At first, there were no legal provisions for this eventuality because the case had simply not arisen before. Since shortages as a rule invite semi-legal activities, the roots of the problem will not be eradicated unless the housing shortage itself disappears. None the less, some legal measures were taken to reduce at least the irritating or harmful aspects of this phenomenon. The property or real estate a family can own was limited to one privately owned flat and one secondary residence or small plot. (Since 1977 state-owned land may no longer be sold to private parties for secondary residences or small plots, but only let on a long lease of ninety-nine years.) Incomes derived from the subletting of real estate must be declared and are taxed. Endeavours are also made to discover the other loopholes in the economic system which open up possibilities for speculation, and to fill them so as to abolish the basis of these incomes. (Such steps can, for example, mean the multiplication of small private businesses in fields where supply is inadequate, or the creation of new – state- or co-operative-owned – enterprises so as to reduce scarcity and thus the profit margin.)

The second problem – a growing inequality in assets, important especially from the point of view of inheritance – is handled mainly by means of various taxes. Inheritance taxes were reviewed and made more progressive in 1974. A number of property taxes were either newly introduced or increased: taxes on cars were raised, highly progressive taxes were imposed on secondary residences and privately owned luxury homes. The underlying rationale of these somewhat unusual taxes on possessions is twofold. They seek to discourage the ostentation of wealth (because of the social tensions created by this, and also because these differences have a tendency to acquire important social overtones). At the same time they reckon with the fact that the incomes derived from these assets are never fully reported, that is they try to compensate for tax avoidance.

The differentiation in accumulated wealth – although it is not comparable with inequalities in wealth where the bulk of national wealth is privately owned – is not a negligible phenomenon. Let me stress that at a higher income level the problem would emerge even if income inequalities were far smaller, or non-existent, because of the variations in the utilization of resources. There are several dilemmas and difficulties involved, and here I am not referring to the frequently mentioned point that the limitations imposed on accumulation for whatever purpose discourage thrift and encourage lavishness or waste. Goods for personal use are extremely varied and if people are encouraged to spend (even if income differences are limited), this stimulates the appearance of new needs and tastes, and contributes to the evolution of more varied, more human, less strained ways of life. In other words, thrift and frugality should not be considered as eternal human values and lavishness or prodigality as moral flaws. (Without wanting to moralize, it is interesting to note that lavishness and prodigality used to be and sometimes still are condemned by the self-righteous well-to-do only when indulged in by people who are poor or at least have only limited means.)

The real difficulty in Hungary lies elsewhere. It has already been stressed that a more radical reduction of income differentials (except in the case of unearned incomes or semi-legal gains) was unwarranted under the present conditions. Such endeavours would actually harm the economic interest, probably' very gravely, because an important factor of stimulation of individual achievement would be invalidated.

It may be, and in fact is, often asked at this point why

individual economic success still plays such an important role in a society where some of the most fundamental social relations have already been transformed in a socialist way and the objective of socialism is close. I do not think that the reason lies in human nature in general, in the 'thirst for gold' so often invoked. But one has to reckon with the fact that Hungarian society is not isolated from other, capitalist parts of the world which constantly radiate 'models' of success and the values underlying them. One must not forget either that a large segment of the population in Hungary was and may still be socialized into respect for these values. Furthermore, although income security has been attained, in many cases standards are low so that accumulation still helps to supplement welfare benefits. Moreover, some needs – dwellings in particular – are not yet accepted as universal and basic needs which must be covered by central funds, so that many people 'accumulate' in order to improve their living conditions or to buy a flat for their children. (The housing problem will be discussed in more detail in Chapters 7 and 8.) What is perhaps even more important is that because of the historical circumstances surrounding the creation of socialist conditions in Hungary, namely a lost war, grave economic shortages which were overcome less than a decade ago, international strains, etc., we do not have as yet real or feasible 'models' of what human well-being will mean in a fully developed socialist society. The replacement – or, better, the enrichment – of material interests and values by more humanized needs and values seems to be a rather long process. The incomes policy will not solve this problem by itself, even if it works perfectly. Nevertheless, the limitation of high incomes and control over the way they are used are thought to be necessary if we are to prevent the massive reappearance of some of the old patterns.

The theme of high incomes has been treated at some length. I do not, however, want to create the impression that this is a topic of primary importance. This is certainly not true for present-day conditions and, because of the factors already described, the problem will probably not acquire alarming dimensions. The really pressing questions are to be found, for the time being, at the other, lower end of the income scale.

6.2 Differentiation by occupational group (or by the nature of the work done)

The differences between pooled family incomes within socio occupational groups depend, to a large extent, on the wage system. There are factors that accentuate the work-related differences. Manual workers tend to have slightly

Table 6/2: Data on the composition of households 1972

Head of household's occupation (economically active only)	Average size of households	Number of		
		regular earners	all earners[a]	children under 15
		out of 100 persons		
Managers, senior administrators, professionals	3·28	58	58	21
Skilled non-manuals	3·25	58	58	22
Office workers	2·94	62	63	17
Total non-manual	3·20	58	58	21
Skilled workers	3·53	54	54	25
Semi-skilled workers	3·59	52	53	25
Unskilled workers	3·55	52	55	25
Total manual outside agriculture	3·55	53	54	25
Manual workers in agriculture	3·56	48	60	22
All types	3·46	53	55	24

Source: A családi jövedelmek szinvonala és szóródása 1972-ben (The Level and Dispersion of Family Incomes in 1972), Central Statistical Office, Budapest, 1975.

[a] The concept of all earners covers, besides full-time regular earners, family helpers and occasional workers.

larger families than non-manuals, and the wage differences depend essentially on the number of dependants, whether children or adults.

A second factor accentuating the differences as we pass from individual to family incomes is the socially rather homogeneous nature of families. Although social mobility between generations is quite high, a large proportion of children still remain close to the social situation of the parents' group and this has a cumulative effect on family income as long as they live at home. In the majority of cases, in families with several earners, the husband and wife are working and there is a strong correlation between their occupational levels. The wife is usually one or two steps behind the husband in terms of skill, wages, etc. Greater differences (in either direction) are rare. Data are available for 1962 which characterize the social homogeneity or heterogeneity of households on the basis of the occupation of all earners. Of all the households with active earners, 63 per cent had more than one earner. In 71 per cent of those households earners belonged to more than one occupational group out of the categories in Table 6/2. This means that 45 per cent of all households were mixed. This seems to be quite a significant proportion. In the majority of 'mixed' families, however, there were either only non-manuals (5 per cent), or only manuals outside agriculture (11 per cent), or again only manuals both in agriculture and outside it (17 per cent). Thus only 12 per cent of all families were mixed in the sense of having simultaneously both manual and non-manual earners.[1] These proportions have probably not changed very much since 1962, so that they still affect income distribution.

There are, on the other hand, factors which weaken the relation between the level of family income and individual wages. Thus, in the majority of households the second earner is a woman, and the range of female wages is more restricted than that of men. Also, the dependants, whether adults or children, have either no income at all, or bring in a uniform sum to the

1. *Társadalmi rétegződés Magyarországon* (Social Stratification in Hungary), Central Statistical Office, Budapest, 1966, p. 118.

pooled family income in the form of the family allowance. (Thus the original wage dispersion is again attenuated.)

As a result of all these components the incomes of the different occupational groups follow the original wage hierarchy, but with a less steep gradient. The per capita income of the best-situated social group is about twice that of the worst-situated group, a much smaller difference than that between highest and lowest wage. This also means that the occupation of the head of the household is only one, and not the strongest, factor in differentiating incomes. The income difference between, for example, the top and the bottom deciles in the case of households headed by active earners was about fivefold in 1962. No doubt events since 1962 have diminished this distance. The higher rewards for responsibility and skill considerably increased the income of senior administrators and managers, but the rise in minimum wages and social benefits was even more important for the two formerly worst-off groups, unskilled and agricultural workers.

Average figures do not, however, reveal the full significance of the differences shown in Table 6/3. Within each social group one finds widely varying incomes, due to wage differentials and even more to demographic factors. With a similar household income, the per capita incomes may still be different because of the number of people living on this income. These factors may, of course, occur everywhere and may accordingly entail all kinds of overlaps and differences independent of the social situation. Nevertheless, the groups which are better situated in terms of knowledge, power, position, etc., may find means of preventing a serious deterioration in their financial situation, while difficulties are harder to obviate at the other end of the social scale. The socially differentiated chances of financial success can be illustrated by several indicators. For instance, despite that far from negligible reduction in income inequality between social groups, it is still true that socially better-off groups are largely over-represented in the highest-income brackets, and that the social composition of the high-income and low-income brackets is very different.

Table 6/3: The evolution of per capita incomes by the occupation of the head of the household

Head of household's occupation (economically active only)	Per capita monthly income, forints		1972 in % of 1962	in % of the income of unskilled workers	
	1962	1972		1962	1972
Managers, senior administrators, professionals	1,265	2,327	184	187	170
Skilled non-manuals	1,050	1,877	179	155	138
Office workers	983	1,719	175	145	126
Skilled workers	899	1,588	177	133	116
Semi-skilled workers	778	1,418	182	115	104
Unskilled workers	678	1,365	201	*100*	*100*
Manual workers in agriculture	719	1,672	233	106	122
Total	839	1,645	196	124	121

Source: Jövedelemeloszlás Magyarországon 1962-ben (Income Distribution in Hungary in 1962), Central Statistical Office, Budapest, 1967; *A családi jövedelmek szinovnala és szóródása 1972-ben* (The Level and Dispersion of Family Incomes in 1972), Central Statistical Office, Budapest, 1975; and own calculations based on the data published therein.

On the whole, the last ten years have had a particularly favourable effect on the situation of the most handicapped groups. To highlight this fact from yet another angle, the decile distribution may be helpful. Table 5/11 (p. 191) showed that inequality measures declined in the decade between 1962 and 1972. In 1962 the average per capita income of the top decile in the best-off social group was *ten* times as much as the average in the bottom decile of unskilled workers. This ratio was reduced by 1972 to about *eight*. Even more important, with an above-average rate of growth in income level, the worst-off groups

Table 6/4: The social composition at different income levels 1972

Head of household's occupation (economically active only)	The percentage distribution of persons belonging to		
	all income groups together	lowest-income group (under 1,000 forints)	highest-income group (over 2,400 forints)
		per capita monthly income	
Managers, senior administrators and professionals	8	1	25
Skilled non-manuals	11	4	18
Office workers	4	3	4
Skilled workers	32	24	24
Semi-skilled workers	17	26	7
Unskilled workers	12	24	5
Manual workers in agriculture	16	18	17
Total	100	100	100
The % ratio of the group	100%	14%	12%

Source: A családi jövedelmek szinvonala és szóródása 1972-ben (The Level and Dispersion of Family Incomes in 1972), Central Statistical Office, Budapest, 1975, and own calculations based on the data published therein.

achieved an acceptable income level. Their standard of living is certainly still low, their budgets are strained, but essential needs are by and large covered, which was less certain in 1962. In fact, their nominal incomes more than doubled while the price index increased by less than 10 per cent – so that the nominal gain was almost equivalent to the real gain between 1962 and 1972.

6.3 What has happened to low incomes?

I do not want to convey the impression that poverty has been done away with. But the trends established must be judged

Table 6/5: Derived characteristics of the decile distribution of per capita incomes

	The per capita average income				Multiplier between the top and the bottom decile	
	in 1962		in 1972			
	bottom	top	bottom	top	1962	1972
	decile					
Managers, senior administrators, professionals	580	2,500	1,110	4,410	4·3	4·0
Skilled non-manual workers	440	1,930	950	3,250	4·4	3·4
Office workers	410	1,860	830	2,990	4·5	3·6
Skilled workers	370	1,700	830	2,860	4·6	3·4
Semi-skilled workers	320	1,460	610	2,580	4 6	4·2
Unskilled workers	260	1,360	550	2,630	5·2	4·8
Manual workers in agriculture	290	1,420	650	3,290	4·9	5·1
Total	300	1,700	630	3,160	5·8	5·0
Multiplier between the minimum and maximum value	9·6		8·1			

Source: Jövedelemeloszlás Magyarországon 1962, ben (Income Distribution in Hungary in 1962), Central Statistical Office, Budapest, 1967; *A családi jövedelmek szivonala és szóródása 1972-ben* (The Level and Dispersion of Family Incomes in 1972), Central Statistical Office, Budapest, 1975; and own calculations based on the data published therein.

favourably. In the first ten years or so after the war, the leadership simply did not face the issue of low incomes or poverty. This would not have been consistent with the whole logic of voluntaristic leadership. Even if the facts had been acknowledged, no real remedy could have been found at that time – with an average of US $200 to 300 per capita national income. It was assumed, then, that poverty, like all other social ills, would automatically disappear with social and economic evolution.

Since the end of the fifties, the practice has been to reckon with rather than ignore the difficulties. It has been realized that full employment and the system of social benefits (still limited at that time) are not sufficient to assure a decent standard of living for all families. Subsequently, efforts have been concentrated on the lower end of the income bracket – with the results described above. All in all, the number of persons (living in the households of active earners) who may be considered as living below some kind of 'subsistence level'[2] dropped from 30 per cent in 1962 to 8 per cent in 1967, and to about 2 per cent in 1972. If we define this level rather more generously (at 800 forints instead of 600), then the above figures are 54 per cent in 1962 and 6 per cent in 1972. This improvement, together with a real reduction in income inequality, makes poverty much less of a burning issue – whether in absolute or in relative terms – than ever before or than in a large number of countries on a similar, or even on a much higher, economic level. None the less, the problem of poverty has not yet been solved and it imposes a threefold task on social policy. By now it is known that the main factors leading to persistent financial difficulties are either purely socio-economic ones, such as low wages connected with lack of skill, etc., or socio-demographic ones, such as a large number of children; chronic inability to work, especially if one never acquired through employment the right to an anticipated pension; a broken family, where one

2. Because of the well-known theoretical and practical difficulties in defining the 'minimum subsistence level' or the 'poverty line', in Hungary there are no officially accepted standards for these concepts. Everyday experience as well as the analysis of family budget data, however, suggest that less than 600 forints monthly per capita income entails serious difficulties, a level between 600 and 800 forints indicates a tight budget and even the next two categories offer only modest possibilities to overstep the boundary between necessary and 'discretionary' expenditures. (These income brackets refer to the situation in 1972.)

parent is left to bring up children alone; and ageing, especially
for those who were on low wages while active.

Hence, the *first* task is to give priority to increasing social
welfare benefits which contribute most efficiently to improving
the situation of low-income groups and to assuring that low
wages increase more quickly than the average. In some cases
this task has been carried out very consistently (low wages, low
pensions). In others, there is some hesitation because of
conflicting interests – as will be shown in section 6.4. in the case
of family allowances. And there are cases for which the full
extent of the need has not been recognized for long, so that the
provisions have remained inadequate. Single-parent families
form such a group: even though they do have preferential treatment in cash benefits now, far greater differentiation in their
favour is necessary. While social policy was somehow a no-
man's land, these more or less marginal or not very large groups
were often forgotten. Since 1974, when a Social Policy Department was formed at the Ministry of Labour, there have been
more systematic efforts to discover such inadequacies of the
social benefit system.

The *second* task is to deal with the factors which are conducive to the maintenance or revival of a way of life which
shows the 'culture of poverty'. The problem of the 'culture of
poverty' – which has attracted much attention in Western countries for several years[3] – must briefly be discussed here. There is
a somewhat populist current, with apparent or real radical
overtones, which consists in the rejection of 'middle-class' values
in judging the life of the poor, stressing, as did Walter Miller,
'that what the middle class called pathology was a viable and
independent culture' and showing, with Oscar Lewis, 'how
much vitality and joy existed alongside the deprivation and
pathology'.[4]

Most recently this current has spread through France, too, as

3. For more about this debate, see, for example, Herbert Gans, 'Poverty
and Culture: Some Basic Questions about Methods of Studying the Life-
Styles of the Poor', in Peter Townsend, ed., *The Concept of Poverty*, Heinemann, 1970.
4. ibid., p. 147.

witnessed by a rather interesting case study about the utilization of space, domestic utensils and resources in a French working-class family. The study stressed the superiority of flexibility and of the lack of formality found in these families over rigid bourgeois rules.[5] Without denying the validity of this approach, and while sharing many of the values held by its proponents, it seems to me that it may be harmful. It carries implications entirely opposed to the original intentions of many of its spokesmen. By accepting the way of life of the poor as 'independent' and valuable, the difference between this sub-group and the other layers of the population becomes qualitative rather than quantitative, a difference in *essence*. If a difference is perceived as generic, it may entail not only separation, but exclusion. Also, the over-valuation of the culture of poverty may be used by some as an excuse for not fighting its causes. That is why I again tend to agree with Herbert Gans when he says that 'data on the extent of poverty and ... on the life styles of the poor are much less important than studies of the economy which relegates many people to underemployment and unemployment',[6] or with Lee Rainwater, who also sees that the best strategy against poverty is to provide people with jobs and to guarantee them the ability to work at decent wages.[7]

In Hungary, the economic conditions which perpetuate the 'culture of poverty' in Western capitalist countries have been radically altered. Some – the problem of guest-workers for instance – do not exist. Others – like ethnicity – were never of prime importance, except in the case of Gipsies, but even in their case the factors of exclusion are weakening. Yet there are still signs of a certain culture of poverty, though it is less distinct and less clustered than in many Western countries. In so far as it exists, it seems to be related to two main factors: bad housing conditions and an accumulation of social, economic and personal disadvantages and anomies.

5. Yvette Delsault, 'L'Économie du langage populaire' in *Actes de la recherche en sciences sociales*, July 1975.
6. Perer Townsend, *The Concept of Poverty*, op. cit., p. 149.
7. Lee Rainwater, *What Money Buys*, Basic Books, New York, 1974.

Inadequate living conditions mean more than just inconvenience in the present. In the majority of cases, the families or individuals living in such conditions doubtless have a low income but not necessarily one which is still below or near the poverty threshold. Nevertheless, the surroundings create an atmosphere which makes it very difficult to build up a stable, secure way of life. What is more, it is hard to improve this situation by means of steady personal effort. The costs of building or buying a flat by private means are so high that they present a serious problem even in higher-income brackets – but they are prohibitive to those with low incomes. Other solutions – like council housing – are scarce, and not exactly predictable. Thus the whole situation forces people to search for means of escaping from the pressures of a reality which is hard to face – any kind of short-lived pleasure or compensation – and discourages any sustained effort towards rationally thought-out goals.

The housing problem, inasmuch as it is conducive to the perpetuation of a culture of poverty, cannot be solved by income measures only, but it is an important task of social policy to press for some kind of solution.

One element of the syndrome producing the culture of poverty in the case of accumulation of handicaps is certainly a low income level or an irregular income. Nevertheless, if the problem reaches certain proportions, a mere increase in incomes may not be a sufficient help. That is where the need for more individualized personal services arises. Up to a short while ago, only a few services of this kind existed. They were often loosely organized or lacked the necessary powers, and many problems were not covered at all. The last few years has seen the start of a number of new specialized services, such as educational counselling, legal advice or family planning services on a national scale, and local arrangements to deal with various issues. Some local councils have started to engage and train social worker-type family visitors who are expected to uncover the problem families and to deal with their problems from all angles. (Up to now there was no network of social workers in the country, though a number of special services like visiting nurses existed.)

In Western European countries and the United States an important debate has emerged in the last decade or so dealing with the underlying social rationale of the professionalization and the spreading of these types of personal social services. In Britain, the United States and France,[8] social scientists and social workers alike have begun to be increasingly concerned with the role of the social services in reinforcing the domination of the ruling class by extending the control of the dominant group to all the areas of life of the target groups. They have also pointed out the harm caused by undermining the self-respect of the 'clients' and have advocated various ways of avoiding this trap. Thus they usually emphasize the social determinants of personal problems and the importance of overcoming them instead of merely concentrating on professional help in the psychological adjustment of the client. They aim at developing the potential for self-help for instance by making people's rights better known.

In Hungary, however, these very real concerns with over-professionalization do not represent a major danger. The majority of social services and benefits have universal scope; material help in cash and kind is seen as far more important than advice or psychological aid; social causes are always seen as primary; the role of the collectivity – at the workplace or the locality – is often emphasized in offering personal help. None the less this issue, which in fact has never yet been discussed in these terms, needed to be made more explicit. This could help to

8. See, in this respect, for Britain: Barbara Wootton, *Science and Social Pathology*, Allen and Unwin, 1959; or Peter Townsend, 'The Future of Social Services', in *Sociology and Social Policy*, Allen Lane, 1975. For the United States: Richard A. Cloward and Frances Fox Piven, 'The Professional Bureaucracies: Benefit Systems as Influence Systems', in *The Politics of Turmoil*, op. cit. For France: the special issue of the review, *Esprit*, on social work: *Normalisation et contrôle social*, No. 4–5, 1972; Jeanine Verdes-Leroux, 'Pouvoir et assistance: cinquante ans de service social', in *Actes de la recherche en sciences sociales*, June 1976, or *Champ Social*, Maspero, 1976.

improve some of the present solutions (such as foster care for children, which could probably be avoided in a number of cases if the family was offered the means of self-help), and would forestall any latent tendencies to over-emphasize the role of personal professional services.

6.4 Large families and family allowances

The size and composition of the family, more precisely the ratio of earners to dependants, is the most important single factor in the explanation of the variance of incomes. The first income survey in 1959 drew attention to the fact that while the income level of the best-paid occupational groups was twice that of the lowest group, the income level of small families was three times higher than that of larger families (that is, one and six persons respectively). It was shown at the same time that large families were considerably over-represented in the low-income groups and their chances of achieving a really favourable economic situation were small.

Two factors contributed to focus attention on the circumstances of large families. One was the continued decrease in the birth-rate from the mid-fifties on, with the inevitable consequences for the rate of natural increase and the age structure of the population. These demographic trends were largely influenced by the legislation concerning birth control. From 1950 to 1956 there was a practically complete ban on legal abortions, raising the birth-rate over 20 per cent. This phase was followed by the lifting of all restrictions on abortion, which was not accompanied either by the propagation of other forms of birth control, or by measures that would have substantially improved the situation of families with children (for example, flats, child-care institutions or financial help). Hence the number of abortions rose to an unusually high level, over 200,000 a year, while the birth-rate touched its lowest level at 13 per thousand in the middle of the sixties, with about 130,000 births. Meanwhile the economic reform had been introduced and had stimulated fresh consideration of the role of material incentives in work achievement. It was realized that family conditions could easily neutralize the wage surplus if there were several children, and that, conversely, a similar standard of living could be attained by very different work performances depending on the size of family. To put it more crudely: if one had a large family, the incentive to do better work and earn a higher wage almost disappeared.

All these elements converged and led to a gradual improvement of the social measures relating to families in general, and large families in particular. In the last few years, a complex family policy has begun to appear[9] endeavouring to combine the different social, economic, and even cultural and moral elements pertaining to the issue. The social policy measures implemented up to now include an acceleration in creating child-care institutions; improvements in their educational and material conditions; and priorities given to families with more than two children in the allocation of housing, of places in child-care institutions, of holiday homes, etc. Considerable efforts are being made, especially by means of a countrywide 'counselling service for families and women' with units attached to hospitals, to spread the idea of family planning and modern methods of birth control – combined with somewhat more rigorous regulations concerning abortions. (The birth-rate has slowly been increasing since about 1967, with a more significant increase in 1974 and 1975, so that it is now about 18 per thousand. In the same period the number of abortions dropped from over 200,000 to 100,000, and modern contraceptives became more widespread.) The child-care grant, the lengthening of paid leave according to the number and age of children and the new

9. This trend is interconnected with the rediscovery of 'family policy' as distinct from population policy. Since 1974, the Ministry of Labour is the body responsible for a more or less autonomous sub-sphere of social policy designated as family policy. While the long-term guidelines of this policy are still under elaboration, it is already fairly clear that the Ministry intends to work in two directions. One set of tasks is connected with assuring adequate living conditions for all families, the other is explicitly addressed to 'problem families' lagging far behind the majority and unable to solve their own problems.

facilities for taking additional leave (sixty days in the first year, thirty days up to the age of three, etc., paid at the rate of sickness benefits) when looking after sick children are also measures which belong to the realm of family policy. One organic part of this set of policy measures is the development of the system of family allowances.

Before the war, family allowances were allocated on a selective basis – but selection then worked in reverse. The system was extended only to civil servants and to large firms, covered about 30 per cent of the population and applied different rules and standards to manual workers and to white-collar employees which were much more favourable for the latter category. The first step, in 1946, was to make allowances uniform and universal, at least for the whole working population. The sums offered, however, were then perforce rather low. They demonstrated the commitment of the regime, but could not offer substantial help. This remained the position until about the end of the fifties: there were only minor increases compensating for the rise in prices, and the allocation was withdrawn in the case of families with a single child.

The first notable increase took place in 1959. It was basically aimed at easing the financial difficulties of large families, and so the increase affected only families with three or more children. The same improvement was extended to two-children families in 1965. The subsequent modifications in 1966 and 1971 also favoured large families and, at the same time, reinforced the universal nature of the measure, covering a larger proportion of the population, including peasants (members of co-operatives). Since 1968, the only criterion for selection used up till then – the steady employment of one parent at least – was also phased out and the right was gradually extended to occasional labourers, industrial apprentices, students in higher education and home workers. The 1973 rise was mainly a compensation for the increase in the price of milk and dairy products: the flat-rate increase in family allowances – and pensions – in fact more than compensated for the rise.

Besides the extension of the circle of beneficiaries, there has been a steady tendency since the end of the fifties to reduce the gap between the level of the allowance of industrial workers and that of peasants. The modifications in 1974 and 1975 were decisive in fully bridging this gap. At the same time, the 1974 change was one element in the social benefit 'package' which aimed at modifying the unfavourable demographic trends. (For the evolution of family allowances see Tables 6/6 and 6/7.)

Table 6/6: Total sums allocated to family allowances

Year	In million forints	As a % of the national income	Total number of families	Total number of children
			receiving the allowance, in 1,000s	
1950	303	0·6	509 (1953)	1,229 (1953)
1955	772	0·8	467	1,210
1960	1,391	0·9	577	1,422
1965	1,560	0·9	612	1,447
1970	2,810	1·1	731	1,597
1974	5,182	1·4	830	1,652
1975	6,426	1·7	905	1,773

The principles and the practical solutions concerning the system of family allowances are fairly well known in a cross-national perspective, thanks largely to the surveys of the ISSA (International Social Security Association).[10] It is possible therefore to compare the Hungarian solution with that of other countries. In terms of the *level* of benefits, since the last increases, Hungary ranks quite favourably. The allowance for three children and over represented, in 1967, 7 per cent of the mean wage in Great Britain, 10 per cent in the German Democratic Republic, 13 per cent in Sweden, 25 per cent in Romania

10. See, for example, Martin Rein, *Children's Allowances: A Comparative Perspective* (mimeo); or E. K. Burns, ed., *Children's Allowances and the Economic Welfare of Children. The Report of a Conference*, New York, 1968.

and Bulgaria, 30 per cent in Czechoslovakia, 42 per cent in France and 36 per cent in Hungary.[11] The coverage of the benefit seems to be satisfactory, too: fully universal systems are practically non-existent, and the criteria for inclusion are comparatively generous in Hungary.

As for other characteristics, such as the age limit and the progression according to the number of children, Hungary follows the majority pattern: the rate is uniform (thus it neither encourages nor penalizes unusually large families) and the allowance is discontinued at the end of the child's secondary studies, including industrial apprenticeship. On the other hand, among the twenty-seven countries covered by the ISSA inquiry, in eighteen countries the allowance was granted from the first child and in four only from the second. Hungary belongs to the latter group. Given Hungary's economic circumstances and income differentiation, the present arrangement seems to be reasonable. The majority of children live in families that are beneficiaries: in 1970, over 60 per cent of children under fifteen lived in families with two or more children. Also, despite the priority given to larger families, their economic conditions are still worse than those of families with one child. However, the issue is still under discussion. Many argue that problems begin with the first child so that families with a single child should also get an allowance. Others, especially those concerned with population growth, see the family allowance as an incentive for having children and would like to concentrate resources on large families. Those concerned with children's economic conditions come to the same conclusion. Therefore it has not yet been decided whether the next priority will be the introduction of family allowance from the first child on, or a further sizable increase for large families.

Another debatable question is the relation between family income and the level of family allowance. Three principles are known to be applied in this case. The allowance may be progressively related to wages, that is it is higher with higher wages on the ground that children cost more at this level, or that

11. Rein, op. cit., and *Incomes in Postwar Europe*, op. cit., Chapter 9, p. 6.

Table 6/7: Rates of family allowance in forints (monthly sums)

Year/ month	In families with children				Surplus per child in larger families	Parents alone[a] with children		Allowance after three children as a % of the average wage
	1	2	3	4		1	2	
	Workers and employees							
1946. X.	10	24	42	64	26–18	10	24	—
1947. I.	18	36	54	72	18[b]	18	36	—
1948. I.	18	40	66	96	34–50[b]	18	40	—
1951. XII.	30	75	135	210	90–210[b]	30	75	20
1953. III.	—	75	180	260	90–210[b]	30	75	19
1959. IV.	—	75	360	480	120	90	240	23
1965. VII.	—	200	360	480	120	90	240	20
1966. II.	—	300	510	680	170	140	340	28
1972. I.	150[c]	300	810	1,080	270	240	540	36
1973. I.	200[c]	400	960	1,280	320	290	640	39
1974. VI.	300[c]	600	960	1,280	320	300	640	36
1975. VII.	300[c]	600	960	1,280	320	300	640	35
1976. VI.	360[c]	720	1,140	1,520	380	360	740	—

					Members of co-operatives			
					72–80–60[b]			
1953. III.	—	—	144	208	—	—	—	—
1959. IX.	—	—	210	280	70	70	140	—
1966. VII.	—	140	210	280	70	70	140	—
1968. VII.	—	200	360	480	120	120	240	—
1972. I.	100[c]	200	660	880	220	220	440	—
1973. I.	150[c]	300	810	1,080	270	270	540	—
1974. VI.	250[c]	500	810	1,080	270	270	540	—
1975. VII.	300[c]	600	960	1,280	320	300	640	—
1976. VI.	360[c]	720	1,140	1,520	380	360	740	—

Source: Hungarian Statistical Yearbooks, and the successive decrees on family allowance.

[a] Or with handicapped children

[b] Varying according to the number of additional children

[c] In the case of families with more than one child, but when the elder children cease to qualify

otherwise the full advantage of (well-deserved) higher wages cannot be felt. The second solution is flat-rate, that is allowances are independent of other income. The third is the inverse relation, that is the allowance is higher with lower wages, or is offered only up to a certain income limit.

The first solution follows an aristocratic bias and is not compatible with the outlook of Hungarian social policy. It openly declares the 'superiority' of higher-class children and accentuates the accumulation of advantages. It seems that the only place where this principle was consistently followed was in Portugal before the change of political regime, though the same idea is at work whenever a separate scheme applies to civil servants. The third arrangement may be rational if funds are limited and the problems of large families are pressing and/or if higher incomes reach a level where family allowances are no longer needed. This solution prevails in the Federal Republic of Germany, in Romania, and – in a special form, with two levels – in Poland. Despite its rationality in that it permits the concentration of resources on the most difficult situations, it has some drawbacks. For one, there is the 'notch problem' treated in detail by M. Rein and others, which means that a rise in wages may entail a drop in the overall income level of the family. The administration of the allowance also leads to a complicated procedure because the family's pooled income has to be checked up. Finally, the negative effect on work incentive of low family allowances is strengthened.

The flat-rate system is no doubt the simplest solution. Furthermore, it does not contradict the logic of wage-differentiation (like the third solution), and it does not confuse the different principles of distribution in order to maintain social advantages (like the first one). It is also the most democratic in the sense that it proclaims the equality of all children, and makes it clear that society accepts a collective responsibility for all children. No wonder therefore that this is the most widespread form, at least *on the face of it*. In reality, however, in a number of countries the first pattern (income-related allowance) reappears unobtrusively, through the child tax allowances, thus distorting the flat-rate effect. Direct tax rates often depend simultaneously on the level of income and on the number of children, so that at a higher income level the saving is greater with the same number of children. This system is no doubt redistributive between smaller and larger families, but has no significant impact on the income distribution. In some countries – for example, in the United States – this is the main form of financial help for larger families, in others the two patterns coexist. (In Sweden and in England the issue has been widely debated, with some resultant changes in the Swedish system.) In Hungary, since income taxes play a minor role and there is no child tax allowance scheme, the problem does not arise.

The successive increases in family allowances had a favourable effect on the relative positions of smaller and larger families. The improvements by and large follow the changes in the family allowances, as may be seen from family budget data.

Table 6/8: Net monthly incomes per head in households according to the number of children[a] (in forints)

Households with	1962	1965	1975	Households with no children = 100 1962	1975	Percentage increase, between 1962 and 1975
No children	1,281	1,409	2,643	100	100	206
1 child	1,002	1,133	2,095	78	79	209
2 children	786	917	1,758	61	67	224
3 children	588	678	1,473	46	56	251

Source: Háztartásstatisztika (family budget data) for the years quoted, and author's computations based on the published data.
[a] All children under 14 and children in school under 18 years of age.

It should be added that the differences in real living standards between smaller and larger families are slightly smaller than per capita data suggest because of the different age-composition and the 'economy-effect' of larger families. In terms of incomes per consumption unit (adult equivalent unit) for the households presented in Table 6/8, the per c.u. income of the families with three and more children attained 56 per cent of the level of families with no children in 1962 and 70 per cent in 1975.

Another sign of a favourable tendency is the reduction in the number of children in the low-income groups. Since larger families are over-represented at the lower income levels, it is obvious that children are to be found there in a relatively large proportion. In 1962, 31 per cent of all persons and 43 per cent of all children (up to the end of secondary studies) were in the lowest income bracket, under 600 forints per month, while in 1972, 18 per cent of all persons and 24 per cent of children were under the 1,000 forints level.[12] (The consumer price index increased only by 9·7 per cent during these years, so that the 1,000-forint level means a better living standard than the former, 600-forint level.)

Despite a considerable improvement in the situation of large families and children, it is still true that families with several children are at a disadvantage, at least in terms of the economic situation. A combination of several unfavourable income factors – such as low wages, a small number of earners and a high number of children within the family – may lead to serious difficulties. That is why further increases in family allowances must be kept on the list of priorities. At the same time it is very hard to determine what would be the ideal level of this benefit. The family allowance signifies that society takes over some of the responsibilities connected with children and provides for some of their needs within the framework of centralized redistribution. The question which is hard or even impossible to answer on theoretical grounds is how far this provision should go.

12. These data are again derived from the large-scale income surveys already quoted since the sample size of the family budget survey does not permit detailed cross-classifications. (This means that there are no data as yet for the period after 1972.) Incidentally, it may be added that for those years for which both types of data are available (family budget statistics and income surveys), the two sets are rather close and they show a similar trend over time.

According to available data, benefits in cash and in kind covered 33 per cent of the total consumption of children under fifteen in 1965 and 40 per cent in 1970. Out of this, 9 per cent and 15 per cent respectively were covered by the cash benefits.[13] To aim for full coverage is, for the time being, unrealistic because of the lack of economic resources. In addition, social or moral arguments can be put forward against full coverage of the cost of children. The fact of having children depends less and less on chance and increasingly on the deliberate choice of parents. Furthermore, children cannot be viewed as a mere financial burden. They make life richer in many human values, too. Hence, it does not seem right to shift the full responsibility for children to society – which would inevitably mean that everybody would contribute as much to the children's maintenance as parents themselves. This argument has some validity as long as income differentials play a major economic role. None the less a further improvement of the present situation is fully warranted.

One last dilemma appears in this connection. It has to be decided whether the increase should affect child-related benefits in cash or in kind. The analysis presented in Chapter 7 will show that central redistribution usually serves redistributive justice better and more easily if allowances are in cash than if in kind. There is also another argument in favour of benefits in cash, namely that they assure the freedom of choice of the beneficiaries. On the other hand, child-care institutions, schools, day care and meals, students' hostels, etc., if of uniformly high standards, may be efficient tools for counteracting social and cultural disadvantages, to make the conditions of early and even of later socialization the same for all. At the same time, they alleviate considerably the parents' burdens and promote (especially in the case of younger children) the emancipation of women. In a socialist perspective it is the arguments in favour of benefits in kind which carry more weight. Central decision-

13. *A gyermekek eltartási és képzési költségei* (Costs of Maintenance and Education of Children), Central Statistical Office, Budapest, 1973.

makers also seem to be more inclined to adopt this solution for the coming years, although the issue is far from being settled.

6.5 Income and ageing

The pre-war pension system was as restricted and socially discriminating as all other types of social services of the time. From official documents it is clear that more effort went into the regulation of begging and the search for the most appropriate forms of private charity than into working out an acceptable pension system. Pensions were granted to about 30 per cent of the working force. However, the level was adequate or even generous only in case of civil servants and of some private pension schemes. Workers got 30 per cent of their previous wage after twenty years of service. Workers who had no stable employment were not provided for, nor were practically the whole of the rural population.

The post-war economic situation prevented an immediate radical improvement. None the less, the reform of the pension system began soon after 1945, and has been continuing ever since, though not at an even pace. The right of all in employment to receive a pension was declared in 1951, and the former discriminatory aspect was abolished then, too. Since this time, strictly the same rules apply to all employees, including civil servants, with the exception of preferential treatment for those working in unhealthy conditions, etc. (This is not true for all countries: in a number of countries civil servants still enjoy exceptionally favourable terms.) The age limits were also fixed in 1951, at sixty years for men and fifty-five years for women. This preferential treatment of women is often criticized[14] be-

14. See, for example, Andrée Michel, 'Problèmes et approches dans les pays industrialisés', in *Women at Work in the Labour Force and at Home*, Research Series No. 22, International Institute for Labour Studies, 1976: 'Toute la politique sociale (des pays socialistes de l'Est) consiste aussi à développer les mesures "protectrices" de la maternité . . . et à multiplier les mesures discriminatoires concernant les femmes, comme la retraite à 55 ans (alors que celle-ci est fixée à 60 ans pour les hommes) afin de maintenir les femmes dans leurs rôles domestiques traditionnels et à en éviter le fardeau

cause of the discriminatory aspect built into it, that is because it emphasizes the lesser value of the female workforce. This argument is, no doubt, valid and the present legislation will slowly have to be changed. However, as the pensionable age limit is not mandatory, the current preference is justified if one takes into account the 'double burden' which women have had to bear and which is only slowly changing.

Pension rights were extended to members of co-operatives in 1958, but their retirement age was five years higher. A compulsory insurance scheme was introduced for the self-employed in 1962. Thus the number of beneficiaries grew as a consequence of this modification in the regulations. The growth in numbers was accelerated by a lengthening of the average life span. From 1950 to 1975 the number of pensioners multiplied by 3·5.

The level of pensions also underwent a considerable change. The two main general criteria for determining pensions – namely the length of employment and the level of former earnings – have remained the same since 1951, but the particulars have frequently been modified. Thus the minimum pension grew from 100 forints in 1951 to 910 in 1975 and 1,040 in 1977. In 1951 the basis of the pension had to be the wage during the last twelve months before retirement, while at present one has the right to choose as the basis the most favourable period out of the last five years before retirement. In 1951, there was a ceiling for pensions – a maximum of 1,000 forints – while now the normal full pension is 75 per cent of the original wage, without an upper limit. For a very long time there were no adjustments – except occasional increases in the minimum pension – but since 1972 there has been an automatic yearly increase of 2 per cent, or at least 50 forints. The 1975 regulations, following the new Social Security Act, introduced other im-

aux hommes' (p. 77). Unfortunately, if one abolished all these so-called discriminatory measures today the burden of women would be increased, because habits – maintained by men and women alike – would follow the legislation only with an enormous time lag. This type of benevolent voluntarism may be extremely harmful.

provements in favour of those on partial pensions (widows for example) or of those who – not having the right to a pension – have access only to social assistance. An important step is the gradual elimination of the difference in retirement age between workers and peasants. Over the period 1975 to 1979 the retirement age of members of co-operatives is being decreased by one year each year, so that in 1980 the 60/55 limit will be universal. A special clause of the regulations adopted in 1975 – similar in essence to those introduced in the last few years in the Soviet Union and in the German Democratic Republic[15] – favours those who continue working after the retirement age. In Hungary manual workers get an additional 7 per cent of the original pension after each additional year, while with non-manuals the addition is 3 per cent. As a consequence of these modifications, the total sum of pensions has been multiplied by more than twenty-five in the last twenty-five years, which means a fifteen-fold rise even after discounting the effect of price increases.

Table 6/9: The overall characteristics of the pension system

| Year | Number of pensioners in 1000s on 1 January of each year | Percentage of pensioners within | | Total sum of pensions in thousand million forints |
		the whole population	the population over retirement age[a]	
1950	502	5·5	40	0·9
1960	759	7·6	40	4·4
1970	1,415	13·8	70	13·0
1975	1,775	16·9	80	26·8

Source: Hungarian Statistical Yearbooks; A lakosság jövedelme ès fogyasztása 1960–1975 (Income and Consumption of the Population 1960–75), Central Statistical Office, Budapest, 1976; census data; and computations based thereupon.

[a] These are approximations because they compare the effective total number of pensions to the number of men over 60 and women over 55, although some of the pensioners are under these age limits.

15. *UN Report on the World Social Situation,* 1974 (E/CN.5/512/Rev.1).

It may be seen from the summary data in Table 6/9 that significant improvements were made only from about the end of the sixties. Before this, low pensions represented a major social problem. In 1968 47 per cent of old people on pension or assistance still got less than 500 forints per month and 30 per cent between 500 and 800 forints, at a time when the national average income per capita amounted to more than 1,000 forints. The data represented in Table 6/10 show that this problem was alleviated in two ways. First, priority was given to the official increases favouring groups which were previously the worst provided for. Second, the composition of the elderly population changed: more people acquired the right to a full instead of a partial pension (or assistance), whether workers, employees or members of co-operatives.

Other forms of old-age assistance underwent a notable change, too. One of the most important institutions is the social welfare home, used mainly by the aged. At the end of 1974 more than 250 homes cared for about 29,000 people, but they were still unable to accommodate all those in need. Since about 1965, new solutions have been introduced which belong to the sphere of personal social services. There are day-care centres for the aged which assure free or subsidized meals, constant medical care and also social contacts, without forcing elderly people to give up their own homes. The centres catered for about 10,000 persons in 1970 and for 16,000 in 1974. About 50 per cent of those attending got free meals, the others subsidized meals.[16] Several forms of home care were also worked out, to give medical and other help to those who were unable to provide for themselves. This scheme covered about 8,000 persons in 1974 with about eighty visits each a year on average.

The Hungarian system of old-age benefits compares quite favourably with other countries, although truly comparative information is scarce. Some years ago Paul Fisher presented detailed data on minimum pensions and their relation to average wages. The rates of minimum pensions varied between 10 per cent (United States and Switzerland) and 40 per cent (Bulg-

16. *Információs Évkönyv* (The Yearbook of Information of the Ministry of Health on Adult Social Care), 1975, pp. 74 and 80.

Table 6/10: Source, composition and average level of old-age pensioners' incomes 1965–75

Source of income	Percentage distribution of beneficiaries		Average monthly sum		
	1965	1975	Jan. 1965	Jan. 1975	1975 (1965=100)
Workers and employees holding pensions – in own right	41·9	45·0	772	1,478	192
– on derivative title	14·7	10·9	441	846	192
Pensions from co-operatives	2·4	13·7	*320*	926	*289*
Assistance from co-operatives	26·6	13·7	*256*	642	*251*
Pensions of self-employed	2·1	3·4	703	1,256	179
Other assistance	12·3	13·3	*484*	1,322	*273*
Total	100·0	100·0	539	1,191	221
Total number of pensioners in thousands (=100%)	1,101	1,748			

Source: Társadalmi szolgáltatások 1960/1971 (Social Services 1960/ 1971), Central Statistical Office, Budapest, 1972, and *Hungarian Statistical Yearbook,* 1974.

aria).[17] The Hungarian rate is by now 35 per cent, which seems to be acceptably high in a cross-national perspective. Its coverage is respectably high, too. Those who do not qualify for an

17. Paul Fisher, 'Les Pensions de vieillesse sont-elles adéquates? (II)', *Revue Internationale du Travail,* Vol. 102, September 1970, p. 308.

old-age benefit (about 20 per cent of the aged) all live in families. None the less, the absence of a separate income in their case is a social problem to be solved, as is the difficult situation of those who are entitled only to partial pensions. A third problem group is composed of those who retired before the new regulations and whose pension is therefore now much lower than it would be under the present system.

On the whole, old-age benefits have been given priority in the last few years. (Between 1965 and 1975, for example, average wages increased by 53 per cent but average pensions by 121 per cent.) With these developments the income structure of the elderly has changed, too, so that pensioners are no longer relegated almost exclusively to the lowest-income groups. With the abolition of the pensions ceiling, the families of the elderly also stand a fair chance of reaching the higher income brackets. Conversely the differences in income between pensioners have also increased, which is hardly justified, and is due to the historical accident of when one was born or when one retired.

Despite the efforts described, the relative weight of pensioners and families of pensioners within the lowest income brackets is growing. Furthermore, the per capita income within the families of the aged is now relatively lower than some years ago. Table 6/11 shows for example that the percentage of persons in the lower-income groups has dropped in the case of families of active earners from 54 to 6, that is to a ninth, while the corresponding figure for pensioners decreased only to one third (from 70 to 22 per cent). This relative deterioration of the situation of the aged has no independent explanation. It is the residual outcome of other, mostly deliberate changes like the rapid rise of social benefits, or the improved earner–dependant ratio in the majority of families, accompanied by a decrease in households headed by pensioners.

The changes affecting the whole income distribution may be seen in a positive light if we remember that there are now few large families, and especially fewer children, in the lower income groups. From another perspective the same changes have to be seen as a relative loss for the elderly. To put the

Table 6/11: Distribution of per capita income in families headed by active earners or pensioners

Per capita monthly income (forints)	Percentage distribution of persons belonging to families headed by			
	active earners	pensioners	active earners	pensioners
	1962		1972	
under 600	30	45	6 }	22 }
600 to 800	24	25		
800 to 1,000	18	15	8	14
1,000 to 1,200	13	8	13	14
1,200 to 1,600	11	6	28	24
1,600 to 2,000	3	1	21	14
over 2,000	1	0	24	12
Total	100	100	100	100
Per capita monthly income on average	840	689	1,643	1,083

Source: Jövedelemelosztás Magyarországon (Hungarian Income Distribution in 1962), Central Statistical Office, Budapest, 1967; *A családi jövedelmek szinvonala és szóródása 1972* (Level and Dispersion of Family Incomes, 1972), Central Statistical Office, Budapest, 1975.

problem more bluntly: as long as there are income differentials, there will always be someone in the low-income groups, and it is usually those who are in some way handicapped. Social policy measures directly affect the composition of the low-income population. The priorities of social policy may help some groups to escape from their low level (the unskilled, single parents, large families, etc.), but others will necessarily remain at or descend to this level. One of the worse dilemmas of social policy is connected with decisions about these priorities. It is practically impossible to make a satisfactory decision because some groups are bound to be affected unfavourably, at least in relative terms. Hungarian social policy in the last few years can be judged harshly because the situation of a large segment of the elderly has not improved as rapidly as that of the others. But this criticism would probably be much more severe if the relative deterioration had affected children instead. The only possible conclusion is that there is probably no way to determine social priorities once and for all. Social policy must, on the basis of relevant and up-to-date information, always concentrate on those whose situation is the worst at any given moment, and who lack resources of their own to improve their circumstances. Some ten or fifteen years ago the situations of both children and old people were rather strained. With limited funds, priority was given first to children. In the last five years the available financial resources have been used mainly in favour of the elderly. The result of these successive steps is that the conditions of both groups have improved, and one can no longer speak about universal problems in either case. However, there remain subgroups within both these sections of the population who have not been able to profit adequately from the general improvement, because of accumulated disadvantages. In the near future social policy priorities will have to be concentrated on them.

There are still other, theoretical rather than practical, dilemmas connected with ageing. Hungarian social policy will have to consider them in more detail as soon as the most urgent practical problems are more or less settled. One of these problems has to do with the relative situation of the aged in general, that is with the justification of the fact that retirement entails a loss in earnings. The other open question is connected with the differentiation of pensions – whether they should be wage-related or not, differentiated or not.

From a purely humanistic perspective it is self-evident that ageing ought not to be financially penalized. On the contrary, it seems desirable to compensate, at least financially, for the increasing difficulties connected with ageing. Such an arrangement is not, however, economically feasible under present conditions in Hungary. There is no real pressure, either, in favour of such a solution, a fact which deserves some explanation. One of the reasons may be found in the historical trend characterizing the situation of the elderly. Some three or four decades ago there were hardly any institutionalized arrangements in their favour. At the same time, the capitalist market economy had already destroyed the majority of the spontaneous social mechanisms which existed before, such as inter-group redistribution in favour of the aged or the still more archaic habit (rare even then in Hungary) of the voluntary self-destruction of the elderly. Thus ageing in Hungary until 1945 meant, for a majority, uncertainty or even destitution. Compared with this state of affairs, the memory of which is still vivid, the recent improvements are seen as significant, and strong complaints are not felt to be really justified. Another factor leading to the same result may be that the practice of relating rewards, even a large part of social benefits, to performance is seen as legitimate under the present conditions by a large majority, while the aged are usually perceived (by themselves as well as by others) as not performing any really 'useful' function. This again means that it does not seem justified (even to those primarily concerned) to claim a much higher share for the aged. The change in this outlook and mood probably depends, in the first place, on the growth of distributable resources. But it may also depend on the emergence of new ways to reintegrate the aged into societal life. It is, however, still uncertain whether there are real opportunities for such a reintegration in a rapidly changing society.

The second question, whether pensions should be work-related or flat-rate, is connected in a way to the first problem. Where there are universal flat-rate old-age benefits, they are usually below the average wage. This may mean that age will bring some improvement to those whose wage was very low (or who had none), but people with average or higher earnings will experience a significant deterioration. In order to avoid this, that is to assure that nobody loses substantially on retirement, the level of the flat-rate benefit should theoretically be close to the highest wages or salaries. This would correspond to the 'humanist' solution referred to above, but is usually an economic impossibility.

There are, however, practical ways out of this impasse. It seems, in fact, that the flat-rate system is acceptable on two conditions. One is contingent on the high economic level of the country. If resources are plentiful, the flat-rate pension or old-age allowance may be fairly high, so that – even if it signifies some loss as compared with the active period – it does not entail financial hardship. If this condition is not met, then the flat-rate old-age benefit works only if various arrangements (credit accounts and especially private pension schemes) allow those with higher earnings to accumulate throughout their active life a reserve which helps to avoid deterioration after retirement. In other words the universal flat-rate redistribution works if it is combined with the exploitation of the former market position, that is if the final outcome is no longer flat-rate, but follows, possibly more sharply, the former pattern of inequality. This conclusion seems to be substantiated by a detailed research study on ageing carried out in three Western countries.[18]

It appears quite likely, then, that the two pension systems (the wage-related and the flat-rate) have not up to now had widely different outcomes as far as the inequality of old-age incomes is concerned. Only the first preserves the former differentiation openly, while the second works more unobtrusively. This suggests that – whether we agree with it in the name of economic necessity, or condemn it in the name of humanism or equity – as long as incomes differ throughout active life, old-age benefits will follow this pattern. It does not seem feasible to impose an entirely different logic on two spheres while the underlying social relations and social forces are identical. It does not follow, however, that the distribution of pensions must copy that of earnings at a lower level. In fact, in some countries – for example, the Soviet Union – there is a reverse relation between the wage level and the pension, reducing the variance

18. E. Shanas, P. Townsend, D. Wedderburn, H. Friis, P. Milhoj and J. Stehouwer, *The Old in Three Industrial States*, Routledge and Kegan Paul, 1968.

of pensions and avoiding very low pensions. In a way, this is a consistent application of the idea of the minimum pension.

If this analysis is valid, that is, if the flat-rate system, which seems to be in accordance with socialist redistribution, cannot be implemented on an acceptable level in Hungary at present and would introduce grave problems if implemented at a lower level, Hungarian social policy can hardly set as its next task the adoption of the flat-rate system. But the spokesmen for social policy must strive for more redistributive elements such as universal old-age benefits and better retirement terms for the low-wage groups or for those who retired long ago. These endeavours are in accordance with the priorities derived from actual needs and also with the requirements of the more general social aim of collective mobility.

Chapter 7

Distribution and Redistribution

7.1 Types of distribution in a historical perspective

Describing the cycle of social reproduction, I started from the assumption that the basic social relations embedded in the social organization of work closely regulate the pattern of distribution and redistribution. In one sense, production and distribution are but two aspects of the same phenomenon, the system of economic relations, or the mode of production. Therefore, as Marx put it, both have a historically transitory character.[1] The concrete historical forms of distribution were studied more closely by Karl Polanyi[2] – or at least the categories he used to describe the patterns of economic integration may easily be understood in this light. He distinguished as dominant forms in one or another historical context reciprocity, redistribution, the household economy and the self-regulating (or price-regulating) market.

Reciprocity, a dominant form in tribal societies, designates the exchange of goods and services where the acts of giving and taking are not regulated by barter or by the motive of gain, but by the whole web of social relations. The exchange itself is 'disguised as a reciprocal distribution of gifts'. Redistribution – a complement to reciprocity in tribal societies, and a basic principle in a number of pre-capitalist systems, especially the archaic empires – consists of the centralized collection and storage of a part of the product, and of its redistribution if the need arises. The allocation of the collected goods does not follow the principles of economic or market exchange, but assures for all

1. K. Marx, *Capital*, Vol. III, Chapter 51: 'Relations of Production, and Relations of Distribution'.
2. Karl Polanyi, *The Great Transformation*, Beacon Press, Boston, 1967, first published 1944, especially Part II, Chapter 4, 'Societies and Economic Systems'.

the members of the community, though possibly in a highly differentiated way, the right to survive. The household economy (*oikos*) – the autarky of the small plot, or production for one's own use – has been an important form since antiquity.

The first two types of distribution especially, but in a way also the third, tend 'to enmesh the economic system proper in social relationships'.[3] Polanyi, like Marx, stresses that full autonomy of economic relations characterizes only the capitalist society. It is only there that economic relations and economic interests appear naked, and come to dominate all other relations and interests.

Although different types of distribution are dominant in different types of society, almost all of them may occur anywhere. Reciprocity as a main organizing force of social life disappeared long ago, but its logic reappears in all our gift-relations, or when personal services are exchanged either on the basis of solidarity or in the form of string-pulling. Most forms of corruption operate according to this logic. That is why Padioleau[4] can speak of 'corruption by exchange of favours' in France. Hence it is hard to evaluate reciprocity in an unambiguous way. In some traditional societies reciprocity, as a dominant form of economic integration, was based on group solidarity and contributed to strengthen the group. It is probably true that in societies permeated by inequality, the solidarity basis of reciprocity weakens, or at least this type of reciprocity – an essentially symmetrical relation – cannot operate across social groups. It is also likely that the character of reciprocal relations is entirely different in more traditional societies where individual economic self-interest is practically non-existent, and in modern market societies where economic self-interest is one of the most important regulators of social life.

The same considerations may be applied, *mutatis mutandis*, to all the other forms of economic integration or distribution.

3. ibid., p. 52.
4. Jean G. Padioleau, 'De la corruption dans les oligarchies pluralistes', *Revue Française de Sociologie*, January–March, 1975.

Barter existed long before the market economy was in full swing, and the self-sufficient small-holding (household economy) as a sporadic phenomenon survives today even in fairly industrialized societies. Redistribution played a not inconsiderable role under feudalism, especially within smaller communities. It almost disappeared in early capitalism, to regain force in more modern times. Its operating principles have always been affected, as with reciprocity, by the basic social relations of any given society. Polanyi pointed out that in a tribal society reciprocity may turn into redistribution (an asymmetrical relation), if 'there is an intermediary in the person of the headman or other prominent member of the group', and may even serve a primitive form of oppression if, as in the case of the Potlatch, the chief 'places the recipients under an obligation, to make them his debtors, and ultimately his retainers'.[5] Babylon under Hammurabi and the New Kingdom of Egypt 'were centralized despotisms of a bureaucratic type, founded on the economy of redistribution'. It is clear that the legal basis of the collection of goods may have been anything from voluntary participation to severe coercion; that the ratio of centrally collected goods may have varied widely; and that the distribution of goods may have followed any pattern from complete equality of shares to marked inequality. Nevertheless, redistribution always retains one characteristic feature, the attempt to assure *the right to live* for the members of a given community. One of the most important aspects of Polanyi's criticism of capitalism is precisely the exposure of its inhuman traits, especially the fact that redistributive practice has been destroyed by the market, while the self-regulating market itself is necessarily incompatible with assuring the institutional right to survive for everyone.

In short, the character of the basic social relations of production and reproduction of social life determines, by and large, firstly, which will be the dominant type or types of distribution and, secondly, what will be the special characteristics of all the different types that co-exist.

5. Polanyi, op. cit., p. 51.

Under the present conditions of Hungarian society it is still true that all the historical types described above have some place – with special characteristics. Considerations of reciprocity regulate some relations in the private sphere, like the exchange of gifts, and they play a certain role on the margins of legality, as an 'exchange of favours'. This phenomenon is largely interconnected with the scarcity of some goods and services. The *oikos* economy is also slowly becoming marginal, although it is still true that about 10 per cent of all the incomes connected with work are yielded by consumption of what the consumer himself has produced. A special issue is raised by the fact that the dominant principle of distribution – distribution according to work, in the form of wages – cannot be directly subsumed under any one of the above categories. As I have already pointed out (in Chapter 2), distribution according to work can no longer be considered, in the absence of an all-encompassing market, as a pure market category. It is still an economic relation, an economic exchange regulated by economic factors and motivated by economic interests. Nevertheless, the basic unequal social relations – primarily the positions occupied in the exercise of power and the level of relevant knowledge one has – affect it in the same spontaneous way as under 'pure' market conditions, accentuating the differences in 'economic' position. On the other hand, the redistributive principle and other deliberate elements derived from social or societal policy already have a more significant impact on the definition of wages than before. Thus, distribution according to work combines in a special way the characteristics of several former types of economic integration – yielding a new form. Perhaps an opposite formulation can also be offered. One may, indeed, suggest that the market, as the dominant form of economic integration and distribution, has disappeared and is only retained as a complementary instrument, regulating some aspects of production and allocation. None the less, some of the forces which unobtrusively regulated the market under capitalist conditions still operate under the present Hungarian conditions, affecting the deliberately adopted or construed types of distribution. They usually operate in a way which is at variance with the officially endorsed and officially applied principles.

The other main form – the very principle of social policy in the restricted sense of the term – is centralized redistribution. This retains, under socialist conditions, its general characteristic of allocating a part of the social product for the sake of integrating the community and of assuring for its members the right to live. It also has some special characteristics under socialist conditions. Before turning to them, however, the over-all tendencies characterizing central redistribution must be at least briefly described.

7.2 Public funds and centrally redistributed incomes – recent trends in Hungary

Central redistribution geared towards the aims of societal and social policy uses a certain part of the social product, which may be called public or collective funds. The collective funds, gathered from the surplus product, are generally used on the initiative of a body representing a more or less large segment of society, to create, purchase and/or allocate goods, services, equipment and facilities which belong to the non-productive sphere (that is, in the Marxist sense, the sphere which yields no profit or surplus product). The utilization of these goods, services, etc., is apparently independent of market forces.[6]

I have not specified the legal status of the owner of the assets used for public purposes and have not excluded private initiative from among the possible initiators of such facilities. In earlier societies many publicly used amenities – for instance, in Hungary, the first public libraries of the eighteenth century, or the Hungarian Academy of Sciences dating from the early nine-

6. A lively debate has been going on for some years about the problems of collective consumption in some Western countries, highlighted for example, by a recent, as yet unpublished, paper: R. E. Pahl, *What is Collective Consumption? A Critique of Castells' Analysis of State Provisions*, draft, January 1977. The authors use various concepts and give different definitions, so I have had to specify how I understand the concept.

teenth century – were created by aristocrats playing the role of Maecenas. This role has not disappeared in contemporary societies. In a number of capitalist countries high praise for 'public spiritedness', and sometimes incentives such as tax reductions, encourage such activities as making gifts to museums. The phenomenon exists even in present-day Hungary, though, because of the limited amount of private wealth, on a reduced scale. Thus collectors or artists often make bequests to museums, and this is still a respected sign of public spiritedness. Childless couples may also leave their small savings to schools as endowments. (This latter gesture is not encouraged by public authorities, but such endowments are not refused.) Despite these examples it may safely be assumed that in contemporary socialist societies, private ownership of public amenities is practically non-existent, and private initiative in creating them is more the exception than the rule.

The goods, services, equipment and facilities in question may be classified in a number of ways depending on the goal of the analysis. It is possible to group them according to their direct function, or the type of need they cover, such as public administration, foreign policy, education, health, culture, etc. (This is a multi-purpose classification serving the most varied purposes.)

Another question related to the type of needs is whether the services offered are related to some 'elementary necessity of co-existence' (as were a number of urban and other services which emerged in the nineteenth century when rapid urbanization required various health measures in order to avoid epidemics) or whether they cover a 'higher order' of needs.

A classification taking into account whether the resources in question are invested in *fixed* assets (roads, hospitals, the building of a ministry) or whether they serve *current* outlays may be important for the management of the services in question, and has implications for the planning of production, of manpower policy, etc.

Approaching the same goods, services and equipment from the perspective of distribution, and of the social and regional inequalities characterizing their distribution (allocation or utilzation), one has to know, among other things, whether the users are individuals, as in the case of cash benefits or medical services, or whether only a group of users may be identified, as with street cleaning, traffic lights or other 'neighbourhood' services, or whether the users are the members of the general public, as with a number of functions of the public administration. (There may be other, mixed categories.)

A further criterion of classification may be whether there are parallel services operating simultaneously in the private and the collective sphere (from schools to transportation and to laundry facilities).

It is no idle speculation to multiply the perspectives from which the composition or utilization of public funds may be analysed. All the classifications mentioned are derived from more or less grave dilemmas related to the past and future development of central redistribution. This is evident if one reformulates the classifications in the terms in which central decision-makers have to face them. Some of the related problems – whether there should be parallel services, what should be the principles of redistribution, etc. – will be discussed shortly in more detail. But one requirement has universal relevance: the public funds must grow continuously, otherwise it is not possible to attain any of the goals of social policy.

No statistical indicators are available that would cover in a global way the various aspects of the evolution of public funds. But the main developmental tendencies can be followed on the basis of a number of special studies.

According to one study, describing the trends between 1960 and 1970,[7] the gross output of branches belonging to non-material production, which roughly corresponds to what I have defined above as the non-productive sphere, made up about one tenth of the gross output of branches of material production. Between 1960 and 1970, the output of non-material branches grew slightly more rapidly than that of material branches, the respective indices being 203·0 and 197·6 per cent (1960 = 100

7. *Társadalmi szolgáltatások 1960–1970* (Social Services 1960–70), Central Statistical Office, Budapest, 1972.

per cent). The various branches showed similar growth rates, except for the services connected with housing (only 159 per cent) and scientific research services (attaining 517 per cent).

By contrast, the value of investment in branches of material production grew more rapidly (in 1970 236 per cent of the 1960 value) than in non-material branches (199 per cent), but the amounts invested in public administration hardly changed (119 per cent), so that in branches more closely affecting the standard of living the growth-rate approached that of material branches. The global amount of fixed assets also increased less rapidly in non-material than in other branches.

The extent to which the output of non-material branches was allocated to the population on an individual service basis or in a genuinely collective way cannot be ascertained. Detailed data only permit one to conclude that many types of equipment or services destined for some kind of collective use did not develop at a desirable pace.

The study quoted identifies a number of fields where evolution has been satisfactory or even spectacular, such as out-patient clinics, nurseries and kindergartens, the network of visiting nurses, educational facilities in small settlements, holiday homes, electricity, water and gas supplies and heating facilities, playing fields for children and sports equipment, especially swimming pools. On the other hand, it points out that many areas are lagging behind the level attained by countries with a similar economic situation, or failing to meet the demands of the population or the standards which seem to be desirable for the promotion of centrally defined social objectives.

Hospital facilities, some types of schooling and school equipment, the sewerage system, refuse disposal almost everywhere outside Budapest and some of the other cities, and the provision and maintenance of public parks are all areas in which Hungary is deficient, in absolute or relative terms. Moreover, many public buildings – hospitals, schools, cultural homes – are in need of repair. One of the major general problems identified in this study is that regional inequalities in the availability of equipment and services prove to be persistent.

It is easier to follow (on the basis of available statistics) the evolution of that part of the public funds which has been allocated in such a way that the users may be individually identified. These benefits or services are considered as part of personal incomes – whether allocated in cash or in kind.

With the growing role of central redistribution, the proportion of social benefits within the total income of the population was gradually increased – attaining 27·3 per cent in 1975. (See Table 5/10, p. 190).

Benefits in cash have gained in importance ever since 1945 although comparable data are available only from 1960 on. Cash benefits made up 38 per cent of all centrally distributed (personal) benefits in 1960, and 53 per cent in 1975.

Of benefits in cash, pensions represent by far the most important component, the two other significant items being family allowances and sickness benefits. Education and health no doubt make up the bulk of benefits in kind. The composition of benefits either in cash or in kind has not altered greatly over time, though the data clearly reveal some shifting priorities, such as the priority given to pensions, the fluctuation in family allowances or, within benefits in kind, the growing role of cultural and holiday services.

7.3 New aspects of central redistribution in Hungary, in theory and practice

7.3.1 *Theory*

The specific characteristics of central redistribution under socialist conditions follow from the overall change in the basic social relations. The most general and long-term features – a new relation between the 'economic' and the 'social' spheres, and the egalitarian principle – have already been described. In a shorter perspective central redistribution has other distinctive characteristics. Some of these have already been mentioned in various contexts. Nevertheless it seems worth while to discuss them in a more systematic way and to ascertain to what extent these features are really operating.

Table 7/1: The main components of social benefits

(a) benefits in cash

Year	Total amount, in thousands of millions of forints	Pensions	Sickness benefits	Family allow-ance	Child-care grant	Scholar-ships	Other allow-ances	Total
				in percentage of the total sum				
1960	8·4	54·9	20·2	17·1	—	2·2	5·6	100·0
1965	12·6	61·3	18·1	12·5	—	2·5	5·6	100·0
1970	22·1	58·9	16·7	12·8	5·4	1·7	4·5]	100·0
1975	45·1	59·5	13·3	14·2	6·7	1·2	5·1	100·0

(b) *benefits in kind*

Year	Total amount, in thousands of millions of forints	Health services	Subsidies on drugs	Nurseries, social homes	Edu- cation	Culture, holiday resorts, sports	Subsidies on canteens	Amorti- zation of state- owned flats	Total
					in percentage of the total sum				
1960	13·5	28·1	6·8	4·4	37·4	7·9	6·1	9·3	100·0
1965	18·1	28·1	9·0	4·2	36·7	6·9	6·7	8·4	100·0
1970	26·2	27·9	10·3	4·3	37·6	6·9	6·2	6·8	100·0
1975	40·0	25·9	11·0	5·0	36·3	11·6	5·3	4·9	100·0

Source: A lakosság jövedelme és fogyasztása, 1960–1975 (Income and Consumption of the Population 1960–75), Central Statistical Office, Budapest, 1976.

(a) The role of centralized redistribution is certainly greater than in the capitalist society which immediately preceded the present socialist one, and its importance is constantly growing. This is, firstly, a direct corollary of the decreasing role of the market. Secondly, it is related to the general trends in the historical development of socialist society, where distribution according to need is constantly gaining ground beside distribution according to work. In this sense it is a concomitant of the gradual evolution towards a communist society. Lastly, the most general aspect of this process is that socialist development should gradually reintegrate the different social relations that have become sharply fragmented under capitalist conditions.

The broadening scope of centralized redistribution thus means that the considerations underlying it do not operate solely in the realm of social policy proper, but permeate all types of economic relations, especially distribution according to work and the prices policy. While under capitalist conditions the logic of the market pervades non-market, and indeed practically all (even non-economic), relations, under socialist conditions it is the redistributive logic that is diffused far beyond the frontiers of centralized redistribution. Obviously, it is a separate and very intricate problem to decide how far the fusion of redistributive considerations and essentially economic considerations should go at any given level of development.

(b) A second important feature of centralized redistribution under socialist conditions is related to the first and also, more directly, to the rising level of social and economic development. Not only is the part of the social product given over to centralized redistribution growing, but the range of needs covered by it and of goods and services encompassed by it is also expanding. The community endeavours to assure for its members not only mere survival, but an ever fuller life, and endeavours to do so *independently* of their economic potential. It would appear that this process of development is far from being at an end. In Hungary for instance, the coverage of basic housing needs should be accepted in the not too distant future as a social obligation. This was done at an elementary level as early as 1945, when the 'right to be housed' was acknowledged, and eviction on any grounds prohibited. Since then, however, the demands not merely for housing, but for good housing have become very strong. To meet these demands within a reasonable time span is possible only by means of central redistribution, as will be shown in more detail in section 8.3.

In addition, non-divisible goods and services, used by some part of the whole collectivity, must grow steadily in order to assure an adequate framework for the enrichment of everyday life.

(c) A third important characteristic is that the claim for centralized redistribution can become a real right only under socialist conditions. The idea that social benefits should be given as of right had also been repeatedly stressed by progressive thinkers in capitalist countries, Richard Titmuss among others. Legal regulations, too, especially in the last few decades, often emphasize that benefits must be seen as individual rights. The change is not so much in the formulations, as in the social foundations of the law.

The social product becomes common property only if the means of production are in public ownership. If the bulk of the means of production and, consequently, of products is owned by private producers, then the *legal* basis of any distribution that runs against the rights and interests of private (whether individual or corporate) ownership can always be challenged. Individual taxation, the most important resource of public funds, is itself strongly influenced by the constantly shifting power relations, so that the proportion of the surplus product accruing to the central budget may easily decrease. In this case, or if the social position of the dominant groups seems to be very secure, then even in capitalist countries with a well-developed system of social policy the power-holders may challenge and sometimes withdraw some of the rights already obtained. Thus, Piven and Cloward[8] show how the unemployment benefits followed the evolution of the balance of power between workers and employers in the United States.

8. F. F. Piven and R. A. Cloward, *Regulating the Poor*, op. cit.

If, however, it is the community that owns the products, then the right to decide their allocation rightfully belongs to the community. In other words, the right to central redistribution is not contingent on the balance of social forces but is stably established because of the ownership relations. Theoretically, there are no 'givers' and 'takers' – the community is giving itself goods from its own resources.

(d) The last specific feature of socialist redistribution is that it ought to have a genuine redistributive impact, in other words it must reduce social inequalities, or at least inequalities in income which emerge in the sphere of production, because of the present state of the social division of work.

Westergaard and Resler observe that 'the "welfare state" does redistribute income. But ... this is redistribution between households at different stages of life far more than it is redistribution between households at markedly different levels of income. It is redistribution within classes far more than it is redistribution between classes.'[9]

Redistribution between households at different stages of life, or with different loads in terms of the number of persons to be provided for, is an entirely legitimate goal of social policy, but in a socialist perspective this is not enough. Redistribution must take place not only within the social classes – or groups defined according to their situation in the social division of work – but also across them. Similarly, regional differences (indirectly and historically related to the social division of work) which deeply affect conditions of everyday life and chances in life must also be reduced by central redistribution.

This formulation does not imply that differences due to distribution according to work must be completely levelled off. Such a claim would deny the rationality of work-related distribution at a time when this still appears as a social and economic necessity. But centralized redistribution may and should reduce the original socio-economic differentiation. However, there are as yet no ways known to define the optimal measure of this reduction.

9. John Westergaard and Henrietta Resler, *Class in a Capitalist Society,* op. cit., p. 68.

Centralized redistribution operates initially through resources which are assured for those who are outside the social division of work. In this case, there is a clear-cut inverse relation between work-related and redistributive incomes because the latter have the explicit aim of complementing income from work. The second type of redistributive income is, theoretically at least, altogether independent from work performance. Benefits cover certain needs (for example, medical care) which may affect the entire population and which have to be covered according to identical standards everywhere. If this aim is achieved, different groups and strata will receive more or less the same amount of this type of redistributive income. Thus the original work-related differences will be lessened, if not in absolute at least in relative terms. A third redistributive effect occurs because essentially economic phenomena like wages or price policies tend also to be influenced by the logic of redistribution, for example, when determining minimum or maximum levels of wages or deciding on price preferences.

Under the present conditions in Hungary, some of the redistributive incomes, although by their very nature they have a levelling effect, do not in practice alter the initial imbalance of the income distribution because the actual amount is work-related (as with pensions or sick pay). The problems stemming from the 'mixed' character of these benefits have already been discussed in connection with pensions.

7.3.2 Reality

ad (a) and (b). Data presented in previous chapters show clearly enough that both of the first two theoretical characteristics – the increasing role of redistribution and the greater range of needs covered – can be recognized more and more clearly in practice.

I would not affirm that all legitimate needs are recognized as rights to share nor that they are covered sufficiently well. None the less, standards of social benefits are raised usually more rapidly than work-related income, and they are gradually being extended to cover the whole population. New needs, such as the home care of young or sick children, or domiciliary relief for elderly people, are also accepted as a basis for sharing. The need for adequate housing is not universally recognized as one to be covered by the collectivity, but selective measures in favour of workers and large families have been implemented over the last few years.

ad (*c*). It is more difficult to point to the social embodiment of the third characteristic, namely that under socialist conditions redistributive benefits cease to be gifts, donations or concessions fought or bargained for, but become *rights*.

One of the problems is connected with retrograde ways of speaking and thinking. A number of the expressions used in connection with social policy which have gained acceptance in Hungarian are not particularly happy ones. It is somewhat awkward to speak about benefits (implying a 'benefactor'), about social care and aid, and – a recurrent phrase in journalism – about 'gifts provided by society', when new social policy institutions are created or results attained. The gift-view was especially characteristic of the period of the 'cult of the personality'. But even nowadays signs of this attitude are easy to find. As late as 1974, a public announcement could be read on the walls of some universities saying that 'students must apply for study grants'. Or in the case of family allowances, besides handing in the official documents, one also has to make an application. These are formalities inasmuch as the claims have to be accepted in every case. If an individual does not know his rights, he will be informed by the university or by the employer of the steps to take. But the wording itself (using the concepts 'benefit', 'application', etc.) is certainly inadequate. The persistence of this view of social benefits as a donation may be discerned in various more or less official documents, as shown in section 2.5.

But conservative ways of speaking are not the only problem. In reality, even though the right to share has become more real and more solidly established, claims – old or new – are not automatically accepted as rights to share, and not only because the economic resources are always limited. We again encounter the problem that developments in socialist redistribution are not automatically followed. In principle, it is indeed the community that makes decisions on the community resources. In reality, however, participation in decision-making is obviously not direct, nor is the community homogeneous. Therefore, the outcome is influenced by the fact that the various groups in the community do not have identical interests, nor do they have the same opportunities to assert their interests. Those groups, for instance, which are especially favoured by the present distribution according to work will not necessarily be enthusiastic about furthering the cause of centralized redistribution, even if they recognize and approve of its historical and social necessity. Since they are likely to participate more directly in decision-making than less favoured groups, they may slow down the spread of redistributive considerations.

It is only in the last few years that different democratic forums have been established which provide an opportunity for the members of the community to discuss openly the kinds of demands and claims which will arise, and to decide which ones should be given priority in redistribution, once they are accepted as rights. The forums in question operate at the level of the firm, sometimes at the local (neighbourhood) level, and some priorities or claims are debated publicly, by means of the mass media. Thus in recent years there have been widespread debates via the mass media, mainly on radio and TV, about the benefits of handicapped people; about the next priority to be introduced in family allowances; about the transformation of motherhood rights into parental rights; about the priorities operating in the allocation of flats; and about the adequacy of the policies applied to overcome regional inequalities.

ad (*d*). The situation is probably hardest to judge in the case of the fourth characteristic, the 'redistributive' effect of redistribution. This can be done only on the basis of detailed statistical evidence. This evidence is entirely lacking for the utilization of public funds where the users cannot be individually identified. As for the other funds, up to now Hungarian data are available only from an earlier survey that attempted to cover all aspects of personal income distribution, including that of social benefits in cash and kind. This survey relates to 1967. The 1972 income survey also covered the whole process of distribution, but not all of the results have been published so far. These, however, confirm the 1967 findings so that inferences based on the earlier data retain their validity.

7.4 How redistributive is redistribution?

7.4.1 *Social benefits in cash*

Although it is true that without pensions and sick-pay benefits income distribution would be much more unequal, it is also clear that these benefits, because their amount is work-related, do not change the original differentiation. The levelling effect of family allowances – although their standard is known to be still unsatisfactory – is greater. The specific impact of these benefits has been shown in Chapter 6 (especially sections 6.4 and 6.5).

Some social benefits, on the contrary, may be expected to increase rather than decrease the degree of income inequality. One grant of this type is the child-care grant described in section 3.3. This grant is used proportionally more by women with lower skills and lower wages than by others, and may therefore increase the number and ratio of people on low incomes. A special complication is that the increase in the differentiation of incomes affects some social groups disproportionately: it is clear that women with low skills and low wages are found mainly in groups whose social situation is less favourable. A similar possibility may arise in connection with another new arrangement, the opportunity to get a pension even if one continues to work after the retirement age. In this case better-qualified people (with originally higher pensions) may be more willing to continue to work. Thereby the inequality of incomes may again grow, not because low incomes are decreasing, but because higher incomes are increasing faster than the average. Both these measures are fairly popular and socially advantageous from many points of view. But their side-effects must not be forgotten.

The overall effect of cash grants on redistribution is thus the outcome of opposite tendencies. For the time being, however, they do have a genuine redistributive effect. In 1967 as well as in 1972 the range of work-related incomes was greater and their distribution more unequal than that of cash grants or of the total disposable income (including both items). This can be illustrated by the so-called inequality ratio, the value of which was 2.32 for work-related incomes and 1.92 for total disposable incomes in 1967.[10]

Benefits in cash had a positive (levelling) redistributive effect not only on income distribution overall, but also as far as the different social groups (defined according to their situation within the social division of work) were concerned. Relatively more cash grants accrued to the worse situated groups – except for the peasantry, to whom very different regulations still applied in 1967. Because regulations have become more homogeneous since, and because of measures like the raising of low pensions, this redistributive effect of cash grants is somewhat more pronounced now than it was in 1967.

With cash benefits the redistributive impact appears not only in relative but also in absolute terms, at least in some respects. For lower-income groups the percentage as well as the absolute amount of the benefits is higher than for higher-income groups. However, across social groups the redistributive effect is only relative.

Thus it is true by and large that benefits in cash are distributed according to 'needs', and that they counteract the work-related differentiation to some extent. Their final impact therefore corresponds to the original intentions of central regulation even if it may be questioned whether their social efficiency is sufficient.

7.4.2 Social benefits in kind

Benefits in kind affect income distribution in a somewhat different way from benefits in cash. Their impact is also varied

10. *A lakossági jövedelmek szinvonala és szóródása* (The Level and Dispersion of the Incomes of the Population), Central Statistical Office, Budapest, 1972.

Table 7/2: Amount and proportion of benefits in cash within the total disposable cash income 1967 and 1972

Groups formed according to the head of household's occupation	Amount per capita forints per month (1967)	% of total income (1967)	Groups formed according to the per capita monthly income in forints	Amount per capita per month in forints 1967	Amount per capita per month in forints 1972	% of total income 1967	% of total income 1972
Managers, senior administrators, professionals	107	6·7	under 600	147 ⎫	261	31·8 ⎫	42·5
Skilled non-manual workers	97	7·0	601–800	150 ⎭		22·1 ⎭	
Office workers	110	8·7	801–1,000	138	268	15·3	29·7
Total non-manual	102	7·1	1,001–1,200	126	249	11·5	22·6
Skilled workers	90	7·7	1,201–1,400	113	224	8·7	17·2
Semi-skilled workers	87	8·3	1,401–1,600	105	212	7·0	14·2
Unskilled workers	86	8·8	1,601–1,800	105	203	6·2	12·0
Total manual outside agriculture	88	8·1	1,801–2,000	89	186	4·7	9·8
Manual workers in agriculture	48	4·2	2,001–2,400	97	189	4·5	8·7
Retired, pensioners	398	43·2	over 2,401	88	188	3·0	6·1
Total	126	11·1		126	220	11·1	13·9

Source: For 1967: *A lakossági jövedelmek színvonala és szóródása* (The Level and Dispersion of the Incomes of the Population), Central Statistical Office, Budapest, 1972, pp. 183 and 188, and computations based on these data. For 1972: *A családi jövedelmek színvonala és szóródása.* (The Level and Dispersion of Family Incomes), Central Statistical Office, Budapest, 1975, p. 71, and own computations based thereon.

owing to a number of factors, the most important of which are the following:

● The various needs covered by the benefits in kind do not occur with the same frequency in the various social groups. Thus, medical services are required especially often by elderly people. Working clothes and special prophylactic foods (if one considers these items as social benefits, which is only partly justified) are required only under special working conditions which apply usually to manual workers. The same holds for reduced tariffs on public transport used by commuters, who are also mostly manual workers.

● There are needs which, though theoretically equal and universal, are not formulated as demands, and not claimed with equal strength by the different groups. The best examples are secondary and higher education. In this respect there is a social and cultural handicap owing to which, despite very considerable central efforts and significant results, children of workers and peasants are still under-represented in secondary and higher education. The fact that some needs are not felt with the same urgency by the various social groups may be accounted for by differences in their objective conditions as well as their values, interest and expectations. These factors have impact not only on higher education but on more elementary demands like places at holiday resorts or even the use of firm canteens.

No doubt, the absence of demands is partly due to financial reasons. In some cases even the reduced, heavily subsidized charges and fees are hard to meet, without taking into consideration the loss of potential earnings and extra costs entailed by continued studies or even holidays spent in 'idleness'. The other reason is probably that, for well-known historical reasons, there are many rights – the right to rest, to be comfortable, to acquire a university degree, etc. – that are far from becoming self-evident as yet.

The same causes act less openly in other spheres, too, especially in the health service. One's attitude to one's own health is conditioned by numerous factors that cannot be dealt with here in detail. (Such factors are, for example, whether it is socially 'permitted' to be ill, or whether one recognizes the signs of the various illnesses or the possibilities and means of their prevention.) Up to now there have been no adequate studies in Hungary in this field – only sporadic information is available. It is, for instance, symptomatic that workers use hospital care relatively frequently while they use outpatient clinics and medicines less frequently than average. Hence it may be assumed that non-manuals (with a higher education level, etc.) consult a doctor at an earlier stage in an illness so that they are sometimes able to avoid hospitalization. It would be even more important to know whether all social groups are equally knowledgeable about symptoms requiring medical treatment. Presumably they are not – with results that can be foreseen – but systematic information about this is not yet at our disposal. The total amount of health benefits is practically the same for workers as for non-manuals. On the face of it this could mean that all needs are being recognized and taken care of. However, this belief is shaken by the mortality data. For example in 1974 the average age at death of male manual workers (active earners at the time of death) was 46.3 years, that of male industrial workers 43·6, and that of non-manuals 49·3 years.[11] The rate of infant mortality was 35·6 per thousand for workers, 29·2 for non-manuals.[12]

The difference in infant mortality rates is more pronounced if the groups are more closely defined, for instance if the educational level of the mother is taken into account. One may conclude that despite a similarity in *manifest* needs, explicit demands and the utilization of available services, the real medical need of workers is greater than average, but it remains latent, inarticulate and unconscious. I do not want to suggest that these differences are caused merely by a variation in the attitude to health. Working and housing conditions, a less complete or less balanced diet, the difficulties of getting prompt

11. *Demográfiai Évkönyv 1974* (Demographic Yearbook 1974), Central Statistical Office, Budapest, 1975, p. 202.
12. ibid., p. 279.

specialized medical care in smaller towns or villages all contribute to causing a shorter life span or a higher infant mortality rate and they would not be radically altered even if fuller use were made of the health services. But one can hardly doubt that this is necessary, precisely because there are more factors damaging to health where objective conditions are worse.

● A third factor which distorts the operation of the redistributive system is that the different groups are not able to assert their interests in the same way. Therefore, their shares may differ even if needs are felt equally consciously and strongly. This factor plays a role especially in the case of those institutions that function well, with high standards, but where there is a shortage in capacity. The demand is then greater than the supply, but the balance cannot be restored by market mechanisms since these are eliminated by subsidized or nominal tariffs. The goods or services in question, where the right is universal but the capacity too small, are distributed either by following the spontaneous operation of underlying power relations, or on the basis of some rationality that is not necessarily socially justified. The two most important benefits of this type are child-care institutions and housing. Among the child-care institutions, the greatest pressure in 1967 was on kindergartens, which had the highest standards and which were socially most important. At that time 50 per cent of all children between three and six years of age were in kindergartens, but the proportion was around 80 per cent for children of managers and professionals and around 40 per cent for children of unskilled workers.[13] In this case again, as with health services, regional differences accentuate social differentiation. (The larger localities are better equipped than the smaller ones, and non-manuals are more likely to be town-dwellers than the other groups.) In recent years several studies have dealt with the social problems and effects of the allocation of housing,[14]

13. Approximations based on the 1967 income survey.
14. Gy. Konrád and I. Szelényi, 'A lakáselosztás szociológiai kérdései' (Sociological Problems in the Allocation of Flats), in *A szocialista városok és a szociológia* (Socialist Towns and Sociology), Kossuth Könyvkiadó,

where again a number of factors operated in favour of groups which were already better-off.

The allocation of scarce resources which are in great demand does not follow the predefined pattern of centralized redistribution, nor is it operated by pure market forces. Both forms have been replaced by some kind of 'hidden' distribution, regulated partly by personal contacts and good 'connections': better-situated groups have better access to the scarce resources (council flats or places in kindergarten) because they have more contacts. They also find it easier to ask. This may be because they are more confident about their own social worth, because they have more favourable social experiences and because they may be in a position to offer, at some future time, reciprocal services. In this case, then, the logic of redistribution is combined with, or distorted by, that of reciprocity. Another part of these goods may be distributed taking into account the social or economic importance of the work done by a given group or individual. A doctor, for instance, may get a house in a village relatively easily because the community needs him and he could not otherwise be expected to settle down. In this case it is the market logic which distorts 'pure' redistribution. It is clear that the first factor, the utilization of contacts based on expectations of reciprocity, is socially and morally objectionable and its impact could perhaps be reduced with stricter administrative control. It is less easy to judge how far knowledge and skill should be accepted as entitlements for sharing in redistribution. In the first case private interests are clearly opposed to public interests, while in the second case the private interests are opposed to some public interests, but not to all. Moral judgement is not justified and hardly helpful in this latter case. Besides the increase of the available capacities, the only adequate solution, a continuous control is needed in order to assure a better balance between various private and public interests and those of the

---

Budapest, 1971; P. Tóth, 'A borsodi gyáriparban dolgozók lakásviszonyai' (The Housing Conditions of Workers in the Industry of County Borsod), *Szociológia*, 1974, No. 1.

society as a whole. The agencies of control must also pay special attention to groups which have more difficulty in articulating and asserting their interests.

Beside these problems, there is a further benefit, peculiar to Hungary, which is working in a way contrary to its original aims. This is the state subsidy of rents. In the years following 1945 rents had been fixed at an extremely low level, mainly because of social policy (redistributive) consideration. It was only much later that it became clear that better-off groups lived in rented flats in a greater than average proportion and that the quality of their flats was also better than average. Therefore the effect of an originally redistributive scheme became reversed and the social benefit added to existing advantages. The yearly amount of this subsidy was, in 1967, around 560 forints in the group composed of managers and professionals, and 70 forints in that of unskilled workers.[15] After central acknowledgement of the problem, rents of well-equipped flats were significantly raised in 1971. This meant some improvement in the disproportional allocation of the subsidy, but the original differences were too big to be eliminated in a single step.

In addition two more factors influence how an individual is able to assert his or her claims. The effect of these is, however, hard to assess numerically. (In any case, they are not taken into account in the income surveys.) The first factor is related, among other things, to the level of information, which varies with social situation. The quality of services offered is not uniform: schools, hospitals and holiday homes vary in quality. Groups that are better informed, who are deliberately looking for information and are able to use personal influence, tend to obtain access to the better institutions. The second factor is connected with the traditional hierarchical content of interpersonal relations, meaning that different clients may be treated differently. Although the official system rejects discrimination or privilege of this type, the old patterns of interpersonal relations are too deeply ingrained to be easily eradicated. The relation between the doctor and the patient is, for instance,

15. *A lakossági jövedelmek szinvonala és szóródása*, op. cit., 1967.

always an unequal one, but the inequality is greater in the case of less educated, less well-off patients. One of the first systematic studies on the role of social criteria in the differential treatment of patients is to be found in the now classic book by Hollingshead and Redlich.[16] It seems that this has remained a problem practically everywhere. Hungary is no exception to this rule, although the roughest aspects have been attenuated. (One has to remember that the medical profession as a whole has become much less closed and exclusive in the last few decades.)

These factors combine to form different syndromes, yielding different types of social benefits with regard to their effect on redistribution, where 'positive' redistribution means a reduction in the inequalities which existed before redistribution took place. The main types are the following:

Type 1

(a) The level of manifest (conscious and articulated) needs is similar for practically all social groups, or at least differences in this respect are rapidly diminishing;

(b) the institutional framework of the benefit (the 'supply') is broad enough;

(c) the level of utilization is similar in the different social groups.

Hence the grant has a positive, levelling redistributive effect, in accordance with the original intentions. (Original income differences are diminished, even if not eliminated.)

Schematically: similar demands + similar utilization
→positive redistribution

Grants that belong to this category, though with some reservations (mainly as far as quality and ready availability are concerned, especially from a regional perspective), are health services and primary schooling.

16. A. B. Hollingshead and F. C. Redlich, *Social Class and Mental Illness*, John Wiley, New York, 1958, especially p. 192 and Chapter 9.

Type 2

(a) The level of manifest (conscious) needs is different in different social groups, and is positively correlated with the social situation – it is 'hierarchized';

(b) the institutional framework of the benefit is broad enough, or at least flexible;

(c) the level of utilization by social groups is none the less different, because of (a) above.

Hence the grant has a negative redistributive effect, contrary to the original intentions.

Schematically: 'hierarchized' demands + differentiated
utilization → negative redistribution

Benefits that belong to this type include grammar schools and technical (vocational) schools within secondary education, all higher education, subsidized holidays and meal-subsidies at place of work.

Type 3

(a) The level of manifest (conscious) needs is similar for all social groups;

(b) the institutional framework of the benefits is not broad enough;

(c) the possibilities for asserting one's interest differ according to social group, with better chances for better-off groups;

(d) the level of utilization by social groups is differentiated.

Hence there is a negative redistributive effect, contrary to the original intention.

Schematically: similar demands + 'hierarchized'
utilization → negative redistribution

Benefits in this category include child-care institutions (primarily kindergartens but also nurseries); school day-care centres to a smaller extent; the centralized allocation of flats at least before the revision of the regulations concerning the allocation of flats in 1971; and also rent subsidies.

Type 4

(a) The level of manifest (conscious) needs differs between social groups, but the needs are inversely related to the social situation, that is they are needs which appear only under specific, usually disadvantaged conditions;

(b) the institutional framework of the benefits is broad enough (or flexible) although its quality is often unsatisfactory;

(c) the level of utilization is differentiated, but it covers the demands, so that it is 'inversely hierarchical'.

Hence the effect on redistribution is positive, mostly in accordance with the original intentions. Some benefits of this type also reduce original differences in an absolute sense.

Schematically: 'inversely hierarchical' demands
+ 'inversely hierarchical' utilization → positive redistribution

We find here industrial apprenticeship within secondary education (although in this case the unequal distribution is not intentional); prophylactic foods (and perhaps work-clothes) under special working conditions; commuters' special tariffs; subsidies for workers' hostels, etc.

● Regional differences operate within all the above types, transmitting or reinforcing the impact of social differences. In Hungary urbanized settlements are generally far better equipped with social institutions and with all kinds of services. At the same time better-off groups live in these areas in greater proportion. Managers and professionals for instance are mainly town-dwellers.

The individual and overall effect of these different tendencies is hard to ascertain because the surveys from which our data are derived did not cover all types of benefits, and did not take into account differences in quality. None the less, the basic conclusions are probably valid. Thus, social benefits in kind have to some degree increased the income differences between social groups while at the same time they have slightly reduced the inequality of the overall income distribution. (See Table 7/3.) This apparent contradiction in the impact of redistribution is easy to explain. One of the main items within benefits in kind is education, which is mostly used by families with children, whose per capita income level is usually lower than average. The other important item is the health service, which is by and large proportionally distributed (type 1), but has a specific income-levelling effect because of the higher demand of old people. It must be noted that, unlike benefits in cash, benefits in kind affect income distribution only in relative terms. The absolute amounts are similar in the different income groups, or even higher in the higher income brackets. The income-levelling effect of benefits in kind may also be shown by the inequality ratios. In 1967 this ratio was 1·92 for personally disposable and 1·81 for all incomes.[17] In 1972 the respective figures were 1·96 and 1·85.[18]

To sum up: social benefits in cash have a positive redistributive, levelling, effect on the original income differentials, both with regard to the overall income distribution and to different social groups. The redistributive effect of benefits in kind is more ambiguous. They reduce differences in incomes to some extent, though less effectively than cash benefits. This redistribution works mostly within social groups, between families with more or fewer dependent persons. But as far as differences between social groups are concerned, benefits in kind accentuate them, since they are even more unequally distributed than work-related incomes. In short, the social impact of cash benefits corresponds to the intended effect reflecting common socialist interests, but this only partly holds for the benefits in kind which leads to a number of dilemmas.

17. *A lakossági jövedelmek . . .*, op. cit., p. 229.
18. *A családi jövedelmek szinvonala és szóródása 1972-ben,* op. cit., pp. 65–6.

Table 7/3: Amount and percentage of benefits in kind within total (cash and kind) incomes

(Data refer to 1967 and 1972)

Groups formed according to the head of household's occupation	Amount per capita per month in forints 1967	% of income 1967	Groups formed according to the per capita monthly income in forints	Amount per capita per month in forints 1967	Amount per capita per month in forints 1972	% of total income 1967	% of total income 1972
Managers, senior administrators and professionals	260	14·1	under 600	156	} 220	25·2	} 26·4
Skilled non-manuals	221	13·7	601–800	167		19·1	
Office workers	220	14·9	801–1,000	171	244	15·9	21·2
Total non-manual workers	235	14·1	1,001–1,200	167	249	13·2	18·4
Skilled workers	163	12·2	1,201–1,400	161	259	11·1	16·6
Semi-skilled workers	153	12·7	1,401–1,600	163	249	9·8	14·2
Unskilled workers	149	13·2	1,601–1,800	163	249	8·8	12·8
Total manual workers outside agriculture	157	12·6	1,801–2,000	157	246	7·7	11·5
Manual workers in agriculture	114	9·0	2,001–2,400	161	243	6·9	10·0
Retired pensioners	185	16·7	2,401 & over	193	246	6·1	7·4
Overall average	166	12·7	Overall average	166	246	12·7	13·4

Source: As for Table 7/2.

7.5 Dilemmas of central redistribution and of the utilization of public funds

The analysis of current trends of central redistribution brings out issues which may for a while have seemed easy to handle, but which prove to have unwanted effects if applied without caution.

The new dilemmas centre around old issues, which have long been debated by social policy thinkers in non-socialist countries. Whether aware of all the intricacies of these debates or not, Hungary – indeed all the socialist countries – applied the principles which had always been voiced by the workers' movement or by those who were closest to it in their convictions. Thus in current Hungarian social policy it has been taken for granted that selection based on means tests ought to be rejected; that benefits in kind promote socialist objectives in a straightforward way; or that market considerations can be, indeed have been, abolished once they have been officially banned.

It now transpires that the outcome of the policies applied does not correspond exactly to the above assumptions. Some, therefore, question the asumptions and the options based on them, advocating more means tests or the official revival of the market in many spheres. Others (myself included) do not question the soundness of the assumptions but realize that their full implementation requires more effort than previously displayed.

Here I shall discuss three such newly emerging, but in fact old, dilemmas, namely:
- whether benefits in cash or benefits in kind are more effective in promoting some of the social goals of social or societal policy;
- what the respective advantages and disadvantages of universal and selective benefits are;
- whether non-market services should be replaced or complemented by market services.

7.5.1 Cash or kind?

Some common arguments against benefits in kind consist in

pointing out that they limit people's freedom of choice, that every individual knows what is best for him and the state should not force alternatives on people.[19] Others affirm that one does not appreciate things (services) which are free or heavily subsidized, so that even the political advantage is lost. Also, wastage is more likely to occur with free or subsidized products – and this point has been illustrated in Hungary with convincing examples for medicines and bread. A strong case is made against benefits in kind on the basis of their distribution, that is that the outcome is contrary to the original intentions – price subsidies, higher education and a number of other benefits reinforce the inequalities of the original distribution.

The counter-arguments to these affirmations are quite well known, and are repeatedly mentioned in this book.

'Free' choice is interfered with practically everywhere, directly (compulsory schooling is just one example) and even more indirectly – through supply itself. In addition, some needs, demands or rights were so thoroughly stifled by the conditions prevailing in pre-socialist societies (in Hungary, the right to health, to education, to rest, etc.) that they are hard to revive without some affirmative action. In a more general way, some needs which are vital if people's chances in life are to be improved either in physical or in social terms may not be recognized as such because they would require a kind of long-term rationality the basis of which has been eliminated by the given socio-economic circumstances. Free availability combined, in rare cases, with legal compulsion – primary schools, vaccinations, some screening examinations – is effective in stimulating use. Thus it may be considered as some kind of 'affirmative action'.

That people do not appreciate free 'gifts' may be true to some extent. But the only real test would be to withdraw free availability and to watch what happens. I hope that no such tests will be tried out in any country on any substantial scale to support my assumption. The assumption is that people may not be

19. Tibor Liska, 'A bérlakás kereskedelem koncepciója' (The Trade of Rented Flats), *Valóság*, 1969, No. 1.

aware all the time of the advantages of free services, but in fact they are deeply appreciative of them.

Wastages certainly do occur, although not only with free goods. Vance Packard accumulated enough examples to show that highly industrialized societies produced lots of waste,[20] not to speak of the squandering of human resources which accompanies job-fragmentation, unemployment and the rest. But even if we concentrate on free goods, we have to acknowledge that losses due to their being free may be much less than losses occurring if they were not, such as uncured illnesses or other unmet needs. Unfortunately – or perhaps fortunately – the two types of losses are incommensurable.

The most difficult question is the socially unequal outcome of the benefits. No doubt, the above logic – what would happen if there were no free services and nothing to encourage people to use them – can be applied here too. I assume, and at least historical evidence largely supports this assumption, that inequalities in the use of health, education, child-care and other services would be a great deal larger if they were not free. It may be objected that in this case the 'natural' tastes and preferences of people would come to the fore, so that their degree of subjective satisfaction would be greater. The argument is clearly circular because I was also assuming that the hierarchy of needs of the more deprived strata was not 'natural' but historically distorted and that deliberate intervention to change this pattern was legitimate and necessary. It may be added that if the funds now channelled to meet existing but perforce unevenly distributed needs (whether to provide for children or to have a surgical operation) were to be distributed among everybody (equally or according to work or in any other way), then everyone's standards would be slightly raised, but special loads would be much harder, sometimes impossible to bear.

The assumption that more market forces would introduce more inequality is no excuse, however, for the unintended operation of benefits in kind. I have already emphasized that a socially more equal utilization could be promoted, first of all,

20. Vance Packard, *The Wastemakers*, Longmans, Green, 1961.

by a substantial increase in the capacity of equipment and services. But it was also suggested that more social priorities should and could be introduced in the allocation of scarce resources. And this is where the problem of universal and selective distribution comes in.

7.5.2 *Universalism or selectivity?*

This dichotomy is misleading inasmuch as it implies that there are only two types of redistributive principles – benefits for all, or benefits only for the poor, based on means tests. It has repeatedly been pointed out by Titmuss, Townsend, Kahn and others[21] that groups in special need can be selected and can be offered services and benefits without such drawbacks of the means tests as stigmatization, self-selection, bureaucratic procedures and the danger of the services themselves becoming poor. I must add here that because universal schemes are costly and may not serve the intended aims, the necessity for means-tested benefits and services continues to crop up again and again in Hungary, but this is a scattered minority view, without any serious impact.

The usual criteria for the selection of groups with special needs have long been youth or old age, and handicap or illness. All of them are demographic rather than social criteria. Therefore all of them, though obviously legitimate bases for sharing if the right to survive is taken seriously, promote redistribution mainly across different stages of the life cycle and only accidentally or marginally across classes or socio-occupational groups (if for instance workers or the poor tend to have more children than others).

It has to be made clear that if we want to achieve more than redistribution within classes according to demographic criteria, then we must accept other criteria of selection. In other words a redistributive effect is likely to occur along a selected dimension

21. Richard M. Titmuss, 'Choice and the "Welfare State" ', in *Commitment to Welfare*, op. cit.; Peter Townsend, *Sociology and Social Policy*, op. cit., p. 136 and passim; Alfred J. Kahn, *Theory and Practice of Social Planning*, Russell Sage Foundation, New York, 1969, p. 200 and passim.

only if special and deliberate efforts are made to channel its action to groups which are worse off on the same dimension. If there are no criteria of selection along social (or class) lines, then universal services will be utilized disproportionately by better-off groups (better-off in terms of money, power, knowledge, connections, 'marketable skills', etc.). The uneven utilization may be aggravated if the right is universal but the capacity of accommodation insufficient, or if the same service operates with varied standards.

In the last few decades there have been signs in many Western countries that this assumption is at work (though perhaps it has never been formulated so crudely). As a consequence 'affirmative action', or 'positive discrimination', or priorities have been applied sometimes in favour of women, or of blacks in the United States, or of some other minority groups, or disadvantaged regions. These criteria, or the disadvantages counteracted by them, are only indirectly related to the social structure (the basic social relations). This means that the basic social inqualities are present – though maybe on a reduced scale – within the target groups (women, or blacks, or localities). As a consequence, whenever one happens to check the impact of the affirmative action, one will inevitably find that the members of the target group profit unequally from the advantage offered to them. (For instance, the difference between the rates of study in higher education for boys and girls will decrease, but the reduction of sexual disadvantage will be much more marked for better-off than for worse-off groups.)

The socialist countries are to my knowledge the only ones up to now which have introduced among their criteria of selection the 'class bias' in some spheres of social and societal policy. The application of the class criterion has been most consistent in higher education. It was applied for a while to give priority in social benefits to workers and employees against all other classes or groups (peasants and other self-employed groups). Recently, it has begun to be applied in favour of workers only, in other spheres such as the allocation of flats and sometimes of places in kindergartens and nurseries. In addition, the income test without the means test is applied fairly extensively, for example in fixing the tariffs for children's institutions, for subsidized holidays or in defining the level of educational grants. (The income test without the means test signifies that the applicants, usually both parents, make a declaration of their earnings, signed by the employer, and no subsequent check is applied.)

The class criterion and the income criterion do, no doubt, have drawbacks. Both run against the work-incentive built into wages, but this cannot be accepted as a valid counter-argument from a socialist perspective (though the extent can be debated). In addition, priority given to workers and peasants (or their children) in education may undermine the self-esteem of the 'privileged'. Moreover, preference given to workers may arouse anger in other groups and therefore weaken solidarity among social groups.

It seems to me, however – and the data about redistribution of all kinds of social advantages confirm this feeling – that the real problem does not stem from the application of the 'class bias', but from its being applied inconsistently, or with clumsy social techniques – and sometimes without a firm conviction that it has to be done. It is another problem – one to which there is no answer valid once and for all – to decide in what spheres and in what ways the class or socio-occupational criterion should be applied. The most difficult problem in this connection is how to favour a class or various social groups without discriminating against any of the other groups.

Priority given to selected social groups or to lower-income groups in the access to services raises the issue of the quality of these services. One has, in fact, to face the problem of whether there is a danger that 'service for the disadvantaged will become disadvantaged services'. It is in this context that the issue of parallel – market and non-market – services comes up.

7.5.3 *The duality of market and non-market, of collective and private solutions*

It is usually assumed that there are three patterns in the allocation of goods and services: market allocation alone; market and non-market allocation operating parallel to one another; and exclusively non-market allocation.

In capitalist countries, market distribution is prevalent in the majority of goods and services, although essentially marketed goods may be complemented by non-market elements like food-stamps, baby clothes, subsidized meals, school milk and the like. With goods allocated mainly through the market, it is usually true that the non-market allocation benefits primarily the poor, and, more often than not, the poor selected by means tests.

The genuine co-existence of market and non-market mechanisms, or the domination of the non-market, is the result of a long process, through which the non-market distribution has slowly gained ground and overall legitimacy, so that it is slowly accepted by all social groups including those who are not poor. For the time being, and overlooking considerable variations among countries, it seems – still in the case of capitalist societies – that it is only in housing that market and non-market elements may be strong simultaneously, while, with the exception of the United States, the market mechanism is weaker than the non-market in health and educational services. In some countries and for some services the market element may be entirely excluded from these services, although there are continuous and sometimes successful endeavours to bring it back.

In Hungary, the three patterns continue to exist, with rather different content and connotations. There are still goods and services which are most purchased (or allocated through the market, but a market which is already 'interfered with'), and for some of them there is also a genuine non-market (partly or entirely free) allocation. This duality exists with children's milk, and with subsidized meals for children and employed people, and used to exist with 'stamps for baby clothes' – now a cash benefit. The difference is that all of them are universal for the target groups – no means test is applied. (In the case of children's school meals some criteria of selection may be applied if the capacity is too small for all the children. Preference may be given to children of working mothers, or of workers in general, or an income test may be applied as a criterion to exclude the best-off.)

Market and non-market elements both have significant weight in housing, in transportation (private cars and very heavily subsidized public transport co-exist), in holiday opportunities, in the care provided for very young children (private nurseries are allowed to operate on a small scale) and some similar services. The allocation of the non-market facilities is marked by the problems discussed in connection with benefits in kind. Transport forms an obvious exception: one opts out of public transport if one has the means for a private car.

For the most basic services – health, including dentistry, education at all levels, kindergartens – the market mechanism is officially excluded. Some duality, is, however, officially or semi-officially reintroduced in the health service in a specific way: it is allowed to operate within, or on the margins of, the non-market system. Thus all physicians and dentists must have a full-time job within the national health system, but they may have some private, paying practice. Since the health service is genuinely universal, this means that the private practice complements the basic or more expensive treatments, or helps to avoid some queuing-up. The semi-official 'market' means tips offered to the health personnel, a specific and difficult question discussed in some detail in Chapter 8.

Having enumerated some instances where a dual system exists, I shall consider more theoretically why duality offers a viable solution in some cases and why it has – or had – to be rejected in others. Let me add that if the non-paying system always had standards identical to or higher than the paying one, the question would not arise, and of course in the ideal situation, where the non-paying service would be sufficiently large *and* of high standards, the private solution would cease to be relevant. (There are no absolute standards for high quality. The criterion of adequate standards is that the public, non-market facilities are attractive enough to compete successfully with the available individual market solutions.)

In reality, however, duality in the provision may easily result in dual standards – which are worse in the collective solution, at least in some segments of it. This danger is certainly increased if the selection of target groups according to income or class is very strong. I take this eventuality into account when spelling out the social implications of parallel solutions and maintain that despite it parallelism may be encouraged in some fields.

Duality, it seems to me, may be encouraged on two conditions. The first is if the need in question is so elementary, so unavoidable, that, if the costs of the individual solution are prohibitive, the collective solution will have to be used, but where the quality of the service does not play a decisive role in shaping the life of the user. A case in point is public transport. Life is of course easier and pleasanter if the means and conditions of public transport are agreeable and comfortable, but lower standards do not necessarily entail lasting harm or far-reaching disadvantages. The opposite holds, for instance, for services in child care, education and health care, where low standards cause lasting harm.

The second condition is that the need which may be covered in a dual way is not basic at all. In this case the life of the individual is not profoundly affected if the particular need does not occur to him for a while, or if it is not covered for a while. The coverage of such needs is optional, so that, if the collective solution is not attractive enough, the worst possible outcome is that the needs in question are not awakened or that the facilities provided are not used at all. No doubt, for the sake of a colourful, creative way of life and of the lessening of social distances, the awakening and the coverage of such needs as sports, recreation or the simplification of some household tasks is desirable and should be encouraged. But no lasting and irreversible harm is caused by the non-utilization of the service or by its socially differentiated use. Progress is simply rather slower than it could be. Again, the opposite holds for health, education and maybe even housing, where under-utilization of facilities or the absence of demands cause lasting and irreversible harm.

Thus, theoretically at least, *duality* of market and non-market solutions must be rejected in the case of basic and elementary needs where the quality of the service is vital for the physical or social life chances of the individual.

The market solution may be acceptable even in these cases if one can be reasonably sure that the need will be covered, even if the service is not free. This seems to apply to food primarily. That is why the 'food-stamp' scheme is not accepted in Hungary. The only direct intervention in nutrition is the heavily subsidized milk delivered to pregnant mothers and small children in urban settings. This measure, however, though quite popular and helpful in encouraging the consumption of milk, is more a remnant of the period when the milk supply was defective than a genuine social policy priority. (It is often criticized, partly on the grounds that it is obsolete, partly because it is an urban privilege. It is hard to suppress because acquired rights are considered inviolable. Thus it may be extended to the countryside – but the issue is not yet settled.)

For other elementary needs where quality counts the only adequate solution is the exclusive role of the non-market, collective system. This holds for all the institutions which intervene in a substantial way in the process of socialization of the child, and for all types of health care.

There is an apparent contradiction between two principles formulated here. I have emphasized that workers or low-income groups must be given priority and must be more strongly encouraged to use the services than others. If there are shortcomings in the quality or quantity of the service, the consistent application of this principle means that better-off groups may be forced out of the non-market system. I have affirmed, on the other hand, that the needs in question are so vital that they must be covered for everybody, all the more so because the present-day socialist system does not want to harm deliberately or to reject any of the existing classes or strata. Therefore in practice two compromises are made.

One is to accept – tacitly, or marginally, or even in a semi-legal way – the duality. This happens in early child care, and in some domains of the health service. I would venture to affirm that this compromise is better than the open and official acceptance of the duality as far as the future of the service is concerned. In a way, the solution does not exist (officially), or inasmuch as it exists it usually works at the expense of better-off and more influential groups. Therefore there is a strong pressure to improve the official collective solution.

The other compromise is to force out the most privileged groups, though perhaps only temporarily. This happens in higher education where second and third chances are offered in the collective system, but *no* paying or individual solution exists.

In fact, there is a third probability – which happens more often than desirable – and this is that the social priorities are not consistently enforced.

Although it is difficult to draw conclusions from what has been said in this chapter, one conclusion can be affirmed without hesitation:

The system of centralized redistribution is an important element of social affairs in a socialist society. If it functions adequately, it contributes to the realization of the long-term goals of societal policy, because it may have a considerable impact on basic social relations. At the same time, it is an important means of solving, in the short term, a great number of acute social problems. It is of great importance, from both aspects, to make the system socially more effective, and to bring its practical operation more in line with its theoretical principles.

Part Four

The Human Use of Goods

Chapter 8

Consumption

The last two chapters of this book are devoted to the final stage of the cycle of reproduction. The material content of this stage consists of the consumption of goods and services. *What* is consumed? This is the question we are concerned with in this chapter.

In the first decades of the creation of socialism in Hungary the tasks of social and societal policy in relation to consumption seemed fairly clear. The explicit goals were to cover the basic needs of the whole population; to assure regular improvement; to prevent extreme differentiation in consumption and, by doing this, to prevent the tensions generated by excessive inequality in this field. It was always emphasized that medical care was included among the basic needs, so that a universal health service had to be built up. It was also an important tenet that man's needs are not only material: the harmonious development of the personality requires a high cultural level so that the policy of consumption had to ensure the availability of all kinds of cultural goods and services.

These postulates were not formulated on a high theoretical level, but rather as rules of thumb directly ensuing from the general theory of a socialist society. It did not seem necessary at that time to define in detail these 'basic needs' – food, shelter and some clothing seemed to exhaust the concept.

If the attainment of these goals was not automatically ensured, societal policy had to intervene. Thus the liberal capitalist standpoint on consumer sovereignty and market forces as the main or sole regulators of consumption was never considered a viable solution.

Intervention seemed to be warranted on at least two grounds. First, despite the deliberate reduction in income inequalities the lower-income groups would have met with serious difficulties in covering even their basic needs if prices had followed the laws of the market. Therefore prices had to be adjusted so as to prevent this. Second, the coverage of certain needs considered as essential by central authorities could not be or would not have been financed out of normal incomes. In some cases – for instance, long illnesses or expensive treatment – the costs would have been prohibitive for the majority of those affected by such problems. More generally, health and cultural opportunities had to be assured as of right. These goods and services, however, never occurred to people as elementary needs or basic priorities because the majority was forcefully discouraged from using them before the Second World War. So if these services had remained paying, their use would have been left to the historically determined, highly divergent initiative of individuals. This would have entailed in social terms an extremely unequal utilization of the services in question. Therefore all those goods and services where equal accessibility was considered desirable had to be made practically free or at least inexpensive in order to stimulate utilization and awaken the needs in question.

Thus, deliberate central intervention took two main forms: a price policy fitting the above aims and complementing the incomes policy, and the widening of the frameworks of free or nearly free social services (health and culture in the first place). Both steps achieved their basic aims, as will be shown in the next sections. Nevertheless, the problems of the orientation of consumption which originally appeared to be transparently simple proved to be rather intricate in practice. In the course of development a number of dilemmas emerged.

The coverage of basic needs sounded a simple task at first. But the difficulties of defining what these needs are at any given moment are obviously innumerable. They are historically shifting and increasing with improving economic conditions. As it happens, insufficient knowledge of the changing needs and aspirations of those concerned, combined with the predominance of more or less well-understood economic interests and the specific group values of those directly participating in decision-making, had introduced quite important biases in the coverage of basic needs. In this connection the most serious problems emerged in the sphere of housing conditions, which will be treated separately in section 8.3. The overall results in the sphere of consumption will be described in section 8.4.

The adequate shaping of the prices policy also raised a number of problems. These dilemmas – connected mainly with the frequent contradiction between economic rationality and the attainment of social goals – will be discussed in section 8.1. Others related to the subsidization of services are treated in section 8.2.

The problems currently experienced and the main results of the policy on consumption will be presented in this chapter. The more general and more fundamental issues connected with further development and with the definition of socialist welfare will be taken up in the final chapter.

8.1 The regulation of prices

The role of the prices policy in orienting consumption is a complex and far-reaching issue. It is at present probably the most contested element in the whole battery of social policy instruments. The theoretical and operational aspects of the prices policy as well as its historical evolution since 1945 have by now been analysed in a number of Hungarian studies.[1] The debates about the functions of the price system have been especially lively since the mid-sixties.

In the prices policy, and in the debates about it, emphasis was laid on the producers' prices, and whether their primary role was to orient productive processes, to provide the interested parties with economic information, or to transmit political and other preferences to the sphere of production. The first role, the orientation of production, was obviously rejected along with the concept – and the reality – of a self-regulating market. The second role of giving information would have been important, but for a number of political and historical reasons producers'

1. For example Béla Csikós-Nagy, 'A Historic Overview on Hungarian Price Policy', *Gazdaság*, 1975, 1.

prices for a long time expressed the real productive processes and relations inadequately. The economic reform made significant endeavours to restore the economic role of prices. It was realized that prices should give information to producers and managers and therefore the almost exclusively centralized system of the definition of prices was made more flexible. Nevertheless, even after this change deliberate social and economic policy preferences continued to be built into the prices, but the scope of these elements was considerably reduced.

The regulation of consumer prices was for a long time treated almost independently from that of producers' prices. If there was any 'economic' element in the regulation of consumer prices, it was the consequence of some centrally defined political or economic aim, such as the harsh treatment of the peasantry at the beginning of the fifties or the forwarding of the interests of forced industrialization in those same years. Thus, both sets of prices were regulated arbitrarily, but the costs of production were not taken into account in setting the consumer prices.

The first centrally regulated consumer price system after the war, introduced in 1946, changed the pre-war price relations in order to assure, at least for workers and employees, the coverage of basic needs. According to the first detailed price statistics relating to 1949, the price level of foods as compared to 1938 was multiplied by 5 to 7, prices of clothing by 7 to 8, those of services, including rent and fuel, by 1·5 to 3·5. The preferences given to culture and health already had some effect at this time, but not very consistently. The price reform of 1951 introduced more rigidity in the regulation of production as well as that of prices. In the case of consumer prices, it tried to remedy the shortage of consumer goods by reintroducing food rationing and increasing food prices. This measure was followed, as has already been shown, by the drop in the real incomes of workers and employees.

From the mid-fifties up to the economic reform in 1968 the whole economic situation, as well as the living standards of the population, steadily improved. There were no significant changes in the price system, only some *ad hoc* adjustments. The overall price level increased by less than 10 per cent between 1953 and 1968.

The economic reform changed the basis for calculating consumer prices. It re-established a connection between the prices of production and those of consumption. The former system of preferences and penalties – favouring basic needs, penalizing luxuries, etc. – was however maintained, by means of indirect taxes (sales taxes and subsidies of consumer prices) operating, from 1968 on, at the level of wholesale trade. The original price, paid by the wholesaler, is determined by the costs of

Table 8/1: The rates of difference between the prices of production and those of consumption, by main groups of consumer goods, in %, 1968

	Turnover taxes (+)	Subsidies (−)
Basic foods		−18
meat		−29
milk and dairy products		−44
fats		−10
Other foods	+ 6	
Beverages, tobacco	+38	
Catering		−16
Clothing	+26	
Technological appliances	+30	
Toiletries	+30	
Cosmetics	+42	
Fuel		−55
Building materials	+ 8	
Pharmaceuticals		−28
Transport, communication		−34
Industrial and personal services		−35
Communal services		−54
Cultural services		−19

production (plus profit), but the retail trade uses the taxed or subsidized prices in its purchases and sales. The total amount of taxes and subsidies is practically the same, the net profits being realized at the place of production.

The consumer price system was also made more flexible in 1968. Instead of all prices being centrally regulated as before, four categories were introduced, namely centrally fixed prices, prices centrally fixed within defined limits, maximized prices, and free prices. The percentage shares of these categories within total consumption were (in 1970) respectively, 20, 28, 30 and 22 per cent.[2]

The price system, by and large, had the intended effects on consumption (see section 8.4.). It complemented personal income distribution. According to the calculations of the Hungarian Central Statistical Office, the purchasing power of lower income groups (per capita income under 600 forints per month) was – in the mid-sixties – about 6–8 per cent higher than that of higher-income groups (with a monthly per capita income over 1,200 forints). The same difference was estimated at 15 per cent by E. Jávorka.[3] Besides its social role, the price system also served to defer the demand for some industrial products, especially durable goods, in which supply was inadequate for a long time. However, the needs for these goods arose gradually at first, and then more rapidly, so that the shortages created considerable tensions from about the mid-sixties on. They were rapidly eased after the economic reform by increased production and importation, and also by decreases in prices and by financial facilities offered to purchasers (credit, purchase by instalment, etc.).

The slow movement of prices was accelerated after 1970, and especially from 1974 on. Several factors contributed to this. To begin with, some of the subsidies were originally rather large. With growing consumption, and the rising production prices of

2. *A népgazdaság irányitási rendszere* (The System of Guidance of the National Economy), op. cit., p. 69.

3. Edit Jávorka, *Életszinvonal a mai társadalomban* (Standard of Living in Present-Day Society), Kossuth, 1970, p. 345.

such goods, a considerable budgetary deficit occurred. In addition, world inflation greatly affected the Hungarian economy mainly because of the extremely important role of her foreign trade. Increased central subsidies protected the population from the immediate and spontaneous impact of the world market, but again this could only be a temporary remedy. Finally, with a rising income level former preferences and penalization seemed to become outdated.

As a consequence, the policy of gradual price changes was adopted. In order to avoid a deterioration in the situation of the population, a new compensatory technique was worked out. For each price increase which affects the majority, and where social interests require the maintenance of the level of consumption, a flat-rate compensation is given to practically everyone. Since 1971, the measure has been applied several times. In 1971, rents were increased by 115 per cent. The families affected were for a while fully reimbursed. In the case of active earners the reimbursement has been gradually lessened with each consecutive salary increase. Pensioners will get the full reimbursement up to the end of their lives. The prices of milk and dairy products were increased by 30 per cent in 1972. As a compensation, salaries, pensions, child-care grants, family allowances and study grants were increased by 50 forints a month. This increase somewhat over-compensated for losses. When the price of fuel was modified, again a monthly 50-forint compensation was built into all salaries, pensions and child-care grants. (There was no compensation when the price of alcoholic beverages was raised.) Again, with the rise of meat prices in 1976, a monthly 60-forint compensation was added to all types of personal income.

The underlying rationale of the flat-rate compensation is obvious. This is a means of reducing income differentials. According to calculations, the balance between the price increase and the compensation, the gain and the loss, was somewhat differentiated according to the composition of families and their level of income. This may be shown by the example of the milk compensation, in Table 8/2.

Table 8/2: Dairy price increases and compensation (per capita yearly sums, in forints)

	Increase in annual expenditure	Annual refund	Net annual effect on income
Workers and employees:			
Low-income group (under 9,600 forints a year)	597	1,191	+594
Medium group (14,400–19,600 forints a year)	828	620	−208
High-income group (over 28,800 forints a year)	896	311	−585
Peasants:			
Low income	360	926	+566
Medium income	489	563	+ 74
High income	580	151	−439
Pensions	451	805	+354

Source: Edit Jávorka, *Árak és jövedelmek* (Prices and Incomes), Kossuth, 1973.

The consumer price system has been used, then, partly to orientate consumption, and partly to complement the policy of income distribution following the principles of central redistribution. Despite its manifest social advantages, its adequacy is questioned with increasing frequency. The arguments are partly economic, partly social.[4] One of the main arguments is that, on the existing and even more on the future income level, incomes policy must be restricted to the regulation of incomes, otherwise the concept of the distribution according to work loses its sense. From another point of view, prices must simulate the market in order to assure a social optimum. Price preferences hinder the evolution of the centrally regulated (socialist) market and disorientate production, and it is therefore preferable to substitute incomes for price subsidies, and income tax for penalization by prices.

4. Some of the economic arguments were reviewed and criticized by Róbert Hoch, 'Életszinvonal-tervezés és ártervezés' (Planning the Standard of Living, Planning the Prices), *Gazdaság*, December 1972.

The counter-argument put forward by Hoch[5] rejects the thesis that there exists a perfect market yielding a 'social optimum'. He also points out that the actual system of taxes and subsidies does not directly affect the socialist market. Finally, he shows that it is still a major task of the socialist state to protect the normal consumption of less well-off groups. Price preferences and disadvantages cannot be replaced by income measures. The target groups of the two policies will coincide only exceptionally. The two policies have separate and partly autonomous functions. This is true – to develop Hoch's arguments – not only for preferences given to basic needs, but also for cultural and health services. As for the replacement of sales taxes by income taxes, the problems stemming from the taxation of income have already been briefly discussed in Chapters 5 and 6.

The other main line of argument questions the social effectiveness of existing preferences. Several important inconsistencies are easy to detect in the system of preferences even if one consults only the concise list presented in Table 8/1, such as for example, the 'penalization' of building materials and toiletries. Also, because preferences relate to groups of goods, subsidies help not only the low-income groups but the whole population. (For example, beef is subsidized as much as pork or even more, although pork is much more popular in low-income groups.) Therefore attempts are being made, on the basis of more detailed calculations, to revise the income-redistributive effect of the present price system. One study[6] questioned the accuracy of earlier calculations and showed that the full effect was contrary to the intended redistributive aim. According to the author of this study, low-income groups have profited even less than those with higher incomes from the system of preferences. He also pointed out that the present system was permeated by illogical traditional elements, such as the heavy taxation of tea, which was a luxury item before the war but

5. op. cit.
6. János Ladányi, 'Fogyasztói árak és szociálpolitika' (Consumer Prices and Social Policy), *Valóság*, 1975, No. 12.

which has recently become a widespread beverage. He acknowledged that the actual methods of price regulation guarantee some protection to the population against inflationary tendencies, but did not see this as a sufficient justification for these methods. He was therefore of the opinion that social aims would be better served by the gradual adjustment of consumer prices to the prices of production.

Both economic and social arguments are at least partly convincing. A price system which is cut off from its economic foundations may lead to wastage and hence shortages of seemingly cheap products, or to a low level of production and hence, again, to shortages in overpriced goods where demand is not stimulating production. Moreover, the system of preferences and penalization may not serve the declared social aims very well because of the inadvertent operation of particular group interests. Similarly, it is true that some preferences or penalizations have already become obsolete or never were consistent. Finally, the role of prices policy in assuring that basic needs are covered loses some of its importance with the rise in income level.

Nevertheless, before accepting the conclusion in favour of 'market prices', one has to take into consideration the counter-arguments already mentioned and also the fact that the abolition of the present price system would have fairly grave side-effects, not to mention the difficulties of compensation in the case of a wholesale price reform. Therefore, while the actual discrepancies between production and consumption prices may be excessive and may need to be reduced, the main elements of the present price system should be retained for a reasonable time. The system of preferences and penalizations will have to be gradually revised so as to eliminate present inconsistencies and social biases. In other words, they have to be restricted to cases in which a general social interest may be clearly and more or less unambiguously defined and applied. In this sense price preferences only complement the system of social benefits in kind, as they follow almost the same logic. This is especially true for goods and services serving health or culture – needs which are unevenly present in the various social groups but the coverage of which has to be made more or less independent of the market power of individuals. Also, price penalizations, if judiciously applied, may effectively help to reorientate consumption in a way consistent with socially desirable goals.

8.2 Priorities given to culture and health

8.2.1 *Culture*

The importance of a more equal distribution of knowledge, information and 'culture' in general has already been stressed in several different contexts. I have also emphasized that the process is long and difficult. Direct stimulation of cultural consumption is ineffectual. The naïve optimism of the first post-revolutionary years, the view that as soon as financial barriers were removed 'culture' would belong to everybody, certainly proved to be unfounded. Nevertheless, the democratization of culture is – as witnessed by statistics on buying and reading books, etc. – somewhat eased if the pursuit of 'culture' does not require heavy financial sacrifices. The conclusion is that cultural goods and services cannot be considered as commodities: the logic of the market has to be rejected in their case.

The subsidization of cultural goods and services out of collective funds is, no doubt, loaded with contradictions. The main users of these goods and services (from books to higher education) are actually those social groups that are better off in economic as well as in cultural terms. Thus, they profit more from these subsidies than any other group. This outcome is contrary to one of the aims of socialist redistribution – that it must be socially redistributive. To avoid this distortion while maintaining the non-market principle in culture, a selective system of cultural subsidies had to be introduced, which again is contrary to some basic tenets and poses the threat of excessive bureaucracy. A choice has to be made, then, between three unsatisfactory solutions: universal subsidies, selective subsidies and no subsidies. The present choice – universal subsidization –

is made in the hope that it will serve a basic long-term goal which, when achieved, will automatically remove the existing dysfunctional aspects, while the other solutions would only aggravate the existing cultural gaps.

As for what the culture in question actually includes, uncertainties are more pronounced in this respect. It is by and large universally accepted in Hungary that the majority of the products of so-called high culture are not to be rejected on the grounds that this was the culture of the former ruling classes, but must be made – potentially at least – accessible to practically everyone. This means the removal of social obstacles to these products. At the same time, the products of so-called mass-culture or even of low culture, which give immediate pleasure to many, must not be discriminated against. The limits of this tolerance are set by products with an anti-socialist or anti-human content – disseminating pornography or the culture of violence, etc. The uncertainty evoked above signifies that – since in judging cultural products aesthetic criteria are always arbitrary, that is socially biased – it may always be disputed whether a given object of culture belongs to a category to be supported without restraint or to one on the verge of acceptability. (These debates woudl probably be less acute if the subsidies in question did not weigh heavily on the common funds.)

With the encouragement and subsidization of all kinds of active cultural practices we are on somewhat firmer ground. These activities, besides being pleasurable, usually serve the unfolding of the individual's abilities and the development of personality. The necessity to support them is hardly contested.

The basic facts about the level and the distribution of social benefits in kind have already been described, but I wish to add some information about the financial aspects and the overall trends of evolution of these services, especially as regards education and health.

From 1970 to 1975, about 7 per cent of the state budget served educational or cultural aims (around 85 thousand million forints over the five years). Of this sum, 77 per cent was allocated to education, 20 per cent to cultural institutions and 3 per cent to sport.[7] The overall increase was considerable throughout the years, but the uneven rate of growth of the various subsidies reflects a changing system of preferences.

Table 8/3: The yearly subsidy from the state budget, calculated for one user of the given service (in forints)

	1970	1974	1974/70 %
One child in a day nursery	13,127	17,827	136
One child in kindergarten	4,379	5,606	128
One child in primary school	2,713	4,618	170
One child in secondary school (day course)	5,878	9,140	155
One student in higher education (day course)	29,367	33,063	112
One theatre ticket (on average)[a]	28	39	140
One cinema ticket (on average)[a]	5	4	80
One book (on average)[a]	2	3	150

Source: A lakosság életszinvonala 1970–1975 (The Living Standard of the Population), Central Statistical Office, Budapest, 1976.
[a] In some of these cases the subsidy varies greatly according to different categories. In the case of books, for instance, works popularizing science or general knowledge as well as almost all types of fiction are heavily subsidized, while detective fiction sells at a rather high price. It should be added that the former, cheaper books are mostly hard-cover and detective fiction almost exclusively paperback.

The improving standards shown by the figures above have not yet eliminated all the inadequacies in education services. The provision of primary schools was for a long time less adequate than that of other institutions, and even now the major problem in this sphere is that the schools in the villages and on the outskirts of cities are relatively less well built and less well equipped than others. They are to become the priority target of educational policy for the next period of development.

7. *A lakosság életszinvonala 1970–1975* (The Living Standard of the Population), Central Statistical Office, Budapest, 1976.

In the field of 'cultural consumption' progress has been spectacular in most branches, justifying financial sacrifices. It is only in the last few years that some cultural activities have shown a regression, in connection with the spread of TV. This regression is, however, far from universal and really only affects the cinema. The spectacular increases in many fields (books, theatre, museums, etc.) suggest that the practice is slowly (sometimes rapidly) spreading to strata other than the best-off.

Table 8/4: Data on cultural consumption

	1950	1960	1970	1975
Number of books published, in millions	20	35	47	74
Newspapers and periodicals, in millions	475	705	1,101	1,249
Visits to theatres, in millions	3·0	6·4	5·6	6·2
Visits to cinemas, in millions	47	140	80	74
Visits to museums, in millions	—	3·6	7·1	11·9
Visits to recreational and cultural centres, cultural programmes	—	10·9[a]	6·8	7·9
Radio owners at the end of the year, in millions	0·6	2·2	2·5	2·5
TV owners at the end of the year, in millions	—	0·1	1·7	2·4
Members of amateur groups, in thousands	—	299[a]	195	223

Source: Hungarian Statistical Yearbooks, 1974 and 1975.
[a] 1962.

8.2.2 *Health*

It is an undisputed basic principle that the conditions for a healthy way of life must be built up. One element of this provision is the development of health services that may be used whether the patient can afford to pay or not. Another is the encouragement of physical exercise or sport. A third is the spread of more wholesome nutritional habits. This last point is particularly relevant in Hungary, where traditional Hungarian cooking was based on the diet of a poor agricultural population. It was, and still is, rich in carbohydrates and fats, poor in vitamins and proteins.

The structure of food consumption is mainly affected by the prices policy already described and to be treated in the next section, so I shall not discuss it here. There are also other means of indirectly influencing diets, such as offering in all public institutions meals which follow the principles of a healthy diet. This opportunity is, unfortunately, not well used. As experiences in canteens show, one reason is, to some extent, that an entirely different cooking strategy from the one people are used to at home is not popular with the users. The major reason is, however, financial. Moreover, a healthier diet requires more time and more energy, and up to now this task has not been a major priority.

Health services are free and universal, with a 100 per cent coverage since the Social Security Act of 1975. Quantitative data show significant though somewhat uneven progress. The number of physicians per 10,000 inhabitants was 11 in 1950, 15·7 in 1960, 22·8 in 1970 and 25·1 in 1974. The last rate is among the highest on an international scale. The number of hospital beds for 10,000 inhabitants increased from 55·8 in 1950 to 71·1 in 1960, and 85·5 in 1974. The latter ratio corresponds to a medium level in a cross-cultural perspective.

Free access is stimulating utilization to a certain extent. Data on the frequencies quoted below were not available for other countries, but it is probably true that with a population of ten million, yearly figures of 132 million outpatient visits, 1·8 million hospitalized cases and 145 million medical prescriptions are high.[8] Preventive services are functioning well for tuberculosis, with 7·4 million chest examinations a year. As a consequence, tuberculosis has ceased to be one of the major killers as it was before the war: the number of deaths caused by TB was around 14,000 in 1938, around 1,600 in 1974.

Qualitative aspects are less reassuring. The regional dis-

8. *Társadalmi szolgáltatások 1960–1971* (Social Services 1960–71), Central Statistical Office, Budapest, 1972. Data in the text refer to 1971.

tribution of health services is far from satisfactory. General practitioners are readily available nearly everywhere, but specialized services are hard to obtain in villages and even in smaller towns. Outpatients clinics are frequently overcrowded and this results in long waits or in examinations which are often perfunctory. Some services, for example those dealing with mental illness, have long been neglected (according to recent information, mental health services are to receive priority in coming years.) Social medicine is in its infancy, and so is prevention – other than for cancer and tuberculosis. Along with the over-utilization of some services and especially drugs, under-utilization in a social sense also occurs in the form of delayed medical examinations, the neglect or misuse of drugs, etc., which in their turn aggravate health troubles.

The health service operates on a district basis with panel doctors and district outpatient clinics. Hospitals also have their catchment areas except for emergencies and special illnesses. Besides the district system, there is a network of doctors attached to the workplaces. School children have regular medical and dental screening examinations and special medical care offered by school medical officers. These arrangements introduce some flexibility and solve some of the problems stemming from the lack of free choice of doctors. Free choice is not accepted because, given the socially unequal distribution of knowledge and information on the one hand, of medical services on the other, there cannot be genuine free choice, and also because it might lead to bottlenecks. The lack of free choice leads, however, to various other problems. The patient may lack confidence in a doctor whom he did not choose. He will try, therefore, to establish a more personal relationship, and obtain more careful services by offering gifts, giving tips to the doctor, or by looking for private paying consultations. These solutions are in blatant contradiction of the principle of a free health service. Various propositions have been put forward to avoid this. Many of them concluded by proposing as a solution the large-scale institutionalization of a dual system, part paying, part free. The experiences of other countries as well as logic suggest that official duality is conducive to extremely serious social consequences, initially a deterioration of the free services and eventually selection. The remedy, then, seems to be worse than the malady and so proposals for a dual health service were not accepted. The only real solution is the improvement of all the elements of the system, including a wage increase for doctors and for the health service personnel in general, which would eliminate the need to search for exceptional care or to seek for personal advantages.

8.3 Housing

Good housing conditions are a prerequisite for a healthy and cultured way of life, not to mention a comfortable family life. The absolute priority of housing among the needs to be covered has been undisputed since about the mid-sixties. But the issue was neglected for too long. As a consequence, of all the aspects of the quality of life the housing problem has been dealt with least satisfactorily.

The inherited housing stock was initially poor: the majority of pre-war flats consisted of one room and a kitchen. Amenities were scarce, overcrowding frequent and rents high. This stock was then heavily damaged during the war. In the first decade after the war the most urgent reconstructions were carried out, but there were no new housing projects. In the first five-year plan (1950–54) the least well achieved target was in the construction of flats. Of the 127,000 flats planned – already a modest provision – less than half were completed. The main improvement in this period was the declaration of the right to housing, combined with the prohibition of eviction and the enforcement of low rents. But the right in itself could not solve the problem of those who did not have flats, except for the compulsory introduction of co-tenancy affecting existing large flats. It only protected those who were already tenants.

The second decade showed a slow improvement. But it was only the fourth five-year plan (1971–5) which recognized housing as a high priority. Insufficient resources and an inadequate technological level still represent obstacles, but progress is certainly far more rapid than ever before. The present rate of construction (around 9 flats per 1,000 inhabitants) is about average among the advanced industrialized countries, whereas in earlier years Hungary was at the very bottom of the international scale.

The new housing stock is composed partly of state-owned and rented flats and mainly of private or semi-private (co-operative) constructions. Housing co-operatives enjoy the most favourable credit terms, but credit is assured to other private schemes, too. Rents, as already mentioned, were increased in 1971, but are still comparatively low. By contrast, the construction of family houses or the purchase of flats constructed by state enterprises is rather expensive, and prices are still rising. Thus a new differentiation is introduced between tenants and new owners. Family budget data for 1974 shows that households in the process of building houses (these may be second homes – data are not broken down according to this criterion) spend more than 30 per cent of all their expenditure on housing, including light and heating, as opposed to the 10 per cent of tenants and owners of existing properties. This means that those who undertake to build a house have to make economies and sacrifices in all possible fields: they usually decide to build or buy a house not because they have all the means or because they prefer this solution to any other, but because that is the only way to get accommodation quickly. Another drawback to this situation is the increasing amount of privately owned housing, which is a dubious advantage in social terms. The housing stock becomes rigid since it is more difficult to sell an old and buy a new flat than to rent another one. Private ownership and scarcity together open up a vast field for speculation. Inequalities of wealth also set in with private flats and houses, creating problems, in particular those to do with inheritance. But the main problem is that low-income families have scarcely any chance of improving their living conditions. More precisely, before the 1971 regulations the distribution of state-owned flats followed the social situation and merit of the

Table 8/5: Data on housing conditions in Hungary

Year	Stock of flats in thousands	New flats per 1,000 inhabitants	Number of persons per 100 rooms[a]	Percentage of				Percentage of flats with			
				1 room flats	3 and more room flats	1 room flats	3 and more room flats	lava-tory	elect-ricity	lava-tory	elect-ricity
				within the whole stock		within the newly constructed flats		within the whole stock		within the newly constructed flats	
1938	—	2·5	257[b]	—	—	62	10	—	—	34	—
1949	2,385	2·4[c]	259	66	5	60	3	11	48	30	65
1960	2,758	5·8	250	61	7	49[d]	6[d]	18	74	50[d]	85[d]
1970	3,142	7·8	200	46	11	15[e]	19[e]	32	91	69[e]	99[e]
1971	3,201	7·3	195	45	11	10	26	33	92	78	99
1972	3,255	8·7	191	44	11	8	30	35	93	80	100
1975	3,472	—	162	38[f]	16[f]	8	33	40[f]	94[f]	89	99

Source: Hungarian Statistical Yearbooks, 1938, 1960, 1971, 1974.

[a] Not including kitchens.

[b] 1941.

[c] 1951.

[d] 1956–60.

[e] 1966–70.

[f] 1973.

claimant more than actual needs.[9] Since this regulation, priority must be given in distributing council flats to large families (three or more children) and to workers, and the conditions governing state loans for private construction have been eased – which again helps to solve the problem. Nevertheless, the number of newly constructed rented flats is still insufficient to cover all the needs and the social 'importance' of the claimant still plays a role. Also, even if loans are less expensive, building a dwelling still requires enormous effort and sacrifices.

One element in the social handling of the housing problem delayed and in some measure still delays its solution. This is the ambiguous attitude public officials have towards housing needs. It has never been clarified whether good living conditions were to be considered as basic and universal needs; as rewards which were to be distributed according to merit; or as a luxury. Or rather, all three considerations have been variously applied, according to the concrete situation. As a consequence, housing is sometimes considered a social benefit, sometimes a subsidized commodity and sometimes purely a market commodity.

This confusion has historical roots. M. Halbwachs analysed workers' consumption at the beginning of this century. He showed convincingly that 'of all economic needs felt by the workers the need for housing is the least well developed'.[10] One of his explanations was that rents were so high that they choked aspirations before they could be formed. Besides 'a small surplus in expenditure allows workers to obtain the luxury of better food for a few days, while better housing requires greater and more lasting sacrifices'. The result was that the worker accepted poor living conditions as the outcome of his free choice.

Halbwachs' observations and his explanation were correct. But since then housing demands have increased in all develop-

9. György Konrád and Iván Szelényi, 'A lakáselosztás szociológiai kérdései' (The Sociological Problems of the Distribution of Flats), *Valóság*, 1969, No. 8

10. Maurice Halbwachs, *La Classe ouvrière et les niveaux de vie*, Gordon and Beach, Paris, London, New York, 1970 (originally published by Alcan, Paris, 1912), p. 445.

ing countries at a spectacular rate. I assume that this increase was greater in post-war Hungary than elsewhere, for the promises of a social revolution in general, and the policy of low rents in particular, eliminated the main factor hindering the emergence of demands, that of the impossibility of fulfilment. Aspirations were born and needs became articulated not slowly and gradually but explosively. But this process was not perceived in this way by society's leaders who acted first as if housing needs were still latent and inarticulate, and later as if they followed a gradual pattern of development. This neglect of real social needs (which, in turn, is explained by voluntarism, forced industrialization, etc.) led to the acute tension already mentioned, the extraordinary disparity between needs and their fulfilment.

The historical background explains why it was an important step forward to acknowledge housing as a legitimate basic need. It would be over-optimistic to believe that following this acknowledgement the demands already articulated will be covered at the desired rate, especially as needs are socially much less differentiated than the available means of meeting them. But improvement is already rather more rapid in the case of badly-off than better-off groups, which means that some signs of collective vertical mobility are appearing in the area of housing. In fact, the housing conditions of workers have improved more rapidly in the last decade than those of non-manuals, so that the absolute differences between them were reduced according to certain criteria. Thus the average size of flats increased, between 1960 and 1973, by 24 per cent for non-manuals, by 27 per cent within the group of agricultural workers and by 33 per cent for workers. The number of flats provided with a lavatory grew by 28, 22 and 35 per cent respectively in the above groups.[11]

It is often argued – by Hungarian economists among others[12] – that the housing shortage is due to the absence of a free and open market. One has to reckon, however, with all the unmet

11. Census and microcensus data, published by the Central Statistical Office, Budapest.

12. Tibor Liska, 'A bérlakás–kereskedelem koncepciója' (The Trade of Rented Flats), op. cit.

needs on the one hand, and current prices and real demand on the other. As a consequence, the belief in the efficiency of the market appears utterly unfounded. On the contrary, housing appears to be a clear case where an increased utilization of central funds and non-market redistribution offer the only sound solution – although this may safely coexist with a limited market.

8.4 Level and structure of consumption

Pre-war Hungary, although an agricultural country, failed to assure adequate nutrition for about one third of its population. It was therefore a major accomplishment – after some rather difficult post-war years – to achieve a satisfactory average level in food consumption relatively rapidly, at least as far as quantitive needs were concerned. The quality of nutrition is still improving, as foods of high nutritional value replace cheaper and nutritionally less valuable foods, but improvement will be slow from now on.

Table 8/6: The per capita yearly consumption (in kilogrammes) of certain foods

	The average for the years 1934–8	1955	1960	1970	1974
Meat	33·2	36·9	47·6	57·6	66·2
Milk & dairy products	102	87	114	110	119
Eggs	5·2	5·7	8·9	13·7	15
Fats	17·0	22·0	23·5	27·7	28·7
Wheat	145	150	133	124	119
Sugar	10·5	24·4	26·6	33·5	37·7
Potatoes	130	102	98	75	66

Source: Hungarian Statistical Yearbooks, 1960, 1975.

On the basis of the average level at the present time, Hungary is among the best-fed countries as far as the calorie intake and the main sources of nutrition are concerned. The only exception is in the consumption of animal protein, which is nevertheless slowly approaching an adequate level. Price preferences could be a useful way to encourage a healthier diet. But this aim, and that of helping low-income families, are somewhat contradictory. The traditionally evolved popular diet based on cereals, potatoes, animal fat and strong spices has become so habitual that there exists a 'taste culture'. If vegetable oil, greens, fruits, etc., were more heavily subsidized than the more popular foods, higher-income groups would profit much more than lower-income groups. The problem is somewhat similar to the subsidization of cultural goods or services, which also favours better-off groups. There is, however, an important difference. In the case of cultural goods, the (financially or culturally) worse-off groups are not penalized. The worst outcome is that they do not use the subsidies. This, however, does not imply that they have to pay extra for what they in fact use. In the case of food, a pattern of subsidies giving preference to healthy but unpopular foods and taking away the subsidies from the popular ones would seriously affect the budget of worse-off groups, because they would be obliged, at least for a fairly long period, while eating habits changed, to buy the non-subsidized foods.

The consumption of industrial products, including clothing, remained at a relatively low level for a longer period. Production and supply were defective and incomes too low to create a strong demand. (The wage and price policies combined to prevent the emergency of needs.) The tensions thus created were similar to those characterizing the housing situation, until the economic reform helped to solve the problem in a few years after 1967. The various deferred needs were covered relatively rapidly, first in urban settings, then, with some delay, in rural areas, too. Labour-saving devices and electric appliances were rather scarce up to the sixties. As Table 8/7 shows, the seventies really saw a leap forward in this respect. We have no comparative data for furniture but a similar rapid improvement may be inferred from sales figures. Everyday experience and market research suggest, however, that the supply of furniture is still insufficient, with a particular lack of modern pieces, which are much in demand. Variety is also poor.

Of all household durable goods only cars continue to be scarcer than in equally or more industrialized countries. This, however, is the result of a deliberate policy. The social costs and harms of motorization were already clear when the car culture reached Hungary. The spread of cars was therefore resisted for a long time, and Hungary never started to produce cars. With rising incomes and the influence of the Western way of life, however, rising aspirations could no longer be repressed.

Table 8/7: The ownership of various durable goods in households of salaried earners and peasants

	Number of appliances per 100 families							
	Workers and employees				Peasant households and dual-income households[a]			
	1960	1965	1970	1975	1960	1965	1970	1975
Radio	96	97	135	161	77	84	103	123
TV	7	50	81	94	0	13	51	80
Tape recorder, record player	12	22	35	57	1	4	9	17
Washing machine	31	59	80	90	8	34	67	85
Vacuum cleaner	8	29	57	76	0	2	15	40
Refrigerator	2	13	53	84	0	1	11	56
Water heater	3	10	23	40	0	0	3	13
Motorcycle	6	12	15	19	7	15	21	32
Car	0	3	9	22	0	1	3	10

Source: Family budget surveys of the quoted years.

[a] These are usually families living in villages with many of the old peasant attitudes although one or two members work outside agriculture.

Strongly voiced claims had to be accepted as legitimate. Subsequently, the massive importation of cars, the construction of highways, etc., began. By now it is clear that private car ownership will grow as rapidly as supply allows. Central action is limited to slowing down the increase by means of high prices, or moderately increased supplies, and to efforts to improve public transport. The aim of slow progress is to escape for as long as possible the worst features of the car-centred society, in the hope that new solutions will be worked out in the meantime – or that, with more time and money, the country may at least be better prepared for the car-culture. Up to now, however, no ways have been found to replace private cars adequately.

Table 8/8: The ownership of various durable goods in the households of manual and non-manual workers

	1964		1975		Non-manuals compared to workers (workers=1)	
	Workers	Non-manuals	Workers	Non-manuals	1964	1975
Radio	96	101	150	177	1·05	1·18
TV	39	54	93	96	1·38	1·03
Tape recorder	16	31	46	71	1·94	1·54
Washing machine	50	63	90	89	1·26	0·99
Vacuum cleaner	15	41	69	86	2·73	1·25
Refrigerator	6	16	79	90	2·67	1·14
Water heater	4	15	30	55	3·75	1·83
Motorcycle	12	10	22	14	0·83	0·64
Car	2	5	14	33	2·50	2·36

Source: Family budget data of the respective years and calculations based on this data.

In the last decade change in the ownership of durable goods was somewhat more rapid for manual workers than for non-manuals – again a small sign of collective mobility. In fact, the disappearance of the gap between the ratio of households in different groups which possessed such goods as vacuum cleaners or refrigerators suggests a convergence in some habits. The main

Table 8/9: The pattern of consumption

	1965[a]			1975		
	Workers	Peasants	Non-manuals	Workers	Peasants	Non-manuals
Average monthly net income per head, in forints	959	912	1,263	1,910	1,832	2,413
Workers =100	100	95	132	100	96	126
Percentage distribution of expenditure:						
Food, drink	47·2	54·7	42·1	40·1	44·4	34·5
Clothing	14·8	12·4	14·9	13·9	11·9	13·0
Rent, construction, light, heating	12·1	15·7	11·2	14·8	16·8	14·4
Household equipment	8·7	7·1	9·6	9·6	9·2	9·2
Health	2·1	1·2	2·8	2·5	1·7	3·2
Transport	4·5	2·3	6·2	6·9	5·1	10·8
Culture, education	5·6	2·5	6·5	5·3	3·6	6·6
Miscellaneous	5·0	4·1	6·7	6·9	7·3	8·3
Total	100·0	100·0	100·0	100·0	100·0	100·0

The indices of structural differences[b] are

between workers and peasants: 0,034 ⎫ for
between workers and   ⎬ 1965
non-manuals   0,021 ⎭

between workers and peasants: 0,020 ⎫ for
between workers and   ⎬ 1975
non-manuals   0,025 ⎭

exception is, again, cars. Motorization is spreading to workers, too, but in their case so far this means the purchase of motor-cycles, which are less expensive. Motorcycles are bought mainly in villages, where they help to make up for the scarcity of public transport.

In some habits the various groups have certainly come closer. This, however, has not affected the whole consumption pattern. More precisely, peasants have come closer to the urban way of life with the industrialization and urbanization of rural areas and the fading away of traditional agriculture. These changes affect not only the dual-income, mixed households (where there is at least one wage-earner and one peasant), but also 'pure' peasant families. Meanwhile, the structure of consumption of manuals and non-manuals has drifted farther apart. This is partly due to the slow change of some socially and culturally determined habits, including not only reading books or going to the theatre, but also, for example, nutrition. Partly, perhaps mainly, the growing differentiation is the consequence of a greater frequency of car-ownership among non-manuals. Car maintenance costs affect the family budget mainly at the expense of food, clothing and household appliances. (Let me add that these reductions, unlike those following the construction of a house, do not mean a notable reduction of absolute standards. Among manuals as well as non-manuals, cars are purchased

---

Source: Family budget data and own computations.

[a] There is no comparable breakdown for earlier years.

[b] The index of structural differences is defined by:

$$I = \sqrt{\dfrac{\sum\limits_{i=1}^{r}\left(p_{i\mathrm{A}} - p_{i\mathrm{B}}\right)^2}{r}}$$

where p_is are relative frequencies, A and B denote the two compared populations, and r is the number of p_is. (This index was worked out by E. Schnell.)

mainly by the higher-income families, so that this item does not require heavy cuts in other fields of consumption.) With the reorganization of the pattern of outlays, cars may introduce a genuinely more open and more varied way of life, affecting the whole family. The use of motorcycles is entirely different from that of cars. Young people may use motorcycles for fun and in groups, but for the adults the motorcycle is mainly used for getting to work and it hardly changes the pattern of family life. Therefore the current tendency of a divergence in the patterns of consumption between manuals and non-manuals is likely to persist for a while.

In the evolution of consumption deliberate interventions have probably had a somewhat lesser role and spontaneous processes a somewhat greater role than in the spheres of production or distribution. This assumption can be logically proved on the grounds that the utilization of resources, and thus consumption, belongs essentially to the private sphere on which central regulations have little direct control. Factual proof is harder to collect – evidence is rather more impressionistic than exact. Some evidence is offered, for example, by the persistence or emergence of status symbols (makes of car, outward marks of 'luxury' homes) which means that the socially divisive nature of consumption is a living tradition. Or, to give another more demonstrable example, the utilization of social benefits in kind or the distribution of flats, as shown earlier, have been heavily influenced by spontaneous social forces at variance with the declared intentions.

Despite the comparatively limited possibilities for public intervention, the majority of explicitly pursued social goals have been approached. In other words, the most basic problems concerning standard of living have been or are in the process of being solved – and this is not a negligible result in a country with the limited economic resources and relatively low economic level of Hungary. But, as previous evidence shows, progress poses new problems.

Chapter 9

Organizing Life in a Socialist Way

9.1 How the question of 'ways of life' emerged

The most pressing needs in Hungary have by and large been covered by now. Hunger, mass squalor, precarious living conditions, general scarcity are problems of the past, and have hopefully been wiped out for ever. The far from negligible hardships which still exist – inadequate living conditions and so forth – are gradually being eased, and already they no longer affect the majority.

On the other hand, a growing section of the population is becoming well-off, even prosperous. The level of production is increasing, many goods are appearing which serve much more than just the bare necessities. How should the new prosperity be used? What aims should be served by the new products?

Up to now, only one 'model of prosperity' has found answers to these questions – that of the advanced capitalist countries. It has evident advantages as compared to earlier stages of capitalism. But it is clear by now that the modern capitalist system does not correspond to a socialist ideal – whether we look at its relation to other parts of the world, or the solution of its inner social problems or, especially, the perspective it offers to people. This is expressed in many ways by the inner critics of the 'affluent society' who personally experience its drawbacks. But the major problems are also perceived by those who observe it only from the outside – as shown for instance by some Hungarian opinions.

In 1969 the Hungarian Commission for Perspective Planning on Manpower and Standard of Living published its hypotheses concerning the orientation of social development for the next fifteen years. A public debate was launched on the issues raised, in which a hundred or so people – mostly professionals – expressed their comments. One of the concerns which frequently came to the fore related to the possible values orientating a socialist way of life. 'It is somewhat disheartening that the forecasts of a socialist country up to 1985 . . . do not say much more than that the structure of consumption will follow a pattern very similar to that of more developed countries . . . If we want more than just to create a kind of bourgeois welfare, then we have to take into account more seriously the specific nature of a socialist country.' Or: 'We cannot but start from a bourgeois way of life and have no idea whatsoever as yet of what will be a socialist way of life based on economic welfare.' And another comment: 'If socialism implies the requirement and the goal of the creation of a new way of life, it cannot be uncritical towards the cultural patterns, values and stereotypes inherited from the past. . . While on the one hand, we cannot force upon people any imaginary utopias of a socialist way of life because this has to emerge from their everyday activity and they themselves have to create it, we cannot on the other hand refuse to influence this evolution in the name of the basic values of socialism.'[1]

The final version of the long-term plan later emphasized certain elements which undoubtedly overstep the traditional boundaries of a 'bourgeois way of life'. Its principal ideas were – besides material progress – to assure a secure and stable life for everybody; to strengthen the open character of society by maintaining mobility at a high level; to enhance the socialist character of income distribution, implying the reduction of the distance between extremes; to build up a more consistent system of preferences in consumption.[2] Later on, in the mid-

1. 'The Hypotheses of the Commission of Perspective Planning on Manpower and Standard of Living' appeared in *Gazdaság*, 1969, No. 2. The content-analysis of the comments was published in the same journal in 1970. My quotations are from Zs. Ferge and K. Rupp, 'The Debate about the Hypotheses of the Long-Term Plans on Manpower and Standard of Living', *Gazdaság*, 1970, No. 4, pp. 65, 66.

2. An important paper on the goals of social planning made public and explicit many implications of these overall goals. It stressed the importance of the decrease in income differentials, of the increase in low incomes, of the growing contribution of society to the support of inactive layers as

seventies the regional dimension was brought in: the need to narrow the gap between the living standards of the various settlements was made explicit in the plans.

It still remains true that the characteristics of a socialist way of life, its chief values and the instruments promoting it have not yet found adequate expression in the social plans. Economic and social planning are of course essentially concerned with those components of economic and social life which can be fairly simply quantified, and in the case of which deliberate social intervention has a clearly traceable *modus operandi*. The qualitative and subtle aspects of the way of life as well as the values themselves usually do not meet these conditions. Technical difficulties are, however, secondary in this case. The real reasons for the delayed appearance of the problems and for the inadequacy of the way in which they were handled in the plans lie elsewhere.

First, the reasons which delayed the emergence of social and societal policy in general also acted in the case of the way of life. It was assumed that once certain basic relations – ownership of the means of production first and foremost – were changed and economic progress was on its way, a socialist way of life, whatever this means, would automatically take shape. More precisely, this assumption implied that under these conditions the only possible outcome was an entirely new way of life. This assumption was built on a simplified conception of the relation of material conditions and social consciousness, positing it as an automatic connection, neglecting the role of traditional attitudes, folk customs, ideals and also the impact of the models presented by Western consumerism. It was also based on a rather simplified view of the material conditions them-

---

particulars of the income policy. In the case of priorities in consumption it emphasized the priority of improving living conditions and of developing health and educational services. Both authors were deeply involved in the preparation of the long-term plans. Róbert Hoch and János Timár, 'Életszinvonalpolitika, fogyasztáspolitika' (Standard of Living Policy, Consumption Policy), *Gazdaság*, 1975, No. 1.

selves as if the way in which production should be increased was self-evident.

Second, there prevailed a long-lasting confusion of values in relation to well-being. The first, post-war and post-revolutionary period was characterized simultaneously by scarcity and egalitarianism. The combination of these two elements inevitably led to a kind of puritanism. The main concern was not well-being, a practical impossibility except for a few, but simply being, the solution of the elementary problems of the many. What is more, all the outward signs of well-being and prosperity were to be found either in the lives of members of the former ruling classes or in those of the 'new rich' who were shrewd or cunning enough to profit from general want. Therefore, signs of prosperity appeared as if they were necessarily inter-connected either with a specific class situation or with an individual mentality, or both, which were incompatible with a socialist system. Hence the asceticism of the period, which was in a way the appropriate attitude under those conditions, took on a heavy ideological load. Thus, as so often happens – a virtue, asceticism, was literally forged out of a necessity.

The need for asceticism declined with improving conditions, but the former ideological orientation did not follow at exactly the same pace. It persisted as a deep conviction especially with the first adherents and most ardent supporters of a socialist transformation. The majority of people, practically all those who had long been exposed to want, could not accept asceticism as the fulfilment of socialist promises. In addition, the young generations who had not lived through the period when asceticism appeared as a socialist value eagerly welcomed the opportunities of an increasingly colourful and comfortable life. But the new tendencies caused disorientation and bewilderment among the partisans of the earlier ideals. They could not but condemn the new values, because they could only equate well-being with a bourgeois way of life – otherwise they would have had to turn against everything they had fought for during long years. Some remnants of these old attitudes still survive, but the most difficult transitory period is over. It is by now clear that well-being or even prosperity do not in themselves represent a danger for socialism and if they can be achieved it is senseless to condemn or negate them in the name of old creeds.

These two circumstances explain why it took so long to face the 'challenge of abundance', to approach in a theoretical way the problems of socialist well-being and a socialist way of life. It is only in the last few years that more and more people have realized that there is a problem here, because there are alternative ways of development, because there is no single predefined solution, because it is not a smooth process 'to lead a society with a differentiated interest structure towards a higher-level synthesis of the present contradictory state of equality and inequality relations'.[3] Since then, politicians as well as social scientists have taken up the issue with increasing frequency, so that some criteria of a socialist way of life are slowly being clarified.[4] First, however, we have to explain the meaning we impute to the concept of 'way of life'.

9.2 The concept of 'way of life'

Throughout this book I have stressed the fundamental role of the basic social relations embedded in the social division of work. This concern is motivated by the conviction that therein lies the key to the transformation of social relations in general and also to the emergence or to the creation of new ways of life. After all, the real aim of a socialist society is not confined to producing more, or to altering the conditions of production, or even to raising the level of consumption, but is to create the conditions for the emergence of new, more meaningful human relations that can be based upon solidarity, and of ways of living characterized by material welfare and the full realization

3. Dr István Hetényi, 'A társadalmi fejlődés és a hosszutávu népgazdasági tervezés kapcsolatáról' (On the Interrelation between Social Development and Perspective Planning of the National Economy), *Társadalmi Szemle*, 1975, No. 3.
4. One of the most recent and most popular works on this issue is: Ferenc Kozma, *Jólét szocialista módon* (Well-Being in a Socialist Form), Kossuth Könyvkiadó, 1976.

of human abilities. This whole set of aims may be conceptualized by means of the notion of 'way of life'.

The concept itself may be defined in various ways. From the perspective adopted here the best approach is the one developed in Hungary by Á. Losonczi.[5] According to her, the way of life must be seen as the system of human activity, organized or geared to maintain life, to satisfy the needs which evolve under changing historical and social conditions. Need and activity are in a strong dialectic relation. Man finds around him a world already filled with the material and other objects created by former generations. Needs are awakened and oriented by these objects, that is they are formed by the social environment. The needs in their turn prompt activity on the part of man, stimulating him to develop abilities which will help to satisfy the needs, to 'appropriate' – in a physical and a spiritual sense alike – the object of the need.

In this relation between the need and the activity both are constantly changing. The activity oriented to a given need develops abilities which will eventually modify the object, create new objects and create new needs. We may add that if various needs are met too easily, without any effort, the impulse for activity may disappear and with it the abilities themselves. If, on the other hand, the fulfilment of a need requires too great an effort, the need itself will be suppressed and will cease to act as a mobilizing force of action and of the unfolding of abilities.

Ways of life are shaped by the interplay of, on the one hand, external economic and social, material and spiritual conditions, which suggest the needs, and, on the other hand, by the ability of man to meet this challenge. His abilities, in their turn, are formed by the same external conditions, which may help or hinder their development.

This conception does not deny the first, biological command of life, the necessity to maintain and reproduce life. It suggests only that man obeys this command according to the historical

5. Ágnes Losonczi, *Az életmódról az időben, a tárgyakban és az értékekben* (On Ways of Life in Terms of Time, of Objects, of Values), Gondolat Kiadó, 1977.

and social circumstances he is born into. If historical stage, or social position, or both, imply strained conditions, then the first commands of the preservation of life – the need to eat, to have shelter, to be covered – will also be practically the last ones. Satisfying them will exhaust all the energies of man. When man's environment is richer, needs will multiply and so will abilities. Undoubtedly, there is a basic hierarchy of needs shaped by the most elementary, essentially biological ones. Nevertheless, even in the simplest, poorest societies – once they are societies – needs acquire social overtones, so that they practically never appear in their crudest form. Customs, rites, folk traditions, norms accompanying the most elementary acts of life appear at the dawn of human history.[6] The social element gradually becomes as strong as the organic or natural drive. That is why human needs are eminently social needs and why they are becoming ever more social.

Of course, this approach is not really new. The social nature of needs and the relation between need and activity are important elements of Marx's theory of social development.[7] The various historical and social tendencies of the evolution of needs, the formation of the hierarchy of needs and the differentiation of these hierarchies according to social conditions was one of the central themes, in a sense *the* central theme, of Maurice Halbwachs's work. I would not affirm that he himself coined the expression 'hierarchy of needs', but certainly his was the first systematic sociological investigation of the subject, as witnessed by his thesis published in 1912.[8] He

6. That is why Maslow's conception seems to be rather too abstract. According to him higher-order needs – security, love, etc. – appear only once the most elementary material ones are satisfied. A. Maslow, *Motivation and Personality*, Harper, New York, 1954.

7 For instance: Karl Marx, *Economic and Philosophical Manuscript* (from 1844), or his *Introduction to the Critique of Political Economy*. Some implications especially relevant for a Marxist approach to the theory of needs were discussed by Ágnes Heller, 'Hipotézis egy marxista értékelmélethez' (Hypotheses to a Marxist Theory of Values), *Filozófiai Szemle*, 1970, No. 5, 6.

8. Maurice Halbwachs, *La Classe ouvrière et les niveaux de vie*, op. cit.

described there how the organic and biological contents of the needs have been supplanted, or at least superseded, by social and cultural elements, a historical process which was paralleled by the variations found among social classes. 'As we pass to groups with a more intense, more organized, more complex social life, we see the needs emptying themselves of their "primitive" contents . . .'[9] As a social consequence, 'on the whole, the workers continue to follow their cultural appetite much more than the higher classes who have much less confidence in their tastes'.[10] Another aspect of this evolution is the appearance of 'new appetites and new satisfactions', a differentiation of needs accompanied by the widening of sensibilities, and the search for new organizing frames for these needs. 'While making our needs more numerous and more complex, society removes us more and more from the exclusive dominance of a *single* need or inclination',[11] and at the same time incites us to arrange these needs in a harmonious pattern. For the higher classes, 'a piece of furniture should not be only comfortable and elegant. It also should look well where it is.'[12]

The various pieces of empirical research on needs, consumption patterns, modes and ways of life – carried out before and after Halbwachs – show, on the whole, two types of social differentiation. There are, on the one hand, continuous tendencies which may be discovered historically and, almost in the

9. 'Ainsi, à mesure qu'on passe à des groupes où la vie sociale est plus intense, mieux organisée, plus compliquée, à mesure aussi qu'on voit les besoins se vider de tout leur contenu "primitif", s'émousser et presque s'évanouir les impressions organiques naturelles et les satisfactions qui en dérivent' (ibid., p. 314).

10. 'En somme . . . l'ouvrier continue à suivre et satisfaire ses appétits organiques plus que l'homme des hautes classes. Celui-ci réfléchit bien plus quand il mange, et se défie bien plus de ses goûts' (ibid., p. 411).

11. 'À compliquer et multiplier ainsi nos besoins, à éparpiller nos désirs, la société nous soustrait de plus en plus à l'empire exclusif d'un besoin ou d'un goût prédominant' (ibid., p. 415).

12. 'Il ne suffit pas qu'un meuble soit commode et élégant, il doit faire bien là où il est' (ibid., p. 414). Or: 'Le plaisir que donne un intérieur bien tenu où, dans les formes et les couleurs, tout est ordre et harmonie, est dans une large mesure, physique' (ibid., p. 413).

same form, within any socially hierarchized society. If we follow an axis going from worse and poorer to better and richer conditions either diachronically or synchronically, we will find a number of similar tendencies: the natural and the biological become less and less visible and appear increasingly in a social and cultural disguise; needs multiply and become increasingly differentiated just like the objects that satisfy them; needs become increasingly articulate and conscious; the inevitable acceptance of the pressure of given conditions is slowly replaced by individualized and deliberate choices between more numerous possibilities in practically all the spheres of life, from consumption goods to personal relations.

Alongside the continuous tendencies we also find another type of differentiation of needs and especially of the patterns of organizing needs in sets. The previously described at least partly quantitative differences turn into qualitative ones. This latter differentiation (as well as the former one, for that matter) is obviously rooted in the class position, in the type of basic, life-sustaining activity characteristic of a group and in the more or less conscious principles and values which underlie the organization and the orientation of activities.

9.3 Variations in the values organizing life in Hungary

These class-related patterns of life have been abundantly studied for a good fifty years. Really systematic studies, attempting to encompass the most important social classes and to give a detailed, historically substantiated and empirically valid account of their value systems and ways of life are, however, scarce.[13] In Hungary, besides an early historical essay by the

13. To mention only some such works: M. Halbwachs, op. cit., and 'La psychologie des classes sociales', published originally as an essay 'Analyse des mobiles qui orientent l'activité des individus dans la vie sociale', in Vol. 1 of a collective work of the same title, ed. Dr H. Arthur and R. B. Liege, Sirey Collection, Thone et Paris, 1938; the two American 'classics', *Middletown* of R. S. Lynd and H. M. Lynd, first published in 1929, and *Yankee City*, by W. L. Warner et al., first published from 1941 on; P. Willmott and

late F. Erdei,[14] the most ambitious and the most exhaustive
research is that already mentioned by Á. Losonczi. She shows
how the past, the former class-bound ways of life and values,
shaped the present, and what continuities and discontinuities
marked the post-war society engaged in a revolutionary transformation. She describes the objective working and living conditions of the most important classes and strata, the constraints
and the freedoms they have to cope with. She shows the various
answers people have found to the pressure of circumstances,
and the organizing principles of life which give structure and
consistence to the various elements. She also endeavours to uncover the central values around which this organization takes
place and how the most essential values are understood or interpreted under varying conditions.

Without going into the details of the findings or the methods
by which they were obtained, some results are worth mentioning in the present context. The most important values which
emerged as orienting everyday morality as well as the organization of everyday life were work, the resources shaping living
conditions and human contacts. But the contents of these values
varied largely with circumstances and so did the secondary principles accompanying the fundamental values. To give just some
examples: for unskilled workers, work is the most important
obligation, the only means of preserving life. It is seen as an
inescapable imperative, something given, not chosen. Its intrinsic features are of practically no interest to the performer of
the job. In this connection there is just one outstanding wish,
that the man who works be respected. This is the only group in
which a significant proportion approaches a basic value in a
'negative' way, by stressing the lack of necessary respect both in
material and in moral terms. The attitude of unskilled workers

---

M. Young, *Family and Class in a London Suburb*, Routledge and Kegan
Paul, 1960; H. Gans, *Urban Villagers*, The Free Press, New York, 1962; and
P. Bourdieu, *Travail et travailleurs en Algérie*, Mouton, 1963
14. Ferenc Erdei, 'A magyar társadalom a két világháboru között'
(Hungarian Society between the Two Wars), written in 1943/4, published in
1976 (*Valóság*, Nos. 4 and 5).

towards material resources is shaped again by the basic strains accompanying their life. Their dominant value is thrift, because otherwise they cannot make ends meet, but a sizable minority is in favour of spending as lavishly as possible – because life would be too dreary otherwise. It is in this connection that it may be interesting to mention that this is the only group where cheerfulness is explicitly mentioned as something important in human contacts. Otherwise human contacts are orientated by family values. This is not unique to this group – in all other strata the role of the family is even more marked. There is, however, a notable difference: unskilled workers form the only group in which class solidarity is very highly praised. This is clearly an inevitable reaction to a situation which can hardly be improved by individual efforts.

At the other end of the social scale, intellectuals (professionals) also organize their life around these values, but they impute to them quite different meanings. Work is no longer perceived as a mere compulsion, nor is it seen as a means to sustain life. They can look on work (because it is, or at least may be, lived as an option) as a value in itself because of its content, its intrinsic interest, its social results. This motive reappears in a significant, although in a much lower, proportion in the case of old peasants and skilled workers. Related to work is the urge to be active in the search for truth by confronting principles and social practice. The only other group where this urge reappears, even more strongly, is the group of skilled workers. Perhaps the most important aspect of these activities (in the case of professionals) is that they are 'self-fulfilling', they help to perfect and to unfold the personality – a trait which is found with a lesser frequency among less qualified non-manuals. There is also another facet to the activities cherished in this group, namely that they contribute to the consolidation of society and are thereby serving general social interests. Not surprisingly this aspect is emphasized, more strongly, by leaders in responsible positions. Material goods are not thought to be important: they are taken for granted, hence moderation or sobriety are held to be the appropriate attitudes towards them.

As for human contacts, the group with which one should identify, with which one should feel solidarity, are more varied than
in almost any of the other groups. Family comes first here, too,
but about half of the people feel that other bonds are almost as
basic or more basic. Class solidarity is not prevalent; there is
instead a strong identification with society as a whole, and an
even stronger one with 'humanity' as such. The last two feelings
are both quite strong, but come in an inverse order in the case
of leaders. On the whole, there is not a single group, however
strained or difficult its circumstances, in which material well-
being would be the only concern. The need for action, meaningful if possible, bringing at least respect or consideration if
there is no choice in the content, is a powerful mover everywhere. The quality of human relations, identification with
others – whether in a narrower or broader circle, whether on the
basis of forced or genuine choices – is also a primary need.

The description above conveys a rather positive, idealized
image of the values of various classes or strata. The values they
cherish and hold in high esteem, though profoundly different,
are all compatible with a socialist morality and mentality. If
everyday attitudes, interests, needs and the values orienting
them followed solely and entirely the values which people de-
clare that they have the way would be paved for the easy
emergence of socialist ways of life. One could then safely
assume that with improving conditions work would increasingly
become a human need and a means of self-realization; that
material goods would lose their enticing character. And although one may regret that well-being would entail the fading
away of traditional class solidarity, one may find comfort in the
spread of the feeling of identification with interests that unite
the whole society. These assumptions also suggest that with improving conditions the present sub-cultural differences, whether
quantitative or qualitative, will diminish because both are rooted
in the present very different conditions.

Unfortunately and obviously, real attitudes do not coincide
with those inferred on the basis of the declared values. This is
not to say that the above description of values was false or

irrelevant. At a certain level of social reality the image is true: this is what people think about their own motives and values. The results above were arrived at on the basis of indirect questions or projective tests, and therefore they can be seen as valid indicators of group values and aspirations. But life is different from the image of life. The present conditions and current mechanisms are conducive to systematic deviations between the two levels. Some examples will show the direction of these deviations:

● Acquisitiveness is practically never seen as an acceptable motivation when people describe their attitudes to goods. In practice, however, large groups are striving for material advantages (as has been shown already). They may be motivated simply by the legitimate desire to increase their own comfort, or may try to assure adequate living conditions for their children. But – and this is where the problem arises – they may aspire merely to accumulate goods for the sake of accumulation itself, or again they may be moved by the desire to 'show off'.

● In the same vein, consumerism is often condemned for several more or less well articulated reasons. Among these reasons we may detect criticism towards consumerism because it deprives life of its human content, or because it is conducive to waste, literally or because of under-utilization.[15] In reality, however, elements of consumerism are gaining ground even in Hungary. This is mainly due to the orientation of production: the quality and variety of the goods offered in fact bear some marks of the 'consumerist' mentality. (How far this is due to the attraction of the 'Western' model, to the pressure of the demand influenced by this attraction, or to the available technology which is usually not 'home-bred' but taken over from technically more developed countries, and how important in the sphere of production the absence of a consistent image of the future is – these questions are hard to answer. My guess would be that all these

15. See in this connection Luc Boltanski, 'L'Encombrement et la maîterise des "biens sans maître" ', *Actes de la recherche en sciences sociales*, February 1976.

elements play a certain role.) At present it would be a gross overstatement to say that consumerism is a widespread danger in Hungary. However, it is clear that if production and consumption embark on this course, a never-ending race will start which may be very hard to reverse. Therefore the present signs of consumerism cannot be viewed with equanimity.

● Individualism, especially its extreme and competitive forms, is practically always forcefully rejected by the interviewees and various forms of group solidarity are praised instead. In real life, however, the more or less negative aspects of individualism are often encountered. More precisely, under the present conditions it is still true that all forms of individualism may take on positive as well negative 'loads' (seen from a socialist perspective). In terms of activity, achievement motivation and the striving for results may be coupled with the urge for climbing, the search for excellence may be mingled with that for (mere) superiority. In terms of material or non-material goods, the search for novelty and variety can lead to the search for invidious distinctions or conspicuous consumption. It may be noted that the latter phenomena, emphatically present in pre-war Hungary, disappeared after 1945 for quite a long period. In the early stages of the popular democratic transformation, and under the conditions of general want, they would have elicited stormy reactions. With spreading prosperity they are more easily tolerated, although the old attitudes still prevail: many signs of conspicuous behaviour or consumption are looked upon with contempt or are made fun of, in other words a dual value-system can easily be detected here.

● Steady, diligent and useful work is seen by a vast majority as the main source of man's personal well-being. Defective work-organization, bad working conditions and/or the lack of material incentives or social respect are, however, conducive to lax work-ethics and so forth.

It is clear that the above attitudes – though understandable and, after all, human – can hardly be seen as eminently socialist ones. When explanations are sought, the 'demonstration effect' is often invoked, meaning by this the attraction of the 'easy way of life' emanating from the surrounding capitalist societies. Another reason is found in the slow change of consciousness, in the fact that traditional attitudes (often related to various interests) are difficult to transform. It would certainly be too easy a way out if we suggested (as implied by the above explanations) that all the sources of 'evil' are external to our actual system. In a sense, though, this is true. All the negative features mentioned above – competitiveness, acquisitiveness, conspicuous individualism – correspond to the logic of former class societies and mainly to that of capitalism. But they would be less frequent, less easily revived and much less dangerous in our society if present conditions did not offer them a convenient breeding ground. The components of this breeding ground are to be found – as already pointed out – in the inequalities which are still built into the division of work; in the problems of distribution, due partly to the unequal relations of production, partly to the still prevailing scarcity of important goods, and finally to the inconsistencies between thought and action in societal policy. These are the facts, and hard facts at that, of the objective reality. An additional factor leading to the present problems is that positive standards are rather hazy, so that the modelling of conditions and attitudes moves on uncertain grounds. Since this problem was discovered, some progress has been made in two directions: in the theoretical clarification of guidelines for future action and in the identification of phenomena which may be seen as germs of future progress.

9.4 A positive approach to the socialist way of life

So far I have identified some of the negative, non-socialist, elements occurring under present-day conditions and tried to show some of their roots. These elements are easily identified because they characterize more emphatically all developed capitalist societies and therefore their socially harmful consequences are rapidly detected. Thus, Hungary knows at least what she must avoid – even if the majority of the phenomena in question have not assumed alarming dimensions just yet. The elimination of evils offers, however, only half of the solution. So we come back to what the positive alternative should be – and this is exactly what we cannot find out in advance, purely on logical grounds. The 'positive' approach does not consist in working out the 'ideal' models for a new way of life. Instead, I apply the logic of previous explanations, the assumptions about social determinants, to the future. I assume that, if certain conditions of social reproduction which led to the present problems are altered further, the outcome will be somewhat different. I do not, of course, think that this new outcome will be 'perfect' – but if our understanding of social processes is at least partly right, then it will be better than the present one. The propositions which follow are thus far from original. They add only one element to the former analysis: they spell out some of the implications, for ways of life and life values, of the changes in social relations which have already been described as desirable on general theoretical grounds.

(a) Although the first condition will by now sound like an *idée fixe*, let me repeat that the reorganization of the division of work is a first condition of changing ways of life and mentalities. This reorganization (along the lines suggested in Part One of this book) may attenuate the socially divisive features of work. Also, by mobilizing more human abilities it may arouse more, and more varied, needs. Further, if work is less narrowing and more meaningful for a widening circle of people, all other spheres of their life can change more easily towards better standards.

(b) On the basis of less asymmetrical work relations the present inequalities of distribution can be reduced with less administrative effort and with less danger of 'hidden' distortions. Besides assuring a higher living standard for large strata, this may help to weaken the present tendencies of invidious differentiation. The basis of distribution is extremely important because by now we know from experience that if only the material resources are distributed less unequally, the former quantitative differences in consumption will be replaced by more symbolic, but not less invidious, differences (not to mention the distortions of distribution already discussed).

(c) Also on this basis redistribution may be more plentiful and more egalitarian. If there is consensus among the members of society that an increasing part of the surplus product should be used to cover the needs of all those unable to work, the sense of security and the feelings of solidarity cannot but grow. Since there are no cross-cultural studies on this issue, my next statement may appear unfounded. It seems to me – on the grounds of personal experience and of data about the accumulation of securities – that the acquisitiveness which undeniably exists in Hungary is much weaker here than in a number of capitalist countries. One of the reasons may be that it pays less. The bases of unearned (capital) incomes have already largely been eliminated and it may be taken for granted that those which still exist will, sooner or later, also be abolished. The other reason is – and here we come back to redistribution – that the sense of security is already fairly strong, much stronger than some decades ago. The sense of security, if deeply ingrained, may weaken acquisitiveness inasmuch as this latter is always partly due to the urge to make reserves in order to avoid financial crises.

(d) The utilization of collective funds may also affect consumption patterns and ways of life more directly. I shall try to identify here those developmental tendencies which are most relevant from this perspective. In doing this some repetition is almost unavoidable, because the distribution and the utilization of the services, equipment, etc., are two aspects of the same process. I shall try, though, to keep overlaps to a minimum.

(i) In relation to types of needs, one important question is what needs should be met (in one way or other) out of collective funds. It has already been pointed out that in the interests of financial security and/or a cultured way of life this circle must be widened under socialist conditions, and the relevant standards must constantly be raised. I have also stressed the point that housing must be counted among these needs – and the sooner the better – because otherwise a sound and secure private life cannot be built up, and consumer habits cannot easily change. We may add here, from the perspective of life values, that if, for instance, adequate housing conditions are assured as of right, if they no longer require huge effort and long-lasting sacrifices, then energies will be released for other purposes and, what is more important, one more cause of the acquisitive tendencies may be weakened.

(ii) In relation to the 'unit' of users, I discussed at length in Chapter 7 the social problems of redistribution of goods or services which are used by (identifiable) individuals. Here I must add that similar problems arise in connection with facilities or amenities related to local units – whether to neighbourhood units or workplaces or any other locally identifiable group. I have already hinted that the standards and the availability of public services, equipment, etc., may be very different according to the social standing of the unit in question (the locality, enterprise, etc.) so that the accumulation of social advantages or disadvantages is thereby reinforced. It is an elementary requirement of a socialist social policy to reverse this trend[16] by means of more universalism and of more selection oriented towards historically disadvantaged groups.

(iii) Widening the frames of services which may be used collectively while parallel individualistic solutions exist may serve various purposes. For the sake of clarity, let me repeat that this parallelism is not unconditionally desirable. In some cases – primarily in education and health care – duality carries very real dangers. The parallel collective services I have in mind here, where duality is to be encouraged, include public transport, some traditional household tasks (cooking, laundry), sport and cultural amenities, holiday homes and so forth. If

16. The unequal, stratified, class-bound character of local (urban) services and facilities has been analysed several times and in detail by, for example, H. Lefebvre, *Le droit à la ville*, Anthropos, 1968, and J. Rex, 'The Concept of Housing Classes and the Sociology of Race Relations', *Race*, 12(3), 1971; R. E. Pahl, *Patterns of Urban Life*, Longmans, Green, 1970, and *Whose City?*, Penguin Books, Harmondsworth, 1976; M. Castells, *La question urbaine*, Maspero, Paris, 1972. A journal started in 1977, *The International Journal of Urban and Regional Research*, is concerned mainly with this problem.

these services or the equipment yielding such services are readily available on a collective basis, and if they are attractive and of high standards, their advantages are manifold. They are certainly less wasteful in funds, in time, in human energy, in terms of material assets, either because they may be used more economically or because they are operated with better technology and better skills. For these reasons they contribute more effectively to the preservation of the environment. All these factors militate against the worst features of 'consumerism'. Besides, if they are within easy reach, they may stimulate utilization (arouse needs) and hence may be habit-forming (sports, for instance). Some of these opportunities – if plentiful and of a high standard – may help in their turn to weaken acquisitiveness. If, for example, holiday homes are increasingly operated in this way, the trend towards the acquisition of secondary residences may decline.

It is often sweepingly implied that this type of collective service helps the formation of communities and is, therefore, a means of attenuating individualistic tendencies. This, however, is not their main advantage – many others have been enumerated above. Moreover, with many of them no such result may occur. The increasing utilization of public transport, even if it is of a high standard or even luxurious, will not form collectives out of the passengers under normal conditions. Neither must one believe that swimming pools will arouse solidarity or collectivist feelings. In some cases however, especially if the frameworks are created on the initiative of a group and/or if they are collectively responsible for operating the service, it may happen that in this activity communal action and feelings are strengthened, that new bonds and new interests are found. As a matter of fact, these forms are slowly making their appearance in Hungarian society with collectively built and run holiday homes, for instance, but there are many other possibilities which are not yet adequately encouraged. I might add that efforts to discover such possibilities are slacker than one would wish.

(iv) The problem of 'elementary' and 'higher-order' needs has already been discussed in connection with the evaluation of individual and collective solutions. The same categories have relevance from another perspective, too. Standards may vary in the case of each and every collective service (equipment, etc.). In practically all former societies the pattern of 'private affluence – public squalor' prevailed, perhaps with the debatable exception of Athenian democracy and, of course, of some establishments in each society which were destined to serve the glory of a sovereign, of some *grand seigneur* or of the state itself. (It may be objected that I proceed to an a-historical generalization, by extending the coverage of a modern phenomenon to former societies, because the quoted phrase – public affluence and private squalor – is attributed to Galbraith, who used it in *The Affluent Society* in 1958. But Ross Terrill[17] reminds us that Tawney used the Latin version of the same expression in an essay written in 1918[18] and may have got it from Matthew Arnold, who took it over from Sallust who put it into Cato's mouth ...)

Deliberate efforts to reverse this age-old pattern first appeared on a large scale in the Soviet Union not long after the Proletarian Revolution, as witnessed for instance by the Moscow underground or other public establishments set up in the first decades, destined for mass use. Hungary adopted the tenet underlying these efforts, that 'workers have a right to the best', after 1945, but it was not followed consistently. It has always been more easily applied to new creations than to existing ones which ought first to have been destroyed, but this was difficult because of scarce economic resources.

In any case, if this principle – that equipment and services created and run by collective funds and used by the collectivity must be of the highest standards possible, that 'public squalor' is inadmissible in any field – is really consistently applied, the impact of such a strategy on ways of life and on the values

17. Ross Terrill, *R. H. Tawney and His Times*, Harvard University Press, 1973, p. 224.

18. R. H. Tawney, 'The Conditions of Economic Liberty', published originally in 1918, reprinted in *The Radical Tradition*, Allen and Unwin, 1964; the quoted phrase appears on p. 111.

orienting them is practically boundless. Even if this sounds repetitive by now, this strategy may be one of the most powerful indirect means of fighting acquisitiveness, invidious distinction, conspicuous consumption, and of promoting frameworks which suggest new ways of living. Besides, it may reinforce the self-respect of all the members of a community, it may give a sense of dignity, and may strengthen the bonds between the individual and the collectivity.

I have spelt out some of the directions – to my mind the most important ones – which are, can be or should be followed by deliberate social action in order to influence consumption, ways of life and the values organizing them in a way consistent with socialist values. If successful, these strategies lead to the following results:

● They promote collective mobility by creating less differentiated frameworks for everyday life and by developing more and more varied needs and abilities in everybody;

● They strengthen or create a basis for social relations that may be a form of solidarity because they weaken the motives for acquisitiveness, competitiveness, invidious attitudes;

● They contribute to the humanization of needs. In fact, on the basis of these two conditions the autotelic, self-contained nature of consumption and of ways of consuming may be restored. In class societies, the coverage of the diverse needs took place in a way which transcended the original aim: the way of covering the need almost always become impregnated with social overtones expressing or accentuating the social difference. Thus the coverage of needs ceased to be an end in itself, but was transmuted into a means of expressing social standing. By the same token, the objects (whether material or not) of need-satisfaction ceased to be simple means to that end. By acquiring symbolic overtones, they themselves became ends, possessing an intrinsic value. The humanization of needs implies the reversal of these trends, which becomes possible if, and only if, the present social determinants, based on basic social inequalities, weaken and the needs, the ways and means of the coverage of human needs, become freer, more autonomous expressions of human personality.

Index

(continued on next page)

(continued on next page)

About the Author

Zsuzsa Ferge is a senior researcher in the Institute of Sociology, Hungarian Academy of Sciences, and a senior lecturer at the University of Eötvös, Budapest.